The Inner Journey
Views from the Islamic Tradition

Series Editor: Ravi Ravindra
Associate Series Editor: Priscilla Murray

Titles in *The Inner Journey* series:
Views from the Buddhist Tradition
Views from the Christian Tradition
Views from the Gurdjieff Work
Views from the Hindu Tradition
Views from the Islamic Tradition
Views from the Jewish Tradition
Myth, Psyche & Spirit
Views from Native Traditions

The Inner Journey
Views from the Islamic Tradition

Edited by William C. Chittick

PARABOLA Anthology Series

MORNING LIGHT PRESS

MORNING LIGHT
P R E S S

Published by Morning Light Press 2007.

Editor: William C. Chittick
Series Editor: Ravi Ravindra
Associate Series Editor: Priscilla Murray

Morning Light Press
323 North First, Suite 203
Sandpoint, ID 83864
morninglightpress.com
info@mlpress.com

Printed on acid-free paper in Canada.

Philosophy
SAN: 255-3252

Library of Congress Cataloging-in-Publication Data

The inner journey : views from the islamic tradition / edited by William C. Chittick. -- 1st ed.
    p. cm. -- (Parabola anthology series)
    Includes bibliographical references.

    ISBN 1-59675-016-2 (978-1-59675-016-6 : alk. paper)

    1. Sufism--Early works to 1800. 2. Philosophy, Islamic. I. Chittick, William C.
    BP188.9.I55 2007
    297.5--dc22
                        2007000511

To the path makers
and the pilgrims on the path

General Introduction to
The Inner Journey: A Parabola Anthology Series

When *Parabola: Myth, Tradition, and the Search for Meaning* was launched in 1976, the founder, D. M. Dooling, wrote in her first editorial:

> *Parabola* has a conviction: that human existence is significant, that life essentially makes sense in spite of our confusions, that man is not here on earth by accident but for a purpose, and that whatever that purpose may be it demands from him the discovery of his own meaning, his own totality and identity. A human being is born to set out on this quest. ... Every true teaching, every genuine tradition has sought to train its disciples to act this part, to become in fact followers of the great quest for one's self.

For over thirty years, *Parabola* has honored the great wisdom traditions of every culture, turning to their past and present masters and practitioners for guidance in this quest. Recognizing that the aim of each tradition is the transformation of human life through practice supported by knowledge and understanding, *Parabola* on behalf of its readers has turned again and again to Buddhist and Christian monks, Sufi and Jewish teachers, Hindu scholars, and Native American and other indigenous peoples, evoking from each of them illumination and insight.

Over the years *Parabola*, in each of its issues, devoted to a central theme of the human condition as it is and as it might be, has gathered remarkable material. "The Call," "Awakening," "Food," "Initiation," "Dreams and Seeing," "Liberation," "The Mask," "Attention": in these and in scores of other issues, a facet of the essential search is explored, always with the aim of casting light on the way.

The purpose of the *Parabola Anthology Series* is to gather the material published in *Parabola* during its first thirty years in order to focus this light and to reflect the inner dimensions of each of these traditions. While every religious tradition has both external and inner aspects, the aim of each is the transformation of the whole being. The insights and understandings that ring true and carry the vibration of an inner meaning can provide guidance and support for our quest, but a mere mechanical repetition of forms which were once charged with great energy can take us away from the heart of the teaching. Every tradition must change and evolve; it has to be reinterpreted and reunderstood by successive generations in order to maintain its relevance and application.

Search carries a connotation of journey; we set out with the hope for new insight and experience. The aim of the spiritual or inner journey is transformation, to become more responsible and more compassionate as understanding and being grow. This demands an active undertaking, and insights from those who have traveled the path can provide a call, bring inspiration, and serve as a reminder of the need to search.

For this series, selections have been made from the material published in *Parabola* relating to each of the major traditions and teachings. Subtle truths are expressed in myths, poetry, stories, parables, and above all in the lives, actions, and expressions of those people who have been immersed in the teaching, have wrestled with it and have been informed and transformed by it. Some of these insights have been elicited through interviews with current practitioners of various teachings. Each of the great traditions is very large, and within each tradition there are distinct schools of thought, as well as many practices, rituals, and ceremonies. None of the volumes in the present series claims to be exhaustive of the whole tradition or to give a complete account of it.

In addition to the material that has been selected from the library of *Parabola* issues, the editor of each volume in the series provides an introduction to the teaching, a reminder of the heart of the tradition in the section, "The Call of the Tradition," as well as a list of books suggested for further study and reflection. It is the hope of the publishers and editors that this new series will surprise, challenge, and support those new to *Parabola* as well as its many readers.

—*Ravi Ravindra*

Contents

THE CALL OF THE TRADITION

Said the Apostle of God—upon whom be God's blessing and peace:
"He came to me while I was asleep,
bringing a silken cloth on which was some writing.
He said: 'Recite'; but I answered: 'What shall I recite?'
Then he so grievously treated me that I thought I should die,
but he pushed me off and said:
'Recite.' I answered: 'But what shall I recite?'
saying this only to guard myself against
doing again to me the like of what he had done to me. He said:
'Recite, "In the name of thy Lord who has created," and so on as far as
"taught man what he did not know"' [Quran 96:1-5].
So I recited it, and that ended the matter, for he departed from me.
Thereupon I awoke from my sleep,
and it was as though he had written it on my heart."[1]

—at-Tabari

The infant Muhammad got lost,
and his nurse Halima, dissolved in tears,
was consoled with the words:
"Do not grieve, he will not become lost to thee;
nay, but the whole world will become lost in him."[2]

—Rumi

Hast thou not seen how God has struck
a similitude? A good word
is as a good tree—
its roots are firm,
and its branches are in heaven;
it gives its produce every season
by the leave of its Lord
So God strikes similitudes for men;

haply they will remember.
And the likeness of a corrupt word
is as a corrupt tree—
uprooted from the earth
having no stablishment.
God confirms those who believe with
the firm word, in the present life
and in the world to come;
and God leads astray the evildoers;
and God does what He will.
Hast thou not seen those who exchanged
the bounty of God with unthankfulness,
and caused their people to dwell in
the abode of ruin?—[3]

—Quran 14:24-28

And first the Vale of Search: an endless Maze,
Branching into innumerable Ways
All courting Entrance: but one right: and this
Beset with Pitfall, Gulf, and Precipice. ...
The only word is 'Forward!' Guide in sight,
After him, swerving neither left nor right,
Thyself for thine own Victual by Day.
At night thine own Self's Caravanserai,
Till suddenly, perhaps when most subdued
And desperate, the Heart shall be renew'd
When deep in utter Darkness, by one Gleam
Of Glory from the far remote Harim,
That, with a scarcely conscious Shock of Change,
Shall light the Pilgrim toward the Mountain Range
Of Knowledge. ...[4]

—Attar

He who approaches near to Me one span,
I will approach near to him one cubit;
and he who approaches near to Me one cubit,
I will approach near to him one fathom,
and whoever approaches Me walking,
I will come to him running,
and he who meets Me with sins equivalent to the whole world,
I will greet him with forgiveness equal to it.[5]

—Hadith Qudsi

The Inner Journey: Introduction

The ritual act whereby one becomes a Muslim consists of performing the first of the "five pillars" in the presence of two Muslims: "bearing witness" (shahadah) that "(There is) no god but God" and that "Muhammad is His messenger." In keeping with the Quranic depiction of the prophets in human history, the Islamic tradition has generally viewed the first of these two statements, which is called the words of *tawhid* ("asserting divine unity"), as an article of faith shared by all prophets and all religions. Differences among religions arise because of diverse second statements. In the Islamic case, this means that Muhammad is God's messenger, though he is one of many messengers over history. In this way of looking at things, all traditions agree on the most basic of truths, which is the unity of the ultimately Real. Each tradition then takes a specific form by emulating its own prophet. It follows that, from the Islamic point of view, the inner journey of Islam replicates the inner journey of Muhammad, just as the inner journeys of other traditions emulate those of their own revered prophets, sages and seers.

Muslims conceive of life as a journey toward a destination. Rooted as they are in the notion of God's unique reality, they know that they have come from the One Real and will go back where they came from. They also know that they have been given sufficient freedom to be called to account for the manner in which they travel the road. Without question they will once again encounter the Real, but whether they meet Him as Merciful or Wrathful, Forgiving or Vengeful, depends upon their own personal journeys.

Life, then, is the path that leads back to God. What makes a human journey an "Islamic" one is the attempt to live in conformity with the Sunna or exemplary model of Muhammad, which means traveling the "straight path" (*as-sirat al-mustaqim*) upon which he was the first to walk. Hence Muslims pray, in every cycle of the daily ritual prayer, "Guide us on the straight path" (Quran 1:5).

The Sunna of Muhammad has two sides to it, one visible and the other invisible. Explaining the right way to travel the visible journey of ritual activity and social interaction has been the task of the jurists, those who have codified Islamic law (the Shari'ah). Bringing out the subtle dimensions of Muhammad's character and explaining how to emulate him on the inner journey has largely been the task of those Muslims known as Sufis, though the philosophers—who looked back to the Greeks for a good deal of their inspiration—also made major contributions.

Tawhid tells us that everything comes from God and everything goes back to Him. But Muslims have always insisted that this coming and going is not only a reference to past and future events, but also to the present moment. "Breath by breath" (*ma' al-anfas*) the universe comes forth from the One, and breath by breath it returns to Him. Each moment is a new creation. This is part of what Sufis mean when they call the universe "the Breath of the All-Merciful."

Human beings stand in the unique situation of having a say in how they go back to God. Unlike plants and animals, they do not simply follow the natural course of events. They also exercise a certain degree of freedom in the way they travel the path. It is this freedom that the tradition addresses, for the function of the prophets is nothing other than to bring the guidance that people need to make wise use of freedom.

The nature of the free journey to God is established already by the two formative events of the tradition: the "night of power" (*laylat al-qadr*), when God sent down the Quran to Muhammad, and the "night journey" (*isra*), also known as the "ascent" (*mi'raj*), when Muhammad rose up to his Lord. Night and day commonly symbolize the hidden and the manifest, the inward and the outward. The Quran descended at night, because it came from the inner realm of the Divine Spirit; in the same way, Muhammad ascended at night toward that same realm.

Muhammad is the human embodiment of the religion. God's Word came down to him so that he could assimilate it and be assimilated by it. The mark of his total and complete assimilation is precisely his ascent to God, which occurred, the tradition insists, in the body. Just as the archangel Gabriel had brought the Quran to Muhammad from God, so Gabriel took him first to Jerusalem, then up through the seven spheres, and finally to the edge of Paradise, where Gabriel told him to complete the journey on his own. "If I fly any further," he said, "my wings will burn off."

The most important ritual act of the religion—the *salat* or daily prayers—is tightly bound up with the night journey. The salat was instituted by God when Muhammad reached His Presence. When he told his Companions about his journey, they asked if they too could travel to God. He replied that the salat is the mi'raj of the believer.

Imagery of the path infuses the tradition. The word typically used to designate the revealed law that governs outer activity, Shari'ah, means literally "wide road" or "avenue." It is complemented by the Tariqah, "the narrow road," which guides seekers on the path of transforming the soul by assimilating the divine Word into their character. The inner journey demands overcoming blameworthy moral traits, acquiring praiseworthy traits, and becoming qualified by the very attributes of God (*at-takhalluq bi akhlaq Allah*).

Sufis often describe the human situation in terms of a circle whose center is the Haqiqah, that is, the Reality, God Himself. The Shari'ah is then the circumference of the same circle, the path that we need to walk in our personal and social lives in order to live in conformity with the Reality. The Tariqah is each radius that leads from the circumference to the Center, from the surface to the interior, from this world to God. This triad—Shari'ah, Tariqah, Haqiqah—is known throughout the far-flung Muslim communities, playing an important role, for example, even in China, where Muslims translate the three terms as *li* (propriety), *dao* (the way), and *chen* (the Real).

Every journey has stages that need to be traversed. In the tenth century Shibli could say of Muhammad, "Two strides and he arrived"—with the first stride he stepped beyond this world, and with the second he stepped beyond the next world into the presence of God. Most teachers, however, have described the journey in terms that make it accessible to emulation. They sometimes number the stages as seven, corresponding to the seven spheres through which Muhammad traveled in the mi'raj.

The great Persian poet Fariduddin Attar provides the best known example of a seven-stage model in his "Conference of the Birds." The birds set off to find the Simurgh, the fabulous king of the birds. Their guide leads them over seven mountains—those of seeking, love, self-knowledge, independence, unity, bewilderment and poverty. Finally, they achieve *fana*, the utter effacement and dissolution of "otherness," the full realization of the "No god" in the formula of tawhid ("No god but God"). Simultaneously they enter into *baqa*, the subsistence of the divine form in which Adam was created, the full realization of the "but God" in the formula. At this point the "thirty birds" (*si-murgh*) who have completed the journey wake up to their own identity with the Simurgh. The seeker, the sought, and the seeking had in fact been one from the outset.

Masters of the inner journey offered diverse depictions of the stages that need to be traversed. Treatises and books on the stations (*maqamat*) or waystations (*manazil*)—two terms denoting the stopping places of a caravan—are common in Islamic literature. The stages may be numbered as seven, ten, forty, one hundred, three hundred, even 1001. In every case, the authors are mapping out the journey in terms of the elimination of negativity, the acquisition of virtue, and the achievement of final unity. The underlying truth of human existence, as of all existence, is the truth of tawhid: There is nothing real but the Real; there is no consciousness but His consciousness, no justice but His justice, no good but His good.

Spiritual masters of many types and vocations have appeared over Islamic history. Not just a few of them felt compelled to unpack the implications of the repeated Quranic injunction to heed the signs (*ayat*) of God, which are displayed not only in the Book's "verses" (the same word ayat), but also in the world around us and the world within. A favorite proof-text was 41:53: "We shall show them Our signs in the horizons and in their souls till it is clear to them that He is the Real." The Quran's stress on the importance of perceiving the *vestigia Dei* in the cosmos and the soul had enormous repercussions for philosophy, the study of nature, and spiritual psychology. In contrast to what happened in the West, these disciplines never broke out of the traditional, symbolist world view. It was not only poets, artists and the common people who preserved a sense of cosmic mystery and the transparency of phenomena, but also the great intellectuals of the tradition.

Investigation of "cosmology" in the proper sense of the word, that is, the study of the whole cosmos, "everything other than God," including all the realms that transcend the merely physical, remained a major field of endeavor over the course of Islamic history, resulting in diverse cosmological schemes. At the same time cosmology was never divorced from "spiritual psychology," which we can also call "cosmic anthropology." Just as the signs in the cosmos point to the divine presence in everything around us, so also the signs in the soul point to God's constant presence in His own human image. The cosmos and human beings were seen as working together in a common task, referred to in the famous divine saying (*hadith qudsi*), "I was a Hidden Treasure and desired to be known, so I created the creatures that I might be known." Humans and cosmos are the twin disclosures of the Divine Reality, with man related more to the "subjective" pole, and the cosmos to the "objective" pole. Only in the human heart can a true unity of subject and object be achieved. It is then that, in the words of another divine saying, "The heart of My believing servant embraces Me."

Parabola has been practically unique among Western periodicals in recognizing that the inner aspirations of Muslims teach us far more about the nature of the Islamic tradition than the residual prejudices of our Christian heritage or the outward vagaries of political events and international relations. The journal has always sought out teachers and scholars who have paid close attention to the deeper aspirations of the Islamic tradition. The choices of its editors made the task of putting together this anthology an easy one.

Given that the basic intuition of tawhid infuses every dimension of Islamic life and thought and that this intuition is also found in other traditions, what makes Islam peculiarly "Islamic" is the specific revelation given to the prophet Muhammad and the manner in which he embodied that revelation. The central role of prophecy is the focus of the first chapter. It is especially important for non-Muslims to grasp this salient dimension of Islamic teachings, given that they commonly imagine that Muhammad plays exactly the same exclusive role in Islam that Christ plays within Christianity. The fact is, however, that the Quran and traditional Islam have always talked about the prophets in the plural and considered their role as an essential part of the cosmic drama, so much so that achieving true human status is impossible without their guidance. In this view, prophecy is coterminous with the human condition, which helps explain why Muslims consider Adam the first prophet and eminently worthy of emulation.

Chapter Two looks at the manner in which the spiritual life has been embodied in traditional Muslim life and society, and Chapter Three focuses on the importance that Islam has accorded to beauty in all domains of life, from architecture and calligraphy to gardens and personal comportment.

Chapters Four and Five deal respectively with the cosmos and the soul, illustrating how discussion of each has never been cut off from consideration of the other. Those who want to accomplish the journey to God need to understand how the external realm reflects the internal realm and provides a map of the stages that we have traversed in coming into this world, and those that we now need to traverse in going back home.

Chapter Six turns to the Tariqah per se. What exactly is the nature of this narrow path to God? Here we have a variety of answers reflecting the views of some of the diverse teachers who have guided people on the path down to the present.

Finally, Chapter Seven turns to one of the better known sides of the Sufi tradition, that of the intoxicating joy that characterizes a number of its best known representatives, especially Rumi.

Islamic Imagery

"God is beautiful," said the Prophet, "and He loves beauty." The Quran says, "He made everything that He created beautiful" (32:7), and it tells people: "Act beautifully, as God has acted beautifully toward you" (28:77). Traditional Muslims strive to follow this instruction in all domains of life. They begin by showing respect and reverence for the revealed Word—by reciting it sonorously, by writing it out in an elegant hand, and by placing it in worthy surroundings. Recitation gives rise to diverse expressions of beauty in sound (poetry, music), writing to the arts of the book (calligraphy, ornamentation, miniatures), and concern for worthy surroundings to beautiful buildings and objects along with dignity in manners (*adab*) and clothing.

For captions regarding these images see pages 317-18

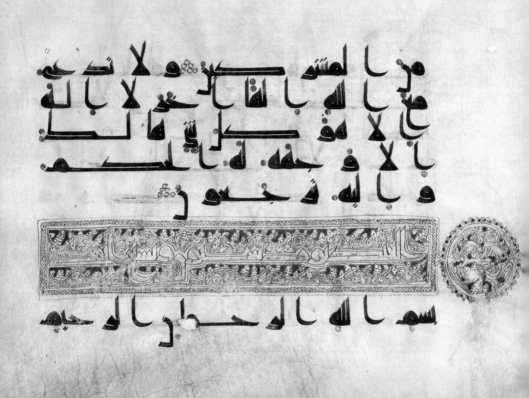

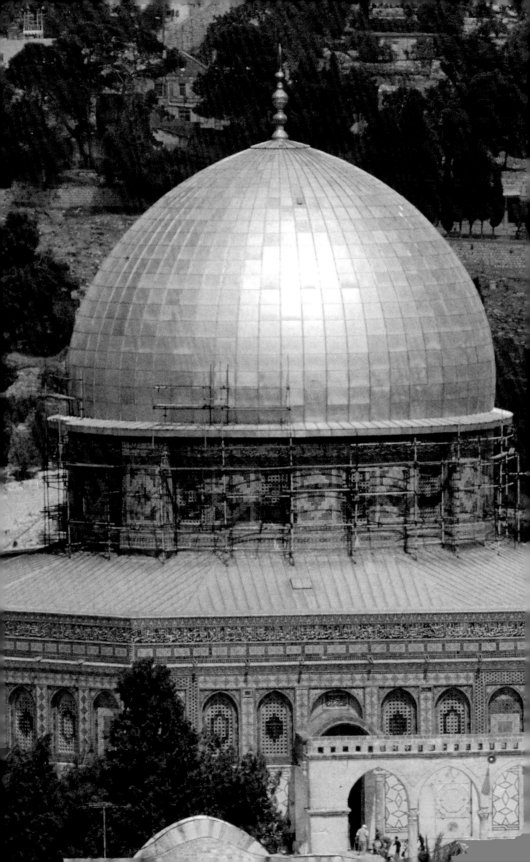

•

PROPHECY

*God has sent on earth a hundred and twenty-four thousand
prophets to teach men the prescription of this alchemy,
and how to purify their hearts from baser qualities in the crucible of
abstinence. This alchemy may be briefly described as turning
away from the world to God, and its constituents are four:
One – The knowledge of self.
Two – The knowledge of God.
Three – The knowledge of this world as it really is.
Four – The knowledge of the next world as it really is.[1]*

—Al-Ghazali

Parabola
Volume: 21.1
Prophets and
Prophecy

THE FIRST PROPHET

Interview with Seyyed Hossein Nasr

Seyyed Hossein Nasr, formerly of Tehran University, is University Professor of Islamic Studies in the George Washington University. Gray Henry, Director of the Islamic Texts Society, U.S.A. interviewed him for Parabola.

Gray Henry: *Professor, may we start with a very large question? What is the essence of prophecy, and why is it needed?*

Seyyed Hossein Nasr: First of all, prophecy is the revelation of some aspect of divine reality in the world of creation. Or, speaking metaphysically, the projection of an aspect of divine reality into manifestation. The world as we see it, of course, is not reality: it is only an appearance of reality, a level of reality. The Divine is reality as such, the absolute and ultimate reality. There is a hiatus, or chasm from one point of view, and nonexistence from the other, between the Divine and its manifestation. From the purely divine point of view, you might say that there is in fact nothing but the Divine, and that is why certain metaphysicians and mystics have asserted that in the One there is only the One. However, from the human point of view, the point of view of creation in which we live, there is the hiatus mentioned.

GH: *Is there any way around that?*

SHN: Indirectly, yes. There is, to speak from an Islamic point of view, a reason for creation. And that is for God to know himself through his own creation. In a "sacred famous saying" of the Prophet, in which God speaks in the first person, He says, "I was a Hidden Treasure. I wanted to be known, therefore I created the world so I would be known." So there is a purpose to creation. And this purpose is to return to the Divine Principle. However, such a return is impossible without the help of the Divine Principle itself. Now the Divine Principle of necessity possesses the quality of mercy. And the Divine Mercy necessitates the providing of this guidance in the ultimate sense for all of creation, but more specifically the human state, to enable men and women to return to the Divine. Hence the necessity of prophecy from the divine point of view.

CH: *That's beautiful. But can you define prophecy for us?*

SHN: The word in English is a much more ambiguous term than it is in Sanskrit, or Arabic, or other traditional languages. In English, the words *prophecy* and *revelation* have become somewhat ambiguous around the edges. Anyone with a vague idea having to do with the future is called a prophet. So are some recent thinkers whose ideas suddenly catch on. For example, some of the nineteenth-century figures who were against all religion are now regarded as "prophets" of the twentieth century! So the term has lost its precise definition. Now in Arabic there's a whole galaxy, you might say, of words to define prophecy. But the one that's the most important is the word which comes from the root *NBY*, that is *nubuwwah*, meaning "to bring news." And the word *nabi*, again from NBY, means "the prophet"; that is, someone who is the harbinger of news from the Divine, who brings something to us from the Divine. So the idea of the connectedness of the prophet to God, and the bringing of news, which is knowledge of something which concerns us, is contained in the etymology of the word *prophet* in Arabic.

GH: *And as you said, it's essential news, because it concerns the very meaning of our existence, our return to the Divine.*

SHN: It's the "Good News." That is, news which has to do, not only with our own nature here in the world— what we are, who we are—but also what we ought to become, where we should be going. Both are contained in this.

GH: *You spoke a moment ago of how prophecy today has taken on another meaning: to do with the future.*

SHN: Yes, and in fact prophecies of the future such as we have in the Old Testament, and as we have in the Revelation of John, and also as we have been given by the Prophet of Islam—about the end of the world, for instance—are necessary, legitimate aspects of the prophetic function. There is no doubt about that. But not everybody who has an insight into the future is necessarily a prophet. There are those who have a kind of vision into the unknown temporal dimensions of existence, who are able to foretell future events without being prophets. In the modern world, no distinction is made between the Divine Order, the spiritual order, and the psychological order. They're all mixed up together—especially the psychological and the spiritual. People oftentimes have an insight into the psychological world or the psychological mechanisms by which things happen, or even elements of cosmic existence, and such understanding is confused with prophetic knowledge, whereas prophetic knowledge comes from God. It cannot come from psychological insight or even "cosmic consciousness," because that kind of "vision" or foresight belongs to the world of manifestation.

GH: *How can we reach the Unmanifest?*

SHN: There is a Persian saying, which I'll translate for you: "The word which arises from the heart settles upon the heart." The person whose words really come from his or her heart utters words with a special resonance. Now, the words of the prophets do not even come from them; they come from God, from the Divine. And therefore, they resonate within a particular level of our own existential reality which is much deeper than either our mental life or our psychological life. They affect the very center of our being. It's not only the content, but also the way, the manner in which words are uttered by the prophets, that reveal the truth.

It's very difficult for us, living in an age of mediocrity, to even imagine what it means to meet a prophet. That's impossible for most of us to imagine, in the same way that even a hundred years ago it was unimaginable for people to think of someone walking on the moon. It was not part of their world of imagination, you might say. For that very reason, it is extremely difficult for us to understand what it is in the message of a prophet, in the words of a prophet, which speaks to us. It is that these words come from the center of our own being, because God is not only transcendent *vis-à-vis* ourselves. He resides also at the very center of our own being. So it's really a call from the deepest center, the deepest layer of our own existence. It's a call to us, from who we really are in the Divine, in the ultimate sense, if I may speak in mystical language. It is our real "I" calling us.

GH: *When that primordial nature— that kingdom of Heaven within— resonates, it also recognizes. We draw out who we really are.*

SHN: "Who we really are." Exactly. Islamic metaphysicians have developed the doctrine that when we employ our intellect in the traditional sense of the term *intellect*, we awaken that divine instrument of knowledge within us. Thus we approach the function of prophecy. That's because each of us has a "prophet" within, by the presence of the intellect within us. And that is why the prophet not only teaches us what to do, but more than anything else, what to know, and how to be, on the highest level. To return to your first question: There is something innate in the prophetic message, which is able to attract, and it differs from the message of a theologian or a mystic or a philosopher since it comes from God Himself. So it appeals to all kinds of people, from the simple shepherd to the deepest mystical or philosophical mind.

GH: *In what does the truth of prophecy consist?*

SHN: The truth of prophecy is nothing other than the source from which it comes, because the Divine is also the Truth, with a capital T. And therefore, the truth of prophecy consists in its conformity to its source. Again to come back to the teachings of Islam about prophecy, Islam claims that a prophet owes nothing to anyone. The modern way of studying history of religion has a prophet being influenced by somebody else, and that other prophet by somebody else. From the traditional point of view, that's utter nonsense. A prophet is chosen by God from on high; you cannot develop yourself into becoming a prophet. In contrast to being a great mystic, or metaphysician, or philosopher, you can neither undergo formal external training, nor even inner purification to become a prophet. God chooses a prophet.

Now God, having chosen a prophet, chooses an instrument for the conveying of His message, which does not have within its nature any element which would defile, subvert, violate, or distort His message. Therefore, the truth of prophecy is in the very nature of prophecy itself, because God is truth, and He is the All-knower, and being merciful, He does not want to present a distorted truth to the world. Prophets do present different versions of the truth to the world, because of different communities that receive the various messages of Heaven. But they never present a distorted version of the truth. And therefore, what a prophet says must of necessity be the truth, because it comes from the source of all truth, through a channel which is chosen by the Truth; by a power which can choose a channel which will not distort His message. So all of those conditions are present metaphysically by the very reality of prophecy.

GH: *Have you gone to Medina to visit the place where the prophet Muhammad is buried?*

SHN: I've had the joy of visiting Medina many times. There one experiences the perfume of paradise in the presence of the Prophet. It is a perfume so powerful that even simple people, who are not aware of the doctrines that are involved, or do not have spiritual experience of a high level, are attracted to it like a magnet. Because, within their hearts, by virtue of the faith that they have in Islam, there is also love of the Prophet. I must add that I've had the singular honor of being inside the tomb itself. Inside the Ka'bah, you are completely on the vertical axis of existence. You're no longer there, in a sense; you experience a state of annihilation, pure transcendence, but in the tomb of the Prophet one experiences paradisal reality!

GH: *Yet most of us fail to heed the true prophets.*

SHN: Yes. The modern world no longer fears God and therefore considers prophecy to be at best a choice, and not a necessity. But the prophetic tradition has to do with reality, and there is no part of reality which is extraterritorial to tradition. You cannot say, "Well, I'll leave God alone if He leaves me alone," because you did not create your own body, your own life, and everything that surrounds you. From the traditional point of view, the reason why we must heed the message of the prophet is that God is not only merciful; He is also just. And precisely because of His mercy, He has sent us a message; we have no excuse for not heeding it. The responsibility is now upon our shoulders. We cannot stand before God on the Day of Judgment and say, "Well, I did not know, because nobody told me."

The grandeur of being human, as well as its great danger, lies precisely in the choice that we have: to heed the call of God, or nor to heed it. And the excuse that one was living on some island and never heard that message is obviated by the fact that prophecy is universal. The last great scripture of this cycle of world history, the Quran, confirms this over and over. And therefore, one cannot say, "I was living in Madagascar and I never heard of any of the religions of the world. Therefore I don't have to heed any call." The message of a prophet is very serious. It concerns our final end, our entelechy, the purpose of our existence, where we are going to go.

GH: *Is prophecy a gift or is it earned?*

SHN: Prophecy is not earned by man. The prophet is chosen by God. He has no choice in accepting the function for which he is chosen. But our participation in the message of prophecy is, first of all, a free choice on our part. And, on the deepest level, to have the blessing of choosing a message of truth is itself a blessing from Heaven. It's based upon Divine Mercy. To be able to have one's eyes open, to see the sun, is itself a great divine gift. So the dichotomy posed in this question is not even there from the human side; whereas from the divine side, it is only a question of divine choice.

GH: *Is prophecy a part of all authentic teaching?*

SHN: Yes, if you take it in the sense of the universal manifestation of God or the Divine Reality, or Divine Principle. It does not even have to be personal. It can be in the form of the illumination of the Buddha. From the Islamic point of view, Buddha is a great prophet.

Prophecy is the origin of all teachings. That is, you never have a single metaphysician, a single mystic, in all of human history (minus the twentieth century in the West, and in the decadent period of Greco-Roman antiquity), who has not related himself, or herself, to the prophetic function. You never had any Taoist sages who were not Taoists, who did not belong to the universe created by Lao Tse. You never had a single Hindu teacher who did not belong to the universe of the manifestations of Vishnu and Shiva, of the great avatars, of Krishna and Rama and so forth and so on. All Confucian sages were Confucian. From the Islamic point of view, one can say that Confucius is a prophet who exercised that function within the Chinese world.

In all traditional societies, including traditional Christian society, the link between the contemporary teacher and the original prophet, the source of prophecy, was always very clear. The teaching might be hidden, but the connection was clear for all to see. Today among so-called modern teachers the teaching is manifest, but the relation between the teacher and the source of his or her teachings is often obscure. So it's a 180-degree subversion, really, of the rapport between the two.

GH: *Doesn't the Quran point out that at all times people have had in their own language a teacher, or a prophet?*

SHN: Islam recognizes different levels of prophecy. Daniel and Moses are both Hebrew prophets, but they're not on the same level. "Verily, to every people we have sent a messenger," says the Quran. But some few prophets were destined, or given the mission by God, to found a new religion as did Abraham, Christ, and the Prophet of Islam.

The Quran is definitely very explicit that God has sent a prophet, in the sense of founding a religion—the highest level of prophecy—to all people. To deny this is to deny the explicit text of the Quran. And there's probably no scripture in the world which is as universal in its assertion of the global nature of religion as is the Quran. It doesn't say that every religion in history has preserved its authentic teachings, because a religious community can decay, like everything else in the world. But it means, in fact, that the phenomenon of religion coming from Heaven, the transcendent source of reality, is universal. It is not bound to any race; it is not bound to a geography or a geographical site; it is not bound to a language; it is not bound to a time. That is, to be human is to be the receiver of revelation. And the key to this is that the first human being, the first *anthropos*, Adam, was also the first prophet. So prophecy is inseparable from the human condition.

Parabola
Volume: 9.3
Pilgrimage

The Hajj

Gai Eaton

And proclaim to mankind the Pilgrimage. They will come to thee on foot and on every swift mount, coming from each distant point that they may experience great benefit.
—Quran 22:27-28

It is said that the religion of Islam is supported by five Pillars. The first is the declaration of faith in the One God and in the messengerhood of Muhammad, the second is ritual prayer five times each day, the third is payment of the poor-due or charity-tax, the fourth is fasting from earliest light till sunset during the month of Ramadan, and the fifth is the Pilgrimage, to be undertaken by every Muslim who is physically and financially able to undertake the journey. Each of these Pillars has its simple and obvious religious function, and each has its symbolic or esoteric significance.

For the ordinary Muslim, it is sufficient to know that he or she acquires great merit in the sight of God by performing the Pilgrimage, and that its performance washes away all past sins. The pilgrim returns home unstained as he was at the moment of birth and able to face the final Judgment—at which every atom of good or ill is exposed and assessed—without fear. The rites are extremely complex and must be carried out meticulously, but the pilgrim is led through them by a qualified pilgrim-guide and does not need to be aware of their deeper significance. This is not an intellectual exercise but a concrete experience in which body, mind, and heart participate. There is, however, one particular aspect of the rites of which even the simplest pilgrim can hardly fail to be aware. This is the aspect of continuity or of "primordiality."

Islam stands or falls, not as one religion amongst others, but as the final religion, the synthesis of the great cycle of revelations or "messages" which began at the time of man's creation and ended with the death of Muhammad. For the Muslim, Abraham was a Prophet of God; so was Moses, so was Jesus, and so were countless others whose names are unknown to us. Each played his part in fulfilling the divine promise that mankind would never be left without guidance through the twisting pathways of life in this world. Muhammad differed from the others only by virtue of the finality of the "message" he brought, and this was neither more nor less than the summing-up of all that had come before; in other words, the Muslim sees Islam not as a new religion, a light suddenly projected into the darkness, but as a "reminder" of the primordial faith, the perennial wisdom. It is for this reason that the other religions must, in one way or another, be reflected within Islam. All are beads in a necklace, and the connecting thread remains unbroken. It is in the rites of the Pilgrimage that this continuity is most apparent.

The Quran tells us that the first Ka'bah was built by Abraham and his son Ishmael but, according to legend, this was only a reconstruction, and the first Ka'bah was built by the first Man, Adam. It is said that after his fall from Paradise, Adam journeyed across the earth to the barren valley of Mecca and was commanded to build, in that very place and directly beneath the Throne of God, a temple around which he must then circle just as the angels circle around the Throne. The heavenly Center had already cast its reflection there in the form of a building roofed with one great ruby and supported by columns of emerald, and it was Adam's task to encompass this vision with an earthly "House" made, so we are told, from stones taken from Mount Sinai, the Mount of Olives, Mount Lebanon, and a fourth mountain called al-Judi upon which, long afterwards, Noah's Ark would come to rest. Even in this legend we can recognize without difficulty the element of "synthesis" so essential to Islam, as we can the element of "imitation" (that is to say the imitation of heavenly models or exemplars) which plays such an important part in the rituals of so-called "primitive" peoples.

But, for Muslims, the Ka'bah is above all Abraham's "House." The Patriarch who stands, as it were, at the source of Judaism and Christianity as he does at the source of Islam, came to the Meccan valley long after Adam's temple had been engulfed by the sands, bringing with him his maidservant Hagar and their little son, Ishmael, and here he abandoned mother and child to the divine Mercy. Distraught and thirsty, Hagar left their son in a sheltered place and followed a track which led between two hillocks, Safa and Marwah. From Safa she saw no sign of water or habitation, and from Marwah she saw none. Seven times she ran between the hillocks (as do the pilgrims today), and then she heard the sound of a voice and hastened back to Ishmael. Beside him stood an angel who now struck the earth with his wing so that sweet water gushed from the ground. This was the spring called Zemzem, from which the pilgrims drink today and every day. Here she reared Ishmael, ancestor of the Arab race.

The boy had grown to manhood by the time Abraham returned, and together they set about rebuilding the sacred House, the Ka'bah, repeating Adam's task as all men must, in one way or another, being of Adam's flesh and blood. Ishmael brought the stones on his back while his father set them one upon another without mortar: "And when Abraham and Ishmael raised the foundations of the House they said,— Our Lord, accept this [service] from us, for truly Thou art the All-Hearing, the All-Knowing" (Quran 2:127). And when he left the Hejaz, never to return, Abraham blessed the Meccan valley and prayed: "Our Lord, I have settled a part of my progeny in a barren valley close to Thy sacred House …" (Quran 14:37). "Our Lord, raise up in their midst a Messenger from amongst them who shall recite to them Thy revelations and teach them the Scripture and Wisdom, and purify them" (Quran 2:129).

Modern man tends to be insensitive to the richness of such stories, poking at them obtrusively with a scholar's finger rather than exposing himself to the meaning contained in seemingly simple images. Certain implications are, however, obvious: the "centrality" of the Ka'bah, directly beneath the Throne of God—that is to say, on the axis which connects this earth with all that is above and beyond it; the "primordiality" of the "sacred House," both Adamic and Abrahamic; and finally, its "connectedness," as though invisible threads attached it to the whole history of humanity. But the first aspect of the Pilgrimage which we must consider relates particularly to the concept of primordiality. This is *ihram*, the state of consecration.

Upon arrival, or, if he has come by sea, before actually landing, the pilgrim has a bath, casts aside the clothing which identifies him in this world, and dons the *ihram* garments, two pieces of unsewn cloth (usually white towelling), one knotted around his waist and the other covering his left shoulder but leaving the right shoulder bare. No one, from now on, can tell whether he is a king or a servant. His status is forgotten, as is his place of origin; even the period of history in which he happens to live has been transcended (no doubt Abraham's generation was clothed much as he is) and, insofar as his former identity has disappeared, he has died to the world he knew. The state of consecration also includes certain "bans." The pilgrim must have no sexual contacts once he has assumed this state, he must not wear jewelry or use perfume, he is not permitted to shave or to cut his hair, and, once within the sacred territory, he is forbidden to kill any living creature (unless it threatens human life) or to uproot any plant. It is not only the territory as such that is sacred; everything within its boundaries partakes of the same other-worldly quality, and it is significant that women—so often veiled in the Arab world—are forbidden to veil themselves while on pilgrimage. It might be said that there is, in the face of a beautiful woman, a foretaste of paradise, something that must be concealed from the vulgar gaze but exposed when the conditions of common life are suspended.

All preparations having been completed, the pilgrim sets out for the Ka'bah in Mecca, crying *Labbayka Allahumma* ("Here am I, O God, at Thy service!") again and again. He is, in a sense, coming home. Throughout his life, assuming that he is pious, he will have prayed five times each day facing in the direction of the Ka'bah and, very possibly, visualizing it in his mind's eye. On his journey he has, so to speak, followed the straight line which always connected his prayer-mat with this building. He is now approaching journey's end, having traveled in body the course previously spanned by mind and heart. The unitarian nature of Islam requires that the whole man should participate in the rites which lead to God for, if the body is left out of any spiritual act, then that act is incomplete; there is no integration, no unity. But the concept of homecoming relates essentially to the esoteric perspective. From this point of view, the human creature is an exile in this world (it is for this reason that our lives here are never entirely free from conflict and disharmony), at home only in close proximity to God. This proximity is, at the very least, prefigured in a place that is primordially sacred, "out of this world." In such a place as this, proximity is realized as concrete experience.

At the same time—and still from the esoteric point of view—the physical journey is neither more nor less than an outward enactment of an interior journey, the journey from the periphery of our being to the center, the Heart which, for Islam, is the point at which the vertical and the horizontal meet, the point at which the Divine intersects with the human. In our everyday experience we are not ourselves; we are exiles from the center in which the two dimensions meet, and we have a passionate desire—expressed, only too often, in irrelevant frenzies—to find ourselves. One way of doing so is to follow, outwardly and in the body, the trajectory which the troubled and dispersed soul must follow if it is to return to its own hidden center, its true selfhood, the Heart.

For the outward to mold the inward, it is not necessary that the individual should be fully aware of what is happening or express his experience in concepts. The pilgrim enters through one of the doorways into the vast amphitheater which has the Ka'bah at its center, and he or she is overwhelmed. This small building has a quality of majesty which even Western sophisticates, despite their need to analyze experience, have difficulty in defining. It is *there*. It *is*. Some may think of the Buddhist term translated as "is-ness"; others will be content with their own astonishment. The Ka'bah is, in fact, a cubic structure some fifteen meters high and twelve by thirteen meters square. It is "clothed" in a canopy freshly woven each year in Egypt, which is embroidered at the hem with verses from the Quran and, elsewhere, with the constantly reiterated Name of God, *Allah*, the golden calligraphy standing out against its dark background like light emerging from darkness. It must be added that the building has been reconstructed many times over the centuries, and yet the pilgrim has the sense of an eternal presence, a massive foursquare solidity which neither earthquake nor tempest could ever shake.

The first rite of the Pilgrimage, which will be repeated on two further occasions in the course of five days, is the *tawaf*, the circumambulation.

The pilgrim circles the Ka'bah, which may now be seen as the perfect image of the "motionless Mover," seven times and, in doing so, he is carried along in a human flood which is reminiscent of the symbolism of the Wheel of Existence turning upon its axis. Life as such may be defined as movement, and movement is of three kinds: towards the goal (centripetal) which represents its finality, or away from the goal (centrifugal) in dispersion and disintegration, or, finally, circular as though attached to the goal by an invisible thread, neither absorbed into it nor losing touch with it. We have, therefore, in the circumambulation, an image of human life when that life is held in balance by the magnetic force of the Principle which resides in the center. It is a short step from this to comparing the circumambulation to the circling of the planets in the "seven heavens," planets which—according to the esoterists—symbolize modalities of the human state in the domain of subtle manifestation, and this is the more apt because the pilgrims' movement is "polar" (that is to say, anti-clockwise). The symbolism of the number seven as such is universal; one need only think of the Biblical text, "God blessed the seventh day and sanctified it. ..." It represents repose in the divine Center, peace and perfection.

On each circuit the pilgrim will, if he can, kiss the Black Stone which is embedded in one corner of the Ka'bah. If the press of people is too great for him to reach it, then he greets it with a raised right hand each time he passes the corner. For the strict exoterist, the only significance of this rite is that he places his lips where those of the Prophet once rested, but many legends surround the stone—which is oval-shaped, about eighteen centimeters in diameter, and set in a mesh of silver wire. According to some, Adam found it in the celestial temple which was the model for the original Ka'bah, but then it was pure white, unstained by human sin. According to others, it was brought from heaven by the Archangel Gabriel, and the scientists say that it is a meteorite, which is merely another way of ascribing to it a celestial origin. For the mystics, it represents "the Right Hand of God," and this lends a special significance to the act of kissing (the Sufi always greets his sheikh, his Spiritual Guide, by kissing his right hand).

Although it is only at the time of the Great Pilgrimage that a vast mass of men and women circle the Ka'bah, there is no time of the year, day or night, when the courtyard is still and the movement ceases, except during the performance of the ritual prayer. This breaks the flow just as—within the individual soul—the flow of thoughts which circle the Heart is halted during the prayer. The circumambulation takes place in time, as do our thought processes, and prayer is in essence outside time or, at the very least, an encounter with the timeless.

But life goes on. The pilgrim, having completed his tawaf, proceeds to the second rite of the Pilgrimage, the *Sa'y*. This is the walking (and, at one point, running) between the hillocks of Safa and Marwah, the same outcrops of rock between which Hagar hastened in search of water for her son. They stand now at the two ends of a covered gallery close to the Ka'bah, and the pilgrim covers the course between them seven times in imitation of Hagar's search. That, at least, is the exoteric explanation of this rite, but the esoterists have explored its significance in much greater depth in the light of certain ancient legends. There is, for example, the story of two young lovers in pre-Islamic times who are said to have profaned the Ka'bah and who were, in consequence, turned to stone, the one at Safa and the other at Marwah. The man's name relates to an Arabic root which has the sense of "regret" and "sadness," while the girl's name suggests "favor and fulfillment," and this is related to the idea that the pilgrim starts his course in a state of sadness on account of his sins and ends it by finding fulfillment and release. There is also a legend to the effect that Adam and Eve, long parted from each other after their fall from Paradise, were reunited here, but not before they had been compelled to stand for a long period, Adam at Safa and Eve at Marwah, forbidden to come together until released by the Archangel Gabriel.

Whatever we make of these stories, the implication is that these hillocks represent the two poles of existence, active and passive, male and female, or, in the Far Eastern tradition, *yang* and *yin*. As he hastens between them, the pilgrim unites the two poles within himself. Duality, which is the source of all movement and all phenomena, must constantly return—or be returned—to Unity, its origin and its end.

Up to this point, we have treated the Ka'bah as the goal of the Pilgrimage, and this is so in the case of the "Lesser Pilgrimage," called the *Umra* or "Visit" (which may be performed at any time of the year). Yet the Prophet Muhammad said, *al-hajj Arafa*, meaning "the Pilgrimage is [to] Arafat," and it is towards Mount Arafat— an up-jutting of stone in the desert beyond Mecca—that the river of pilgrims flows after the rite of the Sa'y has been completed. The pilgrim tents cover the valley and plain around the "mount," and it is here that the Pilgrimage reaches its climax. To understand why this should be so we must necessarily turn to the esoteric teachings.

Anyone familiar with the writings of René Guénon (which may be described as a *Summa* of traditional symbolism) may at once surmise that we are concerned here with the two journeys, the one "horizontal" and the other "vertical," described in traditional metaphysics as also in the mythologies of many different peoples. The first spiritual journey is to the center of the human individuality, the second is towards all that lies beyond this individuality and, ultimately, to Reality as such. The spirit can mount upwards only from one "place"—one "springboard"—and that place is the center which is on the vertical axis joining all possible states of being; or, to put the matter another way, man cannot seek to realize the higher states of being, let alone to be united with his eternal Source, until he has achieved unity and wholeness within himself. Until every aspect of his human nature has been harmonized in relation to the center, the Heart, he is too divided within himself to be capable of undertaking the "second journey."

A number of traditions make a distinction between "Perfect Man" and "Universal Man." The former is one who has reached the conclusion of the first journey, whereas the latter has completed the second, transcending himself and achieving universality. In terms of this doctrine, it may be said that the Ka'bah has two faces. On the one hand it is the center of pilgrimage for those whose religion is called "Islam" and is of significance only to this particular religion; on the other, its connection with Abraham (according to the Quran) and even with Adam (according to legend) makes it a universal center—or simply The Center. The Andalusian mystic, Ibn Arabi, pointed out that the Ka'bah is orientated towards Arafat through the location of the Black Stone in the angle which points that way and, from this point of view, the Ka'bah is like a door opening onto the universal. But the name of the religion itself has this same duality. First we have "Islam" and its followers, the "Muslims"; secondly there is *al-islam*, meaning "submission" or "surrender" (to God), and every creature in this world is *muslim*, that is to say subject to God. Animals "submit" by following their instincts, even a stone "submits" when it falls in accordance with the law of gravity. The only difference is that those who describe themselves as "Muslims" submit willingly and consciously and try to cooperate with divinely willed Destiny which, in any case, none can escape.

For the ordinary pilgrim, who is unlikely to be concerned with metaphysics, the *Wuquf*—that is to say, the "standing" at Arafat—is a prefiguration of the Last Judgment. The vast multitude of which he is one small component now stands before God in this barren desert landscape, just as all men will stand before Him at the end of time, every action they ever did exposed under an all-encompassing radiance.

No more can be said of this since Arafat represents what would be described in certain other traditions as the Void, and the verbal equivalent of this total emptiness is silence. But two other Pilgrimage rites require some brief mention. The first is the animal sacrifice which follows the "standing." On the exoteric level, this takes place in imitation of Abraham's sacrifice of the ram in place of his dearly loved son and is a reminder of the divine mercy which made this substitution possible. On a deeper level, it represents a symbolic sacrifice of the body, and, concerning the animals that are sacrificed, the Quran tells us: "It is not the flesh that reaches God nor is it their blood. It is your piety that reaches Him" (Quran 22:37).

The second of these rites is the stoning of the pillars at Mina, pillars which represent Satan or the forces of evil which operate both within and outside ourselves. This, too, is in imitation of Abraham's action when Satan tempted him to disobey his Lord. Each time Satan approached, so we are told, the Patriarch drove him off by casting pebbles at him. Each pilgrim therefore gathers either forty-nine (seven times seven) or seventy small stones and throws these at the pillars with as much force as he can muster. In doing so he purifies himself. With each throw he destroys—or hopes to destroy—some of the shadows, the temptations and evil impulses within his own soul.

Such are the principal rites of the *Hajj*, the Great Pilgrimage, which each year brings together Muslims of every race "from each distant point" (as the Quran has it) in performance of the fifth Pillar of their religion and in the hope of forgiveness and mercy from God.

Parabola
Volume: 24.2
Prayer and
Meditation

Moses and the Shepherd

Rumi

Moses heard a shepherd on the road praying, "God,"
where are You? I want to help You, to fix Your shoes
and comb Your hair. I want to wash Your clothes
and pick the lice off. I want to bring You milk,
to kiss Your little hands and feet when it's time
for You to go to bed. I want to sweep Your room
and keep it neat. God, my sheep and goats
are Yours. All I can say, remembering You,
is *ayyyy* and *ahhhhhhhhh*."

Moses could stand it no longer.
"*Who* are you talking to?"

"The One who made us,
and made the earth and made the sky."

"Don't talk about shoes
and socks with God! And what's this with *Your little hands
and feet?* Such blasphemous familiarity sounds like
you're chatting with your uncles.

Only something that grows needs milk.
Only someone with feet needs shoes. Not God! Even if
you meant God's human representatives
as when God said, 'I was sick, and you did not visit me,'
even then this tone would be foolish and irreverent.

Use appropriate terms. *Fatima* is a fine name
for a woman, but if you call a man *Fatima*,

it's an insult. Body-and-birth language
are right for us on this side of the river,
but not for addressing the Origin,
               not for Allah."

The shepherd repented and tore his clothes and sighed
and wandered out into the desert.
               A sudden revelation
came then to Moses. God's voice:

You have separated Me
from one of my own. Did you come as a Prophet to unite,
or to sever?
               I have given each being a separate and unique way
of seeing and knowing and saying that knowledge.

What seems wrong to you is right for him.
What is poison to one is honey to someone else.

Purity and impurity, sloth and diligence in worship,
these mean nothing to Me.
               I am apart from all that.
Ways of worshipping are not to be ranked as better
or worse than one another.
               Hindus do Hindu things.
The Dravidian Muslims in India do what they do.
It's all praise, and it's all right.

It's not Me that's glorified in acts of worship.
It's the worshippers! I don't hear the words
they say. I look at the humility.

That broken-open lowliness is the Reality,
not the language! Forget phraseology.
I want burning, burning.
               Be Friends
with your burning. *Burn up your thinking*

and your forms of expression!
Moses,
those who pay attention to ways of behaving
and speaking are one sort.
Lovers who burn
are another.

Don't impose a property tax
on a burned out village. Don't scold the Lover.
The "wrong" way he talks is better than a hundred
"right" ways of others.
Inside the Kaaba
it doesn't matter which direction you point
your prayer rug!
The ocean diver doesn't need snowshoes!
The Love-Religion has no code or doctrine.
Only God.
So the ruby has nothing engraved on it!
It doesn't need markings.
God began speaking
deeper mysteries to Moses. Vision and words,
which cannot be recorded here, poured into
and through him. He left himself and came back.
He went to Eternity and came back here.
Many times this happened.
It's foolish of me
to try and say this. If I did say it,
it would uproot our human intelligences.
It would shatter all writing pens.

Moses ran after the shepherd.
He followed the bewildered footprints,
in one place moving straight like a castle
across a chessboard. In another, sideways,
like a bishop.
Now surging like a wave cresting,
now sliding down like a fish,

with always his feet
making geomancy symbols in the sand,
                recording
his wandering state.
             Moses finally caught up
with him.
         "I was wrong. God has revealed to me
that there are no rules for worship.
                 Say whatever
and however your loving tells you to. Your sweet blasphemy
is the truest devotion. Through you a whole world
is freed.
             Loosen your tongue and don't worry what comes out.
It's all the Light of the Spirit."
              The shepherd replied,
"Moses, Moses,
            I've gone beyond even that.
You applied the whip and my horse shied and jumped
out of itself. The Divine Nature and my human nature
came together.
             Bless your scolding hand and your arm.
I can't say what has happened.
              What I'm saying now
is not my real condition. It can't be said."

The shepherd grew quiet.
            When you look in a mirror,
you see yourself, not the state of the mirror.
The fluteplayer puts breath into a flute,
and who makes the music? Not the flute.
The Fluteplayer!
            Whenever you speak praise
or thanksgiving to God, it's always like this
dear shepherd's simplicity.
               When you eventually see
through the veils of how things really are,
you will keep saying again

and again,
    "This is certainly not like
we thought it was!"

Mathnawi, II, 1720-96, from *This Longing: Poetry, Teaching Stories, and Selected Letters,* translated by Coleman Barks and John Moyne (Putney, VT: Threshold Books, 1988), pp. 19-22.

•

CHAPTER TWO

LIVING IN SOCIETY

The true saint goes in and out amongst the people and eats and sleeps
with them and buys and sells in the market and marries and takes part in
social intercourse, and never forgets God for a single moment.[1]

—Abu Sa'id Abi'l-Khayr

"The Sufi is he
whose thought keeps pace
with his foot."

He is entirely present:
his soul is where his body is,
and his body is where his soul is,

and his soul is where his foot is,
and his foot is where his soul is.

This is the sign
of presence without absence.[2]

—Hujwiri

Parabola
Volume: 9.1
Hierarchy

A Prayer

He who knows, and does not know that he knows:
He is asleep.
Let him become one, whole.
Let him become awakened.

He who has known, but does not know:
Let him see once more
The beginning of all.

He who does not wish to know,
Yet says that he wants to know:
Let him be guided
To safety and to light.

He who does not know,
And knows that he does not know:
Let him through this knowledge, know.

He who does not know, but thinks that he knows:
Set him free
From the confusion
Of that ignorance.

He who knows, and knows that *he* is:
He is wise.
Let him be followed.

By his presence alone man may be transformed.

I who know, and do not know that I know:
Let me become whole.
Let me be awakened.

I who have known, but do not know:
Let me once more see
The beginning of all.

I who do not wish to know,
But still say that I wish to know:
Let me be guided
To safety and to light.

I who do not know,
And know that I do not know:
Let me through this knowledge, know.

I who do not know, but think that I know:
Set me free
From the confusion
Of that ignorance.

He who knows, and knows that *he* is:
He is wise.
Let him be followed.
By his presence alone man may be transformed.

We who know, and do not know that we know:
Let us become one, whole.
Let us be transformed.

We who have known, but do not know:
Let us once more see
The beginning of all.

We who do not wish to know,
But still say that we want to know:
Let us be guided
To safety and to light.

We who do not know,
And know that we do not know:
Let us through this knowledge, know.

We who do not know, but think that we know:
Set us free
From the confusion
Of that ignorance.

He who knows, and knows that *he* is:
He is wise.
Let him be followed
By his presence alone man may be transformed.

.

As with our forebears
So with our successors
So with us
We affirm this undertaking
So let it be.

—Anonymous

This ancient, anonymous prayer is known throughout the Islamic world. According to tradition, it is composed of several hadiths of the Prophet Muhammad, "strung together like pearls on a necklace."

Parabola
Volume: 15.2
Attention

The Revolving Wall

Gai Eaton

There is a Sufi story which I read so many years ago that I have forgotten where I found it. Once upon a time there was a man who had been inattentive throughout his life. After passing through the trauma of death he found himself seated facing a high wall which revolved gradually before his eyes, and it was made known to him that once every thousand years a gate would come level with where he sat, the gate leading into Paradise, momentarily open to him. He must wait in patience for that moment and then seize the opportunity to step into eternal joy. There is, the Quran tells us, just such a wall separating the blessed from the condemned, "a wall wherein is a gate; the inner side encompasses grace and mercy, the outer faces towards perdition" (57:13).

For 999 years, eleven months and many days this man—or this being who had been a man on earth—waited patiently, never taking his eyes from the wall which revolved inch by inch before him. No other thought occupied his mind but the prospect of the Garden, its palaces, its peerless maidens, and its delicious fruits. But there came a moment when some distraction diverted his attention; a memory, perhaps, of the world he had left behind. His attention wavered, and it was in this moment that the gate drew level with the place of waiting and

●

then continued on its unending round. Another thousand years of attentiveness lay before him.

Speaking of those whose attention has been focused elsewhere, the Quran says: "They forgot *Allah*, therefore He forgot them" (9:67). We speak of the insane as having lost touch with reality, and that is a misfortune, but to lose touch with the One Reality is a disaster so momentous that we cannot even assess its extent. This "losing touch," this inattention, is defined by Islam in terms of "forgetfulness." We are born with an awareness of that ultimate Reality. It is embedded in us, indeed—according to the great Andalusian mystic Ibn al-Arabi—it is embedded in all living things, including the animals and the plants. But we are busy. There is so much to distract us in this world, just as the man who sat watching the revolving wall was distracted. We forget and therefore we stand in grave danger of being forgotten.

According to a *hadith qudsi*, one of the sayings of Muhammad in which God spoke directly through his mouth, "I am with My servant when he remembers Me." Significantly, this *hadith* continues: "If he draws near to Me a hand's span, I draw near to him an arm's length; and if he draws near to Me an arm's length, I draw near to him a fathom's length; and if he comes to Me walking, I go to him speedily." To forget God is to be absent from Him, and if this forgetfulness becomes habitual, then the absence is perpetual. On the other hand, the reward for "remembrance," called *dhikr* in Arabic, is beyond measure. To remember is to attend, and attention is not static. It is, by its very nature, an act and therefore a movement towards its object, a movement of the intellect, the will, and the emotions. Life offers no better example of this than the attentiveness of a predatory animal stalking its prey, unless it be that of an archer about to loose his arrow or a rifleman with his finger on the trigger. In this, stillness and movement are one single act.

To pay attention, to wake up, is to be wholly here and now, and it is only here in this place and now at this moment that God is to be found or the encounter with reality consummated. We cannot act in the past, which has been filed away and sealed, or in the unborn future, but, here and now, we are miraculously free to focus attention on the chosen target. This is essentially an act of orientation.

Correct orientation requires the gift of sight if we are to see where we are going. The Quran repeatedly contrasts the "seeing" with the "blind" on the spiritual level and warns us that "those who are blind will be blind hereafter" (17:72), but this is the blindness of those who refuse to see what is truly to be seen, "having hearts wherewith they understand not, and having eyes wherewith they see not, and having ears wherewith they hear not. These are as cattle—No, they are worse. They are the heedless" (7:179). Cattle see well enough, but the focus of their attention is the patch of grass before them.

It can hardly be a coincidence that the Quran speaks of the damned "drinking as the camel drinks" (56:55) and asks, elsewhere: "Is he who goes groping on his face better guided than he who walks upright on a straight way?" (67:22). The reference to those who live only for this world and its patches of grass seems obvious. Those who "walk upright" see what is ahead, far ahead, and they take the path indicated by their orientation. The rest, their attention misplaced, walk on all fours, "worse than cattle" because they have no right to live beneath the human level, the fully sighted level of men and women who walk upright.

The secular world assumes that we were born free, without obligations beyond the social requirements which come with maturity. Islam denies this and condemns those who live as cattle. They have broken a solemn compact. This implication of "pre-existence" is obscure and remains unexplained by exoteric doctrine, but the Sufis, recognizing that an eternal soul or nucleus must have had its beginning before time was created, teach that we have always been "possibilities" within the divine Essence, hidden in a darkness which is also light beyond all imaginable light. It is, then, as hidden seeds that we committed ourselves to acts of worship and of recognition which are, in practice, acts of attention.

All that I have said up to this point invites misunderstanding. It might be supposed that, in paying attention wholly to That which lies beyond this little theater of existence, the Muslim ignores or forgets the world of grassy patches which preoccupies the cattle. He does not ignore it, but he sees it transfigured. He sees phenomena—or hopes to see them—as they really are, that is to say as "signs" of God.

The central principle of Islam is *Tawhid*, Oneness. The barriers which separate one level of reality from another, including the separation of the physical from the spiritual, exist only in our own minds and for our convenience. The Quran tells us to look upon the heavens: "Do you see any rifts? Turn thy vision (upon them) again, and yet again; thy vision will fall back upon thee, dazzled …" (67:3-4). But this is true of the All as such. Between the highest and the lowest there are no "rifts," no separating walls except those that logic requires for its operation. This is made apparent to us, not in the form of a unity which our minds could not comprehend, but through the "signs" which reflect the divine light on earth, and everything is potentially a "sign."

The world is a vast fabric woven out of them. Our attentiveness, if we are wisely attentive, is not to raw objects in their material opacity but to the realities—or the "reminders" of Reality—which shine through them. "See!" says the Quran. "In the heavens and the earth are signs for those who have faith. And in your creation and in all the beasts that He has scattered upon the earth are signs for those whose faith is sure. And in the difference of night and day and the provision which *Allah* sends down from the heavens, thereby quickening the earth after her death, and in the ordering of the winds are signs for people of understanding" (45:3-5).

The rain, the winds, the green earth and the profusion of life upon it— these are great things and bear witness to their Creator. But the Quran tells us also that "*Allah* disdains not to coin the similitude even of a gnat" (2:26), so nothing is too small to be a "sign" and therefore, at least potentially, a door opening onto all that lies beyond this place; and whatever we perceive as a door is worthy of our serious attention. The man who waited a thousand years before the revolving wall might not have had to wait more than a moment if his vision had been more penetrating.

We may, if we choose to do so, go a step further and add that the "signs" are discoverable not only in objects but also in events. If, as Islam teaches, every event has its source in God and is, in fact, a thread in a vast pattern which points back to Him, then nothing that happens is insignificant. This includes the meeting of human creatures one with another, and attentiveness to the other person—who may himself be a "sign" for us—must be seen as a religious duty. There is, indeed, a miraculous quality in the very fact of meeting, given the nature of these egos, each inhabiting its own world, each a unique center protected, as it were, by a circular wall. The fiery stars do not meet. They would explode. Yet men and women meet and even communicate with each other across the vast space which separates them. In doing so they fulfill a destiny established before the foundations of the heavens and the earth were laid down. There can be no such thing as a "chance" meeting—not even an encounter with a stranger in the street—and the fact that we are, for the most part, unaware of this does not affect the issue. The landscape does not vanish because a blind man cannot see it, and our partial blindness, our inattentiveness, does not affect reality, which is what it is.

With the passage of time our sight degenerates, as is the nature of such afflictions. Those who live in teeming cities do not greet one another. In treeless corridors of concrete, awareness of the natural world, and therefore of the "signs" inherent in nature, is lost. Rich beyond the dreams of our ancestors, we are impoverished and increasingly isolated in a selfhood which no longer knows where to seek for doors and windows. This is apparent in the work we do and must do to survive. If anything in this world is trivial, and therefore unworthy of our attention, it is to be found here.

In a traditional Islamic society—and still in many parts of the Muslim world—a commercial transaction is, in the first place, a genuine meeting between persons who exchange greetings, blessings, and news. Only when they have truly *met* and communicated will they get down to the less important business of bargaining. It is hardly necessary to contrast this with a "business meeting" in our sector of the world, a meeting in which there is no meeting because "business" and "private life" are rigidly separated. If coffee is served and cookies are handed around, this means nothing. It is no eucharist. Yet the breaking of bread in company, cementing relationships by the taking of God-given nourishment, was, in the past, a kind of sacrament.

One of the names by which God has made himself known to us in the Quran is *ar-Razzaq*, "the Nourisher," and, as a "sign" to remind us constantly of the spiritual nourishment by which our souls subsist, He gives us the food and drink our bodies need; these are two facets of a single gift. To be inattentive to this gift, whatever form it takes, is ingratitude and heedlessness. Here again we are impoverished, as too is the worker whose hands are no longer skilled in a craft but serve only to press buttons in an automated factory or manipulate articles on a conveyor belt. The craftsman's attention is no less focused than that of the archer and, in every culture in the past, his function has been a sacred one, closely related to prayer.

So much has been lost, and these deprivations have removed the supports of prayer and contemplation. Direct communion with God—or with transcendent Reality—cannot be isolated from the rest of life and, when this is desacralized and trivialized, prayer itself is no longer at home in the world. The events and the things that present themselves to us for our attention materialize out of the void and dissolve back into it, but not before they have pointed away from themselves towards a Center, an enduring Reality, which must then be the object of our full attention. It is in prayer and in what, in Islam, is called *dhikr*—the constant remembrance of God—that the different threads are brought together, multiplicity is absorbed into unity, and dreaming gives way to full wakefulness.

Ultimately the signs to which we have given our attention point away from themselves, as though in an act of self-sacrifice. We attend to them as we attend to a signpost on the road, then we go on our way. Prayer, taken in its widest sense (to include invocation and the various methods of contemplation) is of a different order. Previously, guided by the "signs," we were in motion; now we are in stillness, we are where we belong. But this place of prayer, wherever it may be, is open to the sky and the earth; we have brought with us all that we gathered on the road, both the events and the things, and they are fulfilled through us. Man does not pray for himself alone—sometimes he prays least of all for himself—but for all creation. He alone is articulate, capable of conscious prayer and attentiveness.

Here in the place of prayer and now at the time of prayer attention is, as it were, crystallized by its object, the divine reality which, being what it is, draws us out of ourselves and unifies our turbulent and divided nature. At the same time it reveals the hidden unity of the phenomena, the "signs," with which we have been occupied.

The Muslim is commanded to pray to God "as if you saw Him because, though you see Him not, yet He sees you." At the center, after the wayfaring, attention is mutual between God and man, between eternity and time. Beyond this mutuality it is one single act, transcending all distinctions. The last word is Unity and, after that, there is no more to be said.

Parabola
Volume: 29.2
Web of Life

OUT OF THE HIDDEN ROOT

Baha'uddin Walad

The following are excerpts from the Ma'arif, *a collection of writings by the Sufi religious leader Baha'uddin Walad (1152-1231), father of the mystic poet Rumi. A diary-like record of his inner life, the* Ma'arif *gathers together visionary insights, stories, commentaries on the Quran, gardening and medicinal advice, and musings on many subjects, both earthly and divine.*

Eating a Piece of Bread

While you are eating a piece of bread, try to recall the events that collaborated to let this take place. The oven's heat that baked the bread, the plowed earth before that, sunlight, rain, harvest, the winnowing, the being carried to and from the mill, the complex idea and the building of the mill itself. The many motions of weather in the turning of four seasons. And don't forget the knife that cuts the bread, the metallurgy and the skill of forging that blade, and your teeth, those original grinding devices. Then there's your stomach digesting the crust and there's the rest of your body being nourished, each part in unique ways.

Two hundred and forty-eight bones, five hundred and thirty muscles, three hundred arteries, ligaments, tendons, cartilage, your organs and limbs, your brain. As the bread dissolves, many intelligences within you are deciding and peacefully agreeing on how to divide the benefits. If there were discord, you would feel pain and cry out, but you don't.

Now notice the unified human awareness thoughtfully living inside your body with a soul in communion with other spirit-intelligences. Observe how it sits at the junction of two worlds as a human being looking with kindness on other human beings. Some say this is the culmination of the body's long development and the beginning of the next transformation, that you that live with gratitude for food and thankfulness also for any difficulty, pain, or sudden disappointment, seeing those too as grace, that you live inside and outside time as an angelic breadeating witness taking in this myriad convergence of providential motions and that you are in yourself an individual soul being made from divine wisdom.

Bread and Praise

I was thinking about the piece of bread I have just eaten and the drink of water I have taken. This revelation came: Each bit of bread and taste of fruit has a tongue and a language of praise that gets released when it enters a human body.

The same analogy of transformation extends to the influences that came from the stars and transmuted matter into the elements: earth, air, ether, fire, and water. Those in turn became plants which became animals, then human beings with their flexible way of speaking that can become praise for the compassion as well as the anger of God.

Rigid and Ethereal

Looking at hardpacked clay, the clods in it like rocks, I am amazed at the miraculous variety God grows out of it; not just greenery, but our lives, these intelligent friendships and love, awareness and soul, the method of water inside the ground—there are so many delicate extrusions and enthusiasms pouring through the harsh matrix of this high desert plain. Think of the thick metallic petals that close around the soft cotton fiber.

The mystery arranges what is rigid and what is ethereal so that they work together. If there is a shortage of density, it transforms porous to bricklike, the model being the way climatic moisture loosens a tight-shut seed, then how the plant that grows from that seed draws up and holds *encased* the ambient rain.

Still Growing

Inside and outside my body I see clear cold streams beside the flowers, and after I die, the corpse will find its way back to those and the soft air around them. Our soul-seeds come from the invisible, and here we are, still growing. We fade and go to seed. We die. New seeds slip into the ground of the unseen, each to grow its own unique lineage beside the water. God provides this continuing.

Quran 64:14 reminds us that there may be enemies among those close to us. Be careful, and remember that when you forgive and overlook insults, you are letting grace dissolve resentment.

The Two Trees

The world is a tree growing from a jewelseed planted in raw nothingness. Its roots are water and wind, its trunk the earth. Its branches the sky, its leaf-tips the stars, none of which resemble the original seed. Oak trees do not look like acorns. Each tree, every growing thing, has two roots, one in the visible, another in the unseen. Many acknowledge only this visible. They do not understand that the juice, the taste, the thickness of the trunk, and other qualities come not from this palpable place but from the mystery, out of the hidden root. Now, there is another tree. It has roots here and branches and fruit in the unseen. That is the tree we call surrender, submission, *islam*.

Planets and Plants

By the stars that leave and come back (86:11), by the ground that opens to let plants grow (86:12), planets are both star and plant. They open to let starlight reach into us here, and plants are like planetary bodies, moving through the seasons, and nobody knows where they go when they die.

Someone wakes at dawn confused. Why should the sky be the cause and the earth the affected? Why not the other way?

Every star is a leaf-tip on the sky-tree, whose leaves are the size of a country, with the nightsky turning under the sun's leaf. It will not be surprising in the spirit if a great assembly gathers under a leaf, leaves there being many times the size of this universe.

From *The Drowned Book: Ecstatic and Earthly Reflections of Bahauddin, the Father of Rumi,* translated by Coleman Barks and John Moyne (San Francisco: HarperSanFrancisco, 2004), pp. 9, 24, 75-76, 86, 124, 130.

Parabola
Volume: 25.4
Fate and Fortune

"…AND A LITTLE FROM ABDULLAH"

Carol Ring

Kullu min Allah…
u'shwaya min Abdullah.
(All is from Allah…
and a little from Abdullah.)

The first part of this saying is frequently spoken by elder Bedouin, usually in cases of misfortune, and is accompanied by a shrug of the shoulders. All is from Allah: fortune and adversity, joy and suffering, life and death. All is determined, all is written. There is an Intelligence at work that keeps this vast universe in order and determines the role and path of each particle of its infinitude. Like the cells in a body, we live and die in service of something incomparably larger.

And yet, we have become an odd type of cell that believes unshakably in its own existence as apart from the whole. Today, the "Kullu min Allah" view seems quaintly fatalistic and a disclaimer of personal responsibility. We have come to value above all else our power and our right to determine, if not the outcome of what we do, at least the direction and content of our lives. We believe firmly that we form our own fate. If things seem to go contrary to our wishes, it is because we have not been vocal enough in asserting them, or strong enough to conquer obstacles.

We are not ones to trust in blind forces, and certainly not in any divine representatives of those forces.

If "Kullu min Allah" were the whole story—and until about the end of the Middle Ages it seemed to be the whole story—the only empowerment that could manifest in our lives would come through the all-powerful One, and, on a lesser scale, through His representatives on earth: kings, priests, and other beings high in the hierarchy. When these were true representatives and their moral influence spread throughout society, the earth flourished, and presumably humankind's suffering was alleviated (although a large part of our suffering seems to be inevitable, no matter how well the earth is yielding). But slowly humanity removed the crown from the hierarchy and placed it on its own head, giving consummate authority first to human will, and then eventually to human impulses, unhampered by either reason or conscience. And so, from the old belief in fate and invisible forces, we have swung around to a belief in ourselves as the sole force at work in the universe.

Throughout the ages the debate on fate versus free will has been ongoing, and each tradition has had its say on the way things work. Most have struck a wise compromise, giving the individual a chance to improve his or her lot by doing good while leaving fate in place for the big questions. But the compromise suggested by "and a little bit from Abdullah"—an addition uttered after an appropriate pause, and in a lower voice, generally by younger Bedouin—is particularly apt for all of us. First of all, it gets the relationship right. *Everything* is from Allah—not most things, not only the important things or the good things, but Everything. The grandeur and omnipotence of the Invisible retain their priority: we are under the influence of forces that we neither control nor see, but we have our place as an integral part of the whole. But though everything is still determined from above and perfect submission is our role, there is the addition of "a little bit" that is our own theater of action. It is as if the Everything expands just a little and makes room for a personal effort, which still remains part of the All. The exact nature of the little bit is not specified; each can project his own understanding.

And who does this little bit? Abdullah. The name is a joining of two words, "abd" and "Allah," and means "servant of God." It is not just any one of the myriad personages that inhabit our bodies who is called upon to contribute his share, but the part of us that truly tries to serve something higher.

It is difficult to know whether or not our lives have been determined in advance, whether it is foretold where and when we will be born, when and how we will die, and what we will do in the interim. Some believe, some guess, and some ignore the question. It is even more difficult to stand at one of life's many crossroads, or even one of the little alleyways that are always running across our paths, and wait one second before turning left or right. Is there someone steering the course? Is it the winds of fate or only a momentary impulse? Perhaps it is Abdullah who holds the compass.

Parabola
Volume: 7.4
Holy War

THE SPIRITUAL SIGNIFICANCE OF JIHAD

Seyyed Hossein Nasr

And those who perform jihad for Us, We shall certainly guide them in Our ways, and God is surely with the doers of good.
—*Quran 39:69*

You have returned from the lesser jihad to the greater jihad.
—*Hadith*

The Arabic term *jihad*, usually translated into European languages as "holy war," more on the basis of its juridical usage in Islam rather than on its much more universal meaning in the Quran and *Hadith*, is derived from the root *jhd* whose primary meaning is "to strive or to exert oneself." Its translation into "holy war," combined with the erroneous notion of Islam prevalent in the West as the "religion of the sword," has helped to eclipse its inner and spiritual significance and to distort its connotation. Nor has the appearance upon the stage of history during the past century, and especially during the past few years, of an array of movements within the Islamic world, often contending or even opposing each other and using the word jihad or one of its derivative forms, helped to make known the full import of its traditional meaning, which alone is of concern to us here. Instead recent distortions and even total reversals of the meaning of jihad as understood over the ages by Muslims have made it more difficult than ever before to gain insight into this key religious and spiritual concept.

To understand the spiritual significance of jihad and its wide application to nearly every aspect of human life as understood by Islam, it is necessary to remember that Islam bases itself upon the idea of establishing equilibrium within the being of man as well as in the human society where he functions and fulfills the goals of his earthly life. This equilibrium, which is the terrestrial reflection of Divine Justice and the necessary condition for peace in the human domain, is the basis upon which the soul takes its flight towards that peace which, to use Christian terms, "passeth understanding." If Christian morality sees the aim of the spiritual life and its own morality as based on the vertical flight towards that perfection and ideal which is embodied in Christ, Islam sees it in the establishment of an equilibrium both outward and inward as the necessary basis for the vertical ascent. The very stability of Islamic society over the centuries, the immutability of Islamic norms embodied in the *Shari'ah* (or Divine Law), and the timeless character of traditional Islamic civilization, which is the consequence of its permanent and immutable prototype, are all reflections of both the ideal of equilibrium and its realization. The teachings of the Shari'ah as well as works of Islamic art reflect that equilibrium which is inseparable from the very name of *islam* as being related to *salam* or peace.

The preservation of equilibrium in this world, however, does not mean simply a static or inactive passivity, since life by nature implies movement. In the face of the contingencies of the world of change, of the withering effects of time, of the vicissitudes of terrestrial existence, to remain in equilibrium requires continuous exertion. It means carrying out jihad at every stage of life. Human nature being what it is, given to forgetfulness and the conquest of our immortal soul by the carnal soul or passions, the very process of life of both the individual and the human collectivity implies the ever-present danger of the loss of equilibrium and in fact of falling into the state of disequilibrium, which if allowed to continue cannot but lead to disintegration on the individual level and chaos on the scale of community life. To avoid this tragic end and to fulfill the entelechy of the human state, which is the realization of unity (*tawhid*) or total integration, Muslims, as both individuals and members of Islamic society, must carry out jihad; that is, they must exert themselves at all moments of life to fight a battle both inward and outward against these forces that if not combatted will destroy that equilibrium which is the necessary condition for the spiritual life of the person and the functioning of human society. This fact is especially true if society is seen as a collectivity which bears the imprint of the Divine Norm rather than an ant heap of contending and opposing units and forces.

Man is at once a spiritual and corporeal being, a microcosm complete unto himself; yet he is the member of a society within which alone are certain aspects of his being developed and certain of his needs fulfilled. He possesses at once an intelligence whose substance is ultimately of a divine character and sentiments which can either veil his intelligence or abet his quest for his own origin. In him are found both love and hatred, generosity and covetousness, compassion and aggression. Moreover, there have existed until now not just one but several "humanities" with their own religions and moral norms, and national, ethnic, and racial groups with their own bonds of affiliation. As a result the practice of jihad, as applied to the world of multiplicity and the vicissitudes of human existence in the external world, has come to develop numerous ramifications in the fields of political and economic activity and in social life, and has come to partake, on the external level, of the complexity which characterizes the human world.

In its most outward sense jihad came to mean the defense of *dar al-islam*, that is, the Islamic world, from invasion and intrusion by non-Islamic forces. The earliest wars of Islamic history, which threatened the very existence of the young community, came to be known as jihad par excellence in this outward sense of "holy war." But it was upon returning from one of these early wars which was of paramount importance in the survival of the newly established religious community, and therefore of cosmic significance, that the Prophet nevertheless said to his companions that they had returned from the lesser holy war to the greater holy war, the greater jihad being the inner battle against all the forces which would prevent man from living according to the theomorphic norm which is his primordial and God-given nature.

Throughout Islamic history, the call to the lesser holy war has echoed in the Islamic world when parts or the whole of that world have been threatened by forces from without or within. This call has been especially persistent since the nineteenth century with the advent of colonialism and the threat to the very existence of the Islamic world. It must be remembered, however, that even in such cases when the idea of jihad has been evoked in certain parts of the Islamic world, it has not usually been a question of religion simply sanctioning war, but of the attempt by a society in which religion remains of central concern to protect itself from being conquered either by military and economic forces or by ideas of an alien nature. This does not mean, however, that in some cases, especially in recent times, religious sentiments have not been used or misused to intensify or legitimize a conflict. But to say the least, the Islamic world does not have a monopoly on this abuse, as the history of other civilizations, including even the secularized West, demonstrates so amply. Moreover, human nature being what it is, once religion ceases to be of central significance to a particular human collectivity, then men fight and kill each other for much less exalted issues than their heavenly faith. By including the question of war in its sacred legislation, Islam did not condone, but limited, war and its consequences, as the history of the traditional Islamic world bears out. In any case the idea of total war and the actual practice of the extermination of whole civilian populations did not grow out of a civilization whose dominant religion saw jihad in a positive light.

On the more external level, the lesser jihad also includes the socio-economic domain. It means the reassertion of justice in the external environment of human existence, starting with man himself. To defend one's rights and reputation, to defend the honor of oneself and one's family is itself a jihad and a religious duty. So is the strengthening of all those social bonds, from the family to the whole of the Muslim people (al-ummah), which the Shari'ah emphasizes. To seek social justice in accordance with the tenets of the Quran, and of course not in the modern secularist sense, is a way of reestablishing equilibrium in human society— that is, of performing jihad — as are constructive economic enterprises, provided the well-being of the whole person is kept in mind and material welfare does not become an end in itself; provided one does not lose sight of the Quranic verse, "The other world is better for you than this one" (93:4). To forget the proper relation between the two worlds would itself be instrumental in bringing about disequilibrium and would be a kind of jihad in reverse.

All of those external forms of jihad would remain incomplete, and in fact contribute to an excessive externalization of human beings, if they were not complemented by the greater or inner jihad which man must carry out continuously within himself, for the nobility of the human state resides in the constant tension between what we appear to be and what we really are and the need to transcend ourselves throughout this journey of earthly life in order to become what we "are."

From the spiritual point of view all the "pillars" of Islam can be seen as being related to jihad. The fundamental witnesses, "There is no divinity but God" and "Muhammad is the Messenger of God," through the utterance of which a person becomes a Muslim, are not only statements about the Truth as seen in the Islamic perspective, but also weapons for the practice of inner jihad. The very form of the first witness (*La ilaha illa'Llah* in Arabic) when written in Arabic calligraphy is like a bent sword with which all otherness is removed from the Supreme Reality, while all that is positive in manifestation is returned to that Reality. The second witness is the blinding assertion of the powerful and majestic descent of all that constitutes in a positive manner the cosmos, man, and revelation from that Supreme Reality. To invoke the two witnesses in the form of the sacred language in which they were revealed is to practice the inner jihad and to bring about awareness of who we are, whence we come, and where is our ultimate abode.

The daily prayers (*salat* or *namaz*) which constitute the heart of the Islamic rites are again a never-ending jihad which punctuates human existence in a continuous rhythm in conformity with the rhythm of the cosmos. To perform the prayers with regularity and concentration requires the constant exertion of our will and an unending battle and striving against forgetfulness, dissipation, and laziness. It is itself a form of spiritual warfare.

Likewise, the fast of Ramadan, in which one wears the armor of inner purity and detachment against the passions and temptations of the outside world, requires an ascetism and inner discipline which cannot come about except through an inner holy war. Nor is the *hajj* to the center of the Islamic world in Mecca possible without long preparation, effort, often suffering and endurance of hardship. It requires great effort and exertion so that the Prophet could say, "The hajj is the most excellent of jihads." Like the knight in quest of the Holy Grail, the pilgrim to the house of the Beloved must engage in a spiritual warfare whose end makes all sacrifice and all hardship pale into insignificance, for the hajj to the House of God implies, for the person who practices the inner jihad, encounter with the Master of the House, who also resides at the center of that other *Ka'bah* which is the heart.

Finally, the giving of *zakat* or religious tax is again a form of jihad, not only in that in departing from one's wealth man must fight against the covetousness and greed of his carnal soul, but also in that through the payment of zakat in its many forms man contributes to the establishment of economic justice in human society. Although jihad is not one of the "pillars of Islam," it in a sense resides within all the other "pillars." From the spiritual point of view in fact all of the "pillars" can be seen in the light of an inner jihad which is essential to the life of man from the Islamic point of view, and which does not oppose but complements contemplativity and the peace which result from the contemplation of the One.

The great stations of perfection in the spiritual life can also be seen in the light of the inner jihad. To become detached from the impurities of the world in order to repose in the purity of the Divine Presence requires an intense jihad, for our soul has its roots sunk deeply into the transient world which the soul of fallen man mistakes for reality. To overcome the lethargy, passivity, and indifference of the soul—qualities which have become second nature to man as a result of his forgetting who he is—constitutes likewise a constant jihad. To pull the reins of the soul from dissipating itself outwardly as a result of its centrifugal tendencies, and to bring it back to the center wherein resides Divine Peace and all the beauty which the soul seeks in vain in the domain of multiplicity, is again an inner jihad. To melt the hardened heart into a flowing stream of love, which would embrace the whole of creation in virtue of the love for God, is to perform the alchemical process of *solve et coagula* inwardly through a "work" which is none other than an inner struggle and battle against what the soul has become in order to transform it into that which it "is" and has never ceased to be, if only it were to become aware of its own nature. Finally, to realize that only the Absolute is absolute and that only the Self can ultimately utter "I," is to perform the supreme jihad of awakening the soul from the dream of forgetfulness and enabling it to gain the supreme, principial knowledge for the sake of which it was created. The inner jihad, or warfare seen spiritually and esoterically, can be considered therefore as the key for the understanding of the whole spiritual process, and the path for the realization of the One which lies at the heart of the Islamic message seen in its totality. The Islamic path towards perfection can be conceived in the light of the symbolism of the greater jihad to which the Prophet of Islam, who founded this path on earth, himself referred.

In the same way that with every breath the principle of life, which functions in us irrespective of our will and as long as it is willed by Him who created us, exerts itself through jihad to instill life within our whole body, at every moment in our conscious life we should seek to perform jihad in not only establishing equilibrium in the world about us but also in awakening to that Divine Reality which is the very source of our consciousness. For the spiritual man, every breath is a reminder that he should continue the inner jihad until he awakens from all dreaming and until the very rhythm of his heart echoes that primordial sacred Name by which all things were made and through which all things return to their origin. The Prophet said, "Man is asleep and when he dies he awakens." Through inner jihad the spiritual man dies in this life in order to cease all dreaming, in order to awaken to that Reality which is the origin of all realities, in order to behold that Beauty of which all earthly beauty is but a pale reflection, in order to attain that Peace which all men seek but which can in fact be found only through the inner jihad.

Parabola
Volume: 27.4
War

JUSTICE TO THE ENEMY

Seyyed Hossein Nasr

Not all wars are *jihads*, and Islam has also promulgated certain regulations for conflict in general. First of all, war should be in self-defense and Muslims should not instigate wars, as the … verse, "Fight in the way of God against those who fight against you, but begin not hostilities. Verily God loveth not transgressors" (2:190), demonstrates. If, like the Bible, the Quran does speak of fighting against one's enemies, it must be remembered that Islam was born in a climate in which there were constant wars among various tribes. Still, after ordering Muslims to battle against their enemies, the Quran adds, "Except those who seek refuge with people between whom and you there is a covenant, or (those who) come unto you because their hearts forbid them to make war on you. … So, if they hold aloof from you and wage not war against you and offer you peace, God alloweth you no way against them" (4:90). War can be fought to avoid persecution and oppression or to preserve religious values and protect the weak from oppression. The Quran does mention the biblical "an eye for an eye," but recommends forgoing revenge and practicing charity, as in the verse, "But whoso forgoeth it [that is, an eye for an eye] it shall be expiation for him" (5:45). Also war should not go on indefinitely; as soon as the enemy sues for peace hostilities must terminate, "But if they desist, then let there be no hostility" (2:192).

Of the utmost importance is the injunction that innocent human life must not be destroyed in any warfare, for the Quran says, "Whosoever killeth a human being for other than manslaughter or corruption in the earth, it shall be as if he had killed all humanity" (5:32). The Prophet explicitly forbade attacking women and children and even killing animals or destroying trees during war. His own magnanimous treatment of his most bitter enemies upon his conquest of Mecca has remained the supreme concrete example to be followed. Likewise, Muslims recall to this day how, upon conquering Jerusalem, Umar dealt with Christians and their respected sites of worship with remarkable magnanimity and justice. Needless to say, not all Muslims have followed these precepts during Islamic history any more than have all Jews, Christians, Hindus, or Buddhists followed the injunctions of their religions. But it is essential here not only for Western observers but also for many Muslims who, having lost hope, have fallen into despair and commit desperate acts, to remember what the teachings of Islam as a religion are on these matters. Human nature being what it is, it is not difficult to find reasons why not all Muslims have followed the teachings of their religion in matters of war. What is remarkable is the degree to which over the ages many of the values of this spiritualized chivalry *were* followed, as witnessed over the centuries even by Western invaders, from medieval knights to French officers in Algeria.

Today a new challenge has been created by the invention of modern means and methods of warfare, of weapons of mass destruction causing so-called collateral damage over which no one has control, of bombs that cannot distinguish between combatants and women and children. Now, Islamic civilization did not invent these monstrous technologies, or even the idea of total war involving whole civilian populations, but it is faced with their reality on the ground and, one might add, in the air and at sea. This situation creates an additional challenge of monumental proportions for Muslims, as it does for those Christians in the West who seek to live according to the teachings of Christ, and even for many secular humanists. It is precisely at such a juncture of human history that Muslims are called upon to be most vigilant in defense of what their religion has taught them about jihad and the regulations it has promulgated for any form of warfare. Moreover, any Muslim who has a sense of responsibility before God must be especially careful when he or she carries out an act explicitly in the name of Islam in a world in which inhuman and even infra-human tools of military combat are in the hands of the powerful who dominate the global scene. Although defense of oneself, one's homeland, and one's religion and the overcoming of oppression remain religious duties, the regulations of warfare, especially the protection of the innocent, that is, nonaggression against noncombatants, and dealing with the enemy in justice, also remain part and parcel of the religion and essential to it; they cannot be cast aside with the excuse that one is responding to a grievance or injustice. If one does so, one is no longer speaking or acting in the name of Islam and is in fact in danger of defiling the religion more than its enemies ever could.

As a result of suicide bombings and the extensive use of the term "martyr" in recent years in various Islamic countries, many people in the West have turned to the question of martyrdom in Islam, and some have even described it in the most pejorative manner as an object of ridicule. First of all, martyrdom exists in every religion. Second, Christianity relies particularly on martyrdom and celebrates its martyrs as saints more than Islam does, especially Islam in its Sunni form. It is therefore particularly strange to see some observers in the West speak of martyrdom as if it were a peculiar, solely Islamic concept. The Quran states, "Think not of those who are slain in the way of God that they are dead. Nay, they are living being nourished by their Lord" (3:169), and "They rejoice because of favor from God and kindness and that God wasteth not the wage of believers" (3:171). Therefore, just as Christian martyrs enter paradise, Muslim martyrs are also blessed and allowed entry into the paradisal states. For both, martyrdom is victory over death, and Muslim martyrs share with Christians in asking at the moment of their ultimate victory; "O Death, where is thy sting? O grave, where is thy victory?" (1 Cor. 15:55).

Who is a martyr? In Christianity, at least Catholic Christianity, this question has been decided over the centuries by the Church, but in Islam there is no magical magisterium to decide ecclesiastically who is a martyr. In Twelve-Imam Shi'ite Islam martyrdom plays a more central role than in Sunnism. All the Imams, except the Twelfth (who, according to

Shi'ism, is still alive although in occultation), were martyred, and the martyrdom of the Third Imam, Husayn ibn Ali, who is called *Sayyid al-shuhada*, or the Master of Martyrs, is particularly important in Shi'ite piety. The Shi'ite community has also recognized a number of other martyrs who were clearly killed for religious reasons. In Sunni Islam, likewise, a number of figures have been given the title of martyr over the ages by the Islamic community (*al-ummah*), which is the final arbiter on this matter in Sunni Islam. Sometimes the term "martyr" has also been used more politically for those killed in a religio-political struggle even within the Islamic world and by other Muslims.

The term "martyr" in Arabic is *shahīd*, which is related to the term for the supreme testification (*shahadah*) of Islam regarding Divine Unity. Furthermore, it is truly remarkable that the word *shahīd* is also related to the word *shāhid*, which means "witness," exactly as does the Greek word *martos*, from which "martyr" derives. Even the word "martyr" has therefore the same root meaning in Christianity and Islam. Furthermore, in both traditions the same symbols were often used to describe a martyr. In Shi'ism a martyr is often referred to as the lamp that burns itself but illuminates the world about it; the most famous English Catholic martyr, Thomas Becket, was also called the "bright candle on God's candlestick." In the truly spiritual sense, the shahīd is the person who has borne witness with his or her whole being to Divine Oneness. He or she has made the supreme sacrifice of his or her own life for the sake of God, a sacrifice that has been truly for God and not for any worldly cause. Such people go to paradise because they have given their life in all sincerity to God. In this context it is also important to recall the hadith of the Prophet, "The ink of the scholar is more precious than the blood of the martyr," which means that although martyrdom is such an exalted state, the inner jihad leading to the knowledge of God and His revelation (hence the ink of the scholar) is of even higher value.

But can a person become a martyr by committing suicide? Suicide itself is forbidden by Islamic Law, and those who commit it are condemned to the infernal states because they have taken upon themselves a decision that belongs to God alone. Life can be terminated only by the Giver of life. But suicide as a desperate act to overcome oppression or to defend oneself has manifested itself on the margin of human existence everywhere. Many brave American soldiers in various wars have thrown themselves on bombs, which is an act of suicide, to save others, and we all know of the Japanese kamikazes during World War II. An especially telling case is mentioned in the Bible: Samson commits suicide by bringing the Temple of Dagon down not only on himself, but on thousands of Philistines, including women and children, because his people had been oppressed by the Philistines. Some Jews consider him a hero and a prophet, whereas, interestingly enough, Muslims do not consider him one of the Hebrew prophets.

For Muslims, the difficult question on both moral and religious grounds concerns those who live under appalling oppression and in a state of despair and have no other means of defense except their bodies. Even in such cases the Islamic injunction that one cannot kill innocent people even in war must of necessity hold. As for using one's body as a weapon against combatants, this is an issue that is being hotly debated among experts in Islamic Law in the Islamic world today. Most believe that an act that is certain suicide must be avoided, while some believe that it is permissible as self-defense or for the protection of one's people if it does not involve innocent victims. The great tragedy is the existence of a situation in which young people fall into such a state of desperation that the question of suicide even arises. Here again, as with total warfare, the phenomenon itself, which exists among Hindu Tigers in Sri Lanka, in the case of the person who killed Rajiv Gandhi, and among Palestinians and others, is one of the fruits of modern technology that make what is now called terrorism possible, but about which few are willing to speak. In conclusion, we must remember that there is no peace without justice, and justice implies a constant struggle to establish equilibrium in a world, both within and without, in which forces and tensions threaten chaos and disorder at all times. A Muslim's duty is to seek to establish peace and justice within, and on the basis of the Divine injunctions to establish justice in the world about him through an effort, or jihad, that must avoid outward war and confrontation except when absolutely necessary and in defense. But even in war, regulations set down by the religion must be observed. Today we live in a world full of strife, with powerful economic, political, and cultural wars that occasionally also result in military confrontation. In such a situation Muslims must be vigilant, but also seekers of peace. Some have said that Islam displays a greater combative spirit than other religions. Now, all religions are guardians of the sacred, and Islam, coming at the end of the present human cycle, has a particularly important role in carrying out this duty. Therefore, whenever the sacred is attacked and challenged by the forces of desacralization and nihilism, Islam is destined to display a particularly combative spirit to respond to this challenge. But this response must not be at the expense of destroying the sacred message of Islam itself, based on peace and surrender to the Divine Will. Therefore, Muslims must strive to preserve the sacred and to defend justice, but not by succumbing to the means that contradict and in fact destroy the very reality of not only Islam, but religion as such. Muslims must seek justice, but with humility and charity, not in self-righteousness, ever aware that absolute justice belongs to God alone and that one of the cardinal meanings of the shahadah is "There is no justice but the Divine Justice."

From Seyyed Hossein Nasr, *The Heart of Islam: Enduring Values for Humanity* (San Francisco: HarperSanFrancisco, 2002), pp. 266-72.

CHAPTER THREE

•

ART AND BEAUTY

Die now, die now, in this Love die;
when you have died in this Love, you will all receive new life.

Die now, die now, and do not fear this death,
for you will come forth from this earth and seize the heavens.

Die now, die now, and break away from this carnal soul,
for this carnal soul is as a chain and you are as prisoners.

Take an axe to dig through the prison;
when you have broken the prison you will all be kings and princes.

Die now, die now before the beauteous King;
when you have died before the King, you will all be kings and renowned.

Die now, die now, and come forth from this cloud;
when you come forth from this cloud, you will all be radiant full moons.

Be silent, be silent; silence is the sign of death;
it is because of life that you are fleeing from the silent one.[1]

—Rumi

Parabola
Volume: 18.4
The City

LIGHT FROM THE CENTER

Gai Eaton

Western Orientalists of an earlier period thought they had discovered the secret of Islam in tracing its origins back to the desert: in its poverty and austerity, its wide horizons and open spaces. More recently the tendency has been to stress the social aspects of the religion and to see it as city-bound and most fully expressed in the traditional Islamic city. This is certainly closer to the truth, although the early cities were themselves dots in the vastness of the desert and, to this day, the town Arab instinctively seeks refreshment and renewal in those open spaces. In any case, Islam is a religion which functions in terms of a Center: in man, the Heart and, in the outer world, the holy city. In the five daily prayers every Muslim, wherever he may be, turns his face toward Mecca. His prayer is invalid if he deliberately faces in the wrong direction.

But how can we define a "holy" city? This turns upon the notion of the sacred, once universally understood but, in our time (a time in which centrality has given way to dispersion), devalued and almost forgotten. A sacred place or a sacred object is one in which God makes Himself present or in which the numinous is believed to be present. So far so good, but this remains an ambiguous definition for obvious reasons. God is everywhere present; this has been the view of all the great religions, and it cannot be said that He is less fully present in one place than in another; being indivisible, He cannot be partly here and partly there and, in minor mode, a little bit somewhere else. Where He is, He *is*. It follows that the sacred, whether place or object (or, dare we say, person?), is where we are best able to sense or to perceive the universal presence of That which lies beyond the world of ordinary perception and which infinitely transcends it.

Here again we have to take care not to misunderstand the definition. It might seem to suggest pure subjectivism, in which case my sacred place is not necessarily yours, nor yours mine. An element of subjectivism does indeed come into this. Awareness of the sacred certainly depends upon the alertness and openness of the subjective consciousness to what is *there*. But the initiative belongs to God. It is He—not this or that person—who has chosen the place or the object in which His real presence may be most sharply perceived by those possessed of seeing eyes. Muhammad, the Prophet of Islam and, for Muslims, the "Messenger of God," said that he had come to make our religion "easy for us." The sacred is everywhere, hidden or half-hidden in everything that exists; but the human perception of the sacred has been made "easy" for us by its open crystallization in certain places and objects. It might be said: "You are so short-sighted, so unaware of what surrounds you on every side, that it has become necessary to give it, here or there, an emphatic force which cannot be ignored!"

The sacredness of Mecca, or rather the sacredness of the Ka'bah, to which the city is no more than an appendage, turns upon the factor of primordiality. According to legend, Adam and Eve, separated after the Fall from Paradise, were reunited there, on that holy ground, and Adam was commanded to build "the first temple for mankind," the Ka'bah, in imitation of the central place around which the angels circle perpetually. This is of particular significance if we keep in mind another definition of the sacred: it is that which reflects most directly a heavenly archetype. The Quran however tells us that the original Ka'bah was built by Abraham, with the help of his son Ishmael, and every Muslim must accept—and does accept—the Quranic message. In this case, therefore, the city derives its holiness less from the fact that the Prophet of Islam was born there than from its proximity to the supremely sacred object which lies at its center. Since the sacred is associated with a light which radiates from it, the city might be said to bask in that light.

In the Islamic context, however, we can go a step further and extend the meaning of "holiness." Every Islamic city, if it is what it should be, is a holy city. It is an inhabited center, ordered in terms of priorities determined from above, in which men and women live and fulfill their destinies in harmony with one another, their whole existence dominated by the laws of the religion and directed towards their Last End which is proximity to God in the hereafter. Such a city is blessed. Such a city is home and may justly be called *ad-Dar as-Salam* ("The House of Peace").

Its center is the principle mosque in which, five times each day (and at any other times they choose), the citizens direct their whole attention away from the horizontal dimension—their worldly affairs—onto the vertical dimension, which points to the eternal Center. No house, shop, or office is built so high as to overtop the mosque, for that would be a kind of sacrilege, a reversal of priorities. The Call to Prayer, made from the top of the minaret (an Arabic term which also means "lighthouse"), echoes over the city and pierces through the hubbub of daily life. It is a constantly repeated "reminder" of who we are and where we are and, indeed *why* we are. What is referred to again and again as "remembrance" in the Quran is at the very heart of the religion of Islam, and the Prophet Muhammad himself was sent, not to introduce an innovation in human faith, but, precisely, to "remind" us of the meaning of our existence. So let us say that the ideal Islamic city is the locus of "remembrance."

We must not, however, make too much of a distinction which is purely relative. The horizontal dimension is also sacred, provided that it too is filled with reminders. The city is an image of the world in its entirety and, for this reason, it has a certain self-sufficiency. The laws which maintain order and harmony are not of human devising. They are given in the *Shari'ah*, which derives from the Quran and from the actions and sayings of the Prophet. These laws cannot be changed in accordance with the dictates of the ruler or the whims of the people. The ruler's task is twofold: to defend the city against its enemies and to ensure that the laws are obeyed. For the rest, the community looks after its own affairs. Whereas most European cities (with the exception of London) were planned to facilitate the power of ruler or government, as is exemplified by the wide boulevards of Paris along which an army can march without difficulty, the traditional Islamic city, with its secretive twisting lanes and alleys, excludes such an intrusion. Moreover this is a community and, as such, is committed to mutual support in accordance with Islamic law which insists upon the relief of poverty and care for the sick.

The principal market may be described as the stomach of the city. Yet it is also more than that. In the first place it is where human beings meet each other to negotiate and enter into relationships. Buyer and seller are not merely entering into commercial transactions. They exchange courtesies and they exchange news, they get to know each other; and every meeting between human creatures, opening with the holy Greeting of Peace, is of immense significance in the sight of God and in the context of eternity.

Secondly, the articles on sale (the "goods," in itself a significant term), whether furniture, utensils, or apparel, when they are the work of craftsmen and craftswomen whose labor is also a prayer, have a sacred character. Through their ornamentation, their design or their Quranic inscriptions, they remind those who use them of God, the only Creator.

But there is something else, something immensely important, that is sold in the market: food. One of the Names of God in the Quran is "the Nourisher," and all nourishment, whether spiritual or physical, comes from Him. In the contemporary Western world, overfed and wasteful as we are, we do not find it easy to see any deep significance in the food we eat. It comes from the local supermarket, not from heaven. Yet, rightly understood, it is a powerful "reminder." Here we are in these bodily envelopes which appear closed and firmly sealed, reflecting the isolation of our minds and personalities from other minds and personalities, even if we know in theory that "no man is an island"; but this body depends, every day of its life, upon taking into itself, digesting and absorbing something from outside itself. This is, therefore, a perfect image of the dependence of spirit and soul upon the "food from heaven" which nourishes and sustains us as whole beings.

It recalls also the unitarian doctrine which is the cornerstone of Islam. There is no profane or secular realm. Everything is encompassed by Him who has named Himself the "All-encompassing." The total division which exists in the modern world between home and work and office or workplace cannot be accommodated in this scheme for living, which is why the meeting between buyer and seller is no different in essence from a social encounter. The Muslim is not permitted to split himself into different pieces or conduct his life in separate compartments. His shop in the market is probably also his home. His customers are also his friends, and, before doing business, he invites them to partake of some nourishment. This, in truth, is not only the Muslim way of doing things, it is the human way. In what are commonly called "primitive" societies the exchange of gifts of food is the most profound expression of mutual love or friendship, and in some cultures the climax of the marriage ceremony comes when the bridegroom feeds the bride with a spoonful of food. We love God—or should love Him—because He feeds us; spirit, soul, and body. The fact that we depend upon being fed is one of the most significant facts about our earthly existence. It indicates and reminds us that we *ex*-ist, that is to say we have our being "outside"; outside the fullness of Being, the pleroma, sustained only by our attachment to it through an umbilical cord. This city, this holy city, is then a place of inter-connectedness, of communion, of meeting, in which the priorities are observed, the framework is intact, and the basic needs—spiritual and physical—of every man, woman, and child are met. But everything on earth has its opposite. Are there "unholy" cities? Indeed there are. The world is full of gateways opening either upon what is above or what is below. If the holy city is a gateway to heaven, then it can only be surmised that the unholy city is a gateway to the Fire, the place of enmity, separation, and dispersion.

Look then upon the modern city, the epitome of "civilization," in which enmity, separation, and dispersion are already present. Not only is there universal fragmentation, the complete absence of any organic unity, but the priorities have been reversed. We are sometimes puzzled by the fact that Muhammad, in a saying regarding the "signs of the end"—the end of the world, the end of all things—included "the construction of tall buildings." Yet there is, surely, no mystery here? If we see buildings dedicated to the pursuit of money or personal power and prestige rising high above the mosque or the church, then it is easy to understand that this titanic presumption might presage and merit universal destruction. Seek a church in a Western city and you will discover it like a gemstone, half-buried under pebbles. The orientation of the citizens is no longer upward, the orientation indicated by minaret or spire, but horizontal, exclusively worldly.

The arrogance, pretentiousness, and emptiness of those glass and concrete constructions which dominate our modern cities may remind the Muslim of a Quranic verse in which it is said of him whom God leaves to go astray that: "He causes his breast to be tight and constricted as if he were climbing up to the heavens" (6:125). The heavens, still far distant, mock this puny effort. The "unholy city," dwarfing the people who inhabit it as a giant anthill dwarfs its builders, has not only reversed all traditional priorities; it has negated all human values, for nothing here is built on a human scale. It might be compared to a suit of clothes ten times too big for the wearer. It does not fit us, nor does it belong in the physical landscape into which it has been inserted. It belongs nowhere and to no one. When the sacred is banished from sight, so is the human; so too is all that is natural and God-given. We are left, finally, with a shell fit only for destruction.

Parabola
Volume: 26.2
Light

Divine Unity

Titus Burckhardt

The artist who wishes to express the idea of the "unity of being" or the "unity of the real" (*wahdat al-wujud*) has actually three means at his disposal: geometry or, more precisely, the infinity inherent in regular geometric figures; rhythm, which is revealed in the temporal order and also indirectly in space; and light, which is to visible forms what Being is to limited existences. Light is, in fact, itself indivisible; its nature is not altered by its refraction into colors nor diminished by its gradation into clarity and darkness. In the same way, nothingness does not itself exist except by its illusory opposition to Being; so also darkness is visible only by contrast with light, to the extent that light makes shadows appear.

"God is the light of the heavens and the earth," says the Quran (24:35). The Divine Light brings things out from the darkness of nothing. In the symbolical order in question, to be visible signifies to exist. Just as shadow adds nothing to light, things are real only to the extent that they share in the light of Being. There is no more perfect symbol of the Divine Unity than light. For this reason, the Muslim artist seeks to transform the very stuff he is fashioning into a vibration of light. It is to this end that he covers the interior surfaces of a mosque or palace—and occasionally the outer ones—with mosaics in ceramic tiles. This lining is often confined to the lower part of the walls, as if to dispel their heaviness. It is for the same purpose that the artist transforms other surfaces into perforated reliefs to filter the light. *Muqarnas,* "stalactites," also serve to trap light and diffuse it with the most subtle gradations.

Colors reveal the interior richness of light. Light viewed directly is blinding; it is through the harmony of colors that we divine its true nature, which bears every visual phenomenon within itself.

Among the examples of Islamic architecture under the sway of the sovereignty of light, the Alhambra at Granada occupies the first rank. The Court of Lions in particular sets the example of stone transformed into a vibration of light; the lambrequins of the arcades, the friezes in muqarnas, the delicacy of the columns that seem to defy gravity, the scintillation of the roofs in green tilework, and even the water-jets of the fountain all contribute to this impression.

We have compared this art to alchemy, the well-known theme of which is the transmutation of lead into gold. Lead is the base metallic substance, shapeless and opaque, whereas gold, the solar metal, is in some way light made corporeal. In the spiritual order, alchemy is none other than the art of transmuting bodily consciousness into spirit: "Body must be made spirit," say the alchemists, "for spirit to become body." By analogy, we will say of alchemy, in the manner in which it appears to us here, that it transforms stone into light, which in its turn transforms stone into crystal.

Parabola
Volume: 13.1
The Creative
Response

Echoes of Infinity

Interview with Seyyed Hossein Nasr

Dr. Seyyed Hossein Nasr's books, essays, and lectures have illuminated for many the rich possibilities of the traditional perspective. His most recent book (as of 1988) is Islamic Art and Spirituality *(State University of New York Press, 1987). A scholar who in his writing is himself engaged overtly in the creative act, Dr. Nasr offers unique insight into the nature and role of the creative response. His interview with us took place in the book-lined inner chamber of his offices at The George Washington University in Washington, D. C., where he is University Professor of Islamic Studies. As before, he spoke with authority, remarkable precision, and imagination, demonstrating in action the possibility of engaging in a creative response at each moment.*

—Jeffrey P. Zaleski

Jeffrey P. Zaleski: *In your book,* Islamic Art and Spirituality, *you include an essay on "The Spiritual Message of Islamic Calligraphy," in which you wrote that "Quranic calligraphy issues at once from the Islamic revelation and represents the response of the soul of the Islamic peoples to the divine message." This idea of creativity as a positive response to the sacred differs from the common Western idea of creativity as a Promethean act whereby humanity imitates God and even attempts to usurp His powers. In the Islamic tradition, what role does the creative response play in regard to humanity's relationship with God?*

Seyyed Hossein Nasr: In the Islamic world, there is no idea of Promethean creativity, that is, man acting not only independently of God but often against the Will of Heaven—stealing the power of creativity and then going on his own and creating whatever he will out of his own individualistic level of existence, or out of his own ego, or out of his own limitations. The Islamic tradition sees creativity always related to man's relationship with God. Man receives from God, first of all, his being; secondly, all the qualities that make him human—including the power of creativity. Thirdly, man receives from God life itself, which makes possible the manifestations of these qualities which are contained ultimately in the Divine Names and Qualities themselves. Therefore, art, in the real sense of the word, is seen in the Islamic world as always coming from man's submission to God, allowing, in a sense, the Divine Qualities to manifest themselves through man, rather than man inventing his own qualities or his own creative works as a veil which would somehow hide the Divine. The traditional conception of man in Islam is a centered one: man has a center that he carries within himself. That center is the heart, where both the intellect—in the traditional sense of the word—resides, and where ultimately the Divine Mercy resides. The Quranic message is always addressed to the heart. There is the famous Islamic saying, "The heart of the believer is the throne of the Divine Compassion." It is from this center that there issues the creative élan, the creative vitality. Man finds the center within himself. The work of art is not a center for man. It is man himself who is centered, and through this relationship between him and God, which in fact comes from his own center, man is able to disseminate the Qualities of the Divine in the world about him—of course, on the human level, because God remains God and man remains man. There are no human qualities which do not derive ultimately from the Divine Qualities.

JZ: *In the same essay on Quranic calligraphy, you write that "the saint is himself a work of sacred art." Are the laws that govern the science of sacred art and the laws that govern the science of sainthood one and the same? Also, is it possible to create a work of sacred art without a corresponding inner development?*

SN: I said that man himself—the saint—is the supreme work of art because all things are created by God. Man, in a sense, is God's greatest creation. He contains all the perfections of creation within himself. The saint is the fullness of man—to be a saint is to be fully human. We are all subhuman, from the traditional point of view. The norm is the saint. And therefore in his being the theomorphic nature of man is chiseled out through spiritual discipline, and therefore he represents the perfect work of art. In the rest of us, that perfection is there but it's veiled by our human nature. Occasionally it manifests itself, but in the saint the veil is cast aside and the full nature of being human comes out.

Now the laws, you might say, which make a saint a saint are not exactly the same as sacred art but they're very deeply related to it, in the sense that sacred art has ultimately a supra-individual inspiration. It comes from the world beyond the individual ego—the world of the spirit. And therefore it is related very closely to the spiritual experience of sainthood. Not that the techniques and method are the same, but the original inspiration comes from the same world. That is why, for example, in Christianity the origin of the icon is related to St. Luke, or the angel, not simply to a human being who in the first century may have painted an image of Christ. Therefore, there is an inner link between sanctity and sacred art, and also a profound affinity between the two. Sacred art is based upon a sacred science of the cosmos—both the macrocosm and the microcosm—and the metacosmic reality. Now sanctity—not in all of its modes, but in its sapiential mode—is related precisely to the realization of such a knowledge. And therefore, the knowledge that is at the heart of sapiential sanctity is intimately related to the knowledge that lies at the heart of sacred art. And that is why when this kind of sanctity is destroyed or diminishes, sacred art loses its center and gradually decays. There have been several instances of it in human history, the two most blatant ones being that of late antiquity and postmedieval European art.

As for the question whether it is possible for a person who is not himself a saint to produce sacred art, the answer is, "Yes, it is possible." Because once the norms are given—the symbolic language, the imagery, the technique, and the discipline of the creation of a particular art that originate from the source of the sacred—and once you have the master-disciple relationship in a traditional society, it is possible for those techniques to be transmitted without the disciple fully understanding their complete import. In a sense the art is then greater than the maker of it. But even in that instance, there is the need for a certain amount of moral and spiritual conformity, because one would never be able to become the disciple of a master craftsman, in the traditional world, without a certain amount of moral qualification. That does not make that person a saint, but it makes him a person who's on the way of gaining spiritual perfection through his métier, through his art. So you have these two relationships. At the beginning of sacred art it is the spiritual master who brings the spiritual reality down from the archetypal, spiritual world into the manifested world—whether it be a calligraphic style or in another tradition an icon or sacred images. That's at the beginning of it. But once that art is in the world, that art is higher than the individual who devotes himself to it, and who through that art gradually gains spiritual perfection. And therefore it is possible, in fact, to create a sacred work of art without even being fully aware of all the profound symbolic meanings contained therein.

JZ: *What about in a nontraditional society, such as America today? Or, going back a bit, late nineteenth-century Europe. People speak of artists such as Van Gogh, or, more recently, Mark Rothko, as having a spiritual dimension in their art. And today many artists are trying to relate their art to the sacred, but outside of the context of a revealed tradition. Are these artists deceiving themselves? Can sacred art be created within a nontraditional society like ours?*

SN: It cannot be created, as far as I can see. Sacred art cannot be created outside of the traditional culture for which it was meant. However, it is possible for cosmic qualities, spiritual qualities, to be reflected through art which is not itself of a traditional nature. This can be seen, for example, in Western music. The real sacred Western music is the Gregorian chant. From the Renaissance onward, we gradually hear what's called secular music, which at the beginning is impregnated very deeply by religious and spiritual values. And this continues until the period of Bach. Some of the partitas of Bach, which are not supposed to be so-called religious work, in fact have a spiritual substance to them. And even in the post-Bach period, when Western music becomes more and more worldly, humanistic, titanic—especially with Beethoven and Wagner—occasionally you hear through the purely humanistic, and even at times narcissistic, personalities who created this romantic music, cosmic and spiritual qualities. That is possible. But one cannot create a work of sacred art without the traditional cultural framework. One can try to reflect certain spiritual qualities and there are some painters, such as Van Gogh, the Impressionists, in whose paintings there is something of the cosmic beauty reflected without the painting being traditional art or sacred art.

JZ: *So there is something in these artists that responds to, let's say a higher truth.*

SN: That is true, but sometimes, in fact, the higher truth, the life of the spiritual world, even shines in certain artists in spite of themselves.

JZ: *That was often true of Beethoven.*

SN: Yes, and even more than Beethoven, of Mozart, whose late works—*The Magic Flute*, or *The Requiem*—have a content that does not correspond to the kind of worldly person one would expect Mozart to be and indeed, from what we read about him, he was. And also with Beethoven there is an excessive exteriorization. In a sense, something like the Ninth Symphony should never have been composed because it exteriorizes moods and treasures that really belong to inwardness. And that is not always positive. For someone who is sensitive, the late quartets of Beethoven or the Ninth Symphony could be the cause of spiritual ecstasy, perhaps. That's a possibility. But that's not the common, everyday audience, and the work itself brings a kind of exteriorization with it. But there must have been something in the soul of this man, who after all was a believer, that occasionally permitted these cosmic qualities to pierce through the work, although he was consciously rebelling against the classical tradition of music. He "freed" music, but also broke down the semi-traditional, classical structure upon which the music was based until his time.

JZ: *What about those of us who are not artists, or not craftspeople? What about someone working in a library, or working in a factory? What are the possibilities then to share in a creative response, to express creatively a response, to the world and to the sacred?*

SN: The possibility is there because ultimately everything that we do is art, either good art or bad art. Mankind does three things. There are three elements that are connected with our everyday existence. One is acting. One is making. And then there's the ground of these, which is being. We exist. Usually we're not aware of that existence. It takes a great deal of meditation and contemplation and self-discipline to be able to simply exist. That's a very difficult thing. Occasionally during the day we fall back into the ocean of our own existence, but usually we either act or make. Theoretically, everything that we make and every action that we take should be a form of art. Everything should be a response to the Divine. A person who has already realized a very high spiritual state, even if he's eating his lunch—that in a sense is a response to the Divine. And even the joy he receives from walking, from breathing, from eating—the very elemental aspects of human life—are no less than the joys of great so-called creativity, in the modern sense of art. In fact they are much greater, because he's always responding to God.

That ideal is not easily obtainable, but below that ideal, for ordinary human beings working in the library or walking in the train station, if there is an inner spiritual life, a spiritual practice, a spiritual discipline, then every moment of life, in a sense, is a response. And one that can manifest itself—if not perfectly at every moment as in the case of the saint—at certain moments of time. In the case of the person in the library, it isn't that the way that he or she puts the books on the shelf is as creative as, for instance, painting something on the wall. But the manner of acting, the spiritual intention behind it, the perfection one tries to achieve no matter what one does, making one's work a gift to be presented to God—even making one's living in difficult circumstances—can always be sanctified. It is possible for this creativity to manifest itself, even though outwardly it would not be called art today.

JZ: *You speak of the perfection one tries to achieve in whatever one does. In your new book you write often of beauty and its creation. There seems to be something within which orients us towards beauty, towards the perfect, and there's an urge in us to be artists.*

SN: Yes, as Coomaraswamy said quite rightly, the artist is not a special kind of man; every man is a special kind of artist. There is in all of us an urge, a need for beauty. First of all in art—I'm using the word traditionally, because today there are certain people who think art has nothing to do with beauty. But of course it does, in the traditional sense of the word. There is something in us which seeks beauty, and the reason for that is twofold. First of all, we still carry within ourselves the perfect nature with which we're created. In Western Abrahamic traditions, it's called a paradisiacal nature: Adam in Paradise before he fell. So we carry something of the memory of the Edenic state. And therefore we have a kind of thirst for what we really are. We are looking for ourselves, and that self always was impregnated by beauty. It was inundated, that self in Paradise, by beauty. Secondly, as a consequence, since we cannot evade being what we are, there is something of the Infinite in us. Inwardly, our being opens up to the Infinite. We're not a closed world. Having fallen into the world of finiteness, we are always thirsty for that infinitude. All of our rebellion against finiteness, including the desire for freedom, and being unhappy with what we have, comes from that. It's very rare that human beings become happy with attainment, material attainment, or even nonmaterial attainment; as in the case of famous actors or actresses, most of whom are psychologically ill—to put it mildly. For some reason they have not attained felicity. The more we run it seems that felicity is somewhere beyond the horizon. The reason for that is that only the infinite can bring us the sense of finality, and therefore contentment, in the ultimate sense, and peace, in the ultimate sense. Beauty is really a kind of echo of that infinity. Beauty for a moment breaks the bond of limitation, breaks the chain with which we are shackled, and therefore our soul thirsts for beauty. There are different modes of beauty, there is a hierarchy of beauty, but even the lowest form of beauty is alive and leads to the Ultimate Beauty which is the Beauty of God. And the more contemplative and spiritual a person is, the more he or she is sensitive to the freeing power of beauty. Beauty frees. It also, of course, makes us drunk. It inebriates. And the reason that we like this inebriation is that for a moment we forget the limitations of our own ego. Why do humans get drunk? Because they want to forget themselves. And physical drinking is nothing compared to spiritual drinking in which one is able to go beyond oneself. Beauty has tremendous power of achieving that. However, it's also very dangerous because of this power. It's a double-edged sword. If the soul is not disciplined, instead of this beauty being a ladder leading to the Ultimate Beauty which is God, it can pose in fact as a decoy. It can disperse the soul even more, and prevent the integration of the soul by having the soul become attracted to a limited form of beauty, but blind to the ultimate form of beauty. And that's why some religions, especially Christianity, have saints who have shunned the expression of beauty. In Islam, it's the other way, especially in the Sufi tradition, which almost always emphasizes the positive spiritual character of beauty. And Islam as a religion emphasizes beauty and as a civilization was always based on the attempt to create beauty. Beauty is a way of access to God.

JZ: *In the Western tradition those considered great artists—Beethoven, Shakespeare, Dostoyevsky—focused not only on the spiritual or the sacred in their art, but also very much on the all-too-human. Dostoyevsky, for instance, wrote about child abusers, about extremes of ugliness; and it seems as if it was necessary for him to know that side of humanity too in order to create his final, wise testament. How important is self-knowledge to the pursuit of the creative response? Is it necessary to know the lower as well as the higher?*

SN: It certainly is necessary. Somewhere, there are people who, like eagles, fly right to the higher, to the sun, and who do not need to examine the labyrinth of human life, and the labyrinth of the psyche, which is extremely complicated. But certainly in a total civilization that is necessary; somewhere along the way this has to be examined, and every civilization has done it. In traditional civilizations, the labyrinth of the psyche is always subordinate to the spirit. What happened in the West is that, often, the exploration of what you call the all-too-human was done with total indifference to the source of the human state, which is the spirit, which is God. This was a child of Renaissance humanism, which matured a century or two later, in literature especially. There are vast novels in which one immerses oneself to run away from both the world of nature—God's creation—and religion. One creates a world as a substitute, one spends one's whole life creating mammoth novels with false characters. In a sense, that is falling into the labyrinth without ever coming out. Now there are exceptions, and I think that Shakespeare should not at all be classified with the later figures, because Shakespeare is sort of the tail end of sacred art, certainly religious art of the deepest kind in Western literature. Although he came during the Elizabethan period, he really belongs to the medieval conception of literature, because although Shakespeare has incredible insight into human character, it's always with the aim of integrating human character in its final journey. As pointed out so well by Martin Lings in his well-known book on Shakespeare, the works of Shakespeare help us to gather unto ourselves the little sparks of our soul in different nooks and crannies before we depart from this plane. But with the famous novelists of the nineteenth century who wrote the gigantic novels—Dostoyevsky was one who was very sensitive to religion in many ways; he was very perceptive and has certain passages which have helped people become attracted to religion—most of these novelists, even those with a great mark of genius from a purely human point of view, were pulled by a kind of humanistic narcissism, which in a sense tried to substitute the human world for the Divine World. It was no longer a religious humanism, it was a kind of rebellious humanism. So one can go on for one's whole life reading these novels and have it be no more than a phantasm which does not help a person to realize himself or herself spiritually. It's not like reading the Mahabharata epics, or medieval literature. It's not like reading Dante. The medieval Western writer and the traditional writer in other civilizations always wrote both with the vision of creativity and the salvation of his soul in mind. These two became more or less divorced in much of modern literature, especially in the novel, and therefore it's possible to study the human world *ad infinitum* without ever getting out of it. It's this which traditional literature tries to avoid. It also has the deepest insights into the human world. Look at the stories of the North American Indian: unbelievably deep insight into human nature, but it always relates this human nature to the world of the spirit. It's an illusion to deal with the human state as a purely independent order of reality.

JZ: *You're a writer yourself. You deal with the challenge of creativity. How do you prepare for the act of writing?*

SN: I do not distinguish between so-called creative writing and scholarly writing, because they really go together. I also occasionally write poetry and some literary writings, but most of my works are either scholarly or metaphysical or philosophical—but a kind of literary style comes into them. So what I answer probably concerns everyone who writes. Each person to whom God has given the gift of creativity, in the sense that you use the word, has a kind of rhythm which pertains to his own inner nature. My answer must be somewhat personal, on this level. God has given me a great gift for concentration. When I want to write something, the ideas begin to simmer in my mind, and I draw from two things. Either I'm writing a scholarly article, let's say on a particular philosopher, and I have to refer to his writings, to his books and the page numbers, etc., the scholarly underpinning of the writing. Or I'm writing a metaphysical or philosophical or mystical essay which does not need this scholarly apparatus. But in both cases, whether I draw from my own intellectual powers and memories, or whether I have to go to the library and look up new footnotes and so forth, once that source is ready, then it begins to simmer within me. And whether I'm walking, or even sometimes talking, that essay or that book is being spun in my mind. And then I usually sit down and I pray. As a Muslim I pray five times a day, but besides that I do a kind of special contemplative prayer to cleanse myself, prepare myself, and then somehow what was prepared in my mind flows upon the page. I have very little trouble. All the work is done beforehand, and once I put the pen in my hand I always have trouble keeping up with my mind. I never type my writings; I always use an old-style pen with ink, not a ballpoint pen. I still write with a traditional instrument, and I write very, very fast because everything is ready in my mind and it just flows through.

JZ: *Yes, it seems that the creative process operates on a different level than that of our usual thought. And it seems as if there's an element of surrender to the creative process, allowing it to happen. In this regard, what do you think of art such as surrealist art or art which attempts to tap into dreams, which are certainly apart from our usual waking consciousness?*

SN: That can be a very dangerous art. Much of surrealism is really ill-named. *Sur*, from the French and Latin, means "above," and certainly this art, for the most part, is not above realism, but is sub-realism. If we call the ordinary waking state real—and that's an acceptable philosophical definition of real, although of course ultimately that's not what's real—and if we call that art realism which emulates the external forms of nature—the paintings of Ingres or the famous classical school of the eighteenth century—then you have two worlds, one which is above and one which is below. There is the world which is above the physical world—the spiritual world—and then there's a subrealist world which is the world of the subelements of the psyche, which in fact is where all the mud of the pond assembles, that is, the most negative, and oftentimes dangerous, elements of the human psyche. And the art which tries to bring that out? Oftentimes it's like freeing the dragon without having Saint Michael to slay it. It can be a powerful psychological art which also helps in the decomposition of the psyche, which brings about agitation. Usually it's not beautiful, although occasionally there may be a beautiful image. But it is not really visionary art, not visionary in the sense the American Indians or Asian Indians had. There are specific treatises in Sanskrit on how the yogi has first a vision of the archetype and then brings that into the world of forms. That belongs to the archetypal world, above the so-called real external world. Tapping into these dreams is oftentimes going into the subreal world. Now, the other element which is problematic with this art is that there are five billion people on the surface of the earth. Why is it that the dream of A is so interesting, and why not that of the other five billion people? What's so interesting about a particular psyche, about my expressing my ego, my individual I? There's a megalomania connected with so much of modern art. In the old days, even in the classical period of painting, you tried to paint perhaps a tree, so that there was something objective vis-à-vis you. Or before that you tried to paint the archetype, the universal archetype, as in medieval art. But now you're supposed to express your dreams, your individual imaginary forms, and from the artistic point of view, one can say, "So what? Why this?" And of course, the traditional point of view is opposed completely to the idea of art for art's sake. This is insanity from the normal point of view. Art must reflect the cosmic quality of virtue or beauty or truth.

JZ: *In your essay "Sacred Art and Persian Culture" you wrote that "the function of art, according to its Islamic conception, is to ennoble matter." That's wonderful—and succinct. Regarding this matter that is ennobled—which in the Islamic world would range from dinnerware to home design: does it automatically transmit an effect on all who perceive it? If someone not trained in a tradition were to walk into a mosque, would that person necessarily be affected? Or is training necessary to receive what sacred art has to offer?*

SN: There are degrees and levels. Usually art has its own language, and in the same way that you or I cannot understand Sanskrit unless we have studied it, it is not always so easy to be able to enter into an art world and to understand its language fully. It requires training—like learning a language—to fully appreciate the artistic message of a civilization or tradition alien to oneself. But this being said, this ennobling of matter nevertheless allows certain cosmic qualities, certain forms of beauty, to reflect through matter. And even if that's not totally appreciated, it is appreciated to a great extent by those who come into contact with it. That's why ninety percent, let's say, of American tourists who go from a Mid-western state into the Alhambra, as soon as they enter they say "Oh, how beautiful." That's their first comment. They've not fully understood the whole message, the very complicated geometric symbolism and the calligraphy and what the calligraphy says, but nevertheless there is the immediate impact of an ambience in which the inner structure of matter is brought out. Its opacity is changed to a transparency. But there are a small number of people who are themselves almost totally opaque vis-à-vis art forms alien to them. That can happen. Look at many of the white people when they first came to America. They had no appreciation whatsoever of the art of the American Indians. And look what was destroyed before gradually people began to realize that this was a very beautiful form of art.

JZ: *You're aware of course that Peter Brook is currently staging the* Mahabharata *in New York. Are there any artists working today, outside of the traditional revealed religions, whose work you would recommend?*

SN: This is a difficult question to answer. I know Peter Brook very well personally, from the old days when he used to come to Iran and we had days and days of discussion about sacred art and sacred theater and how it is possible to bring some of those elements into the modern situation. I've not seen the *Mahabharata*, but he's brought at least some people to an awareness that there are other forms of art than the usual humanistic art which they have been surrounded by. As far as music is concerned, there are people who write classical music which has a certain amount of qualities to it, although it's certainly not traditional music. And certainly for literature, I would say T. S. Eliot and Ezra Pound are two great poets of the English language who sought to recreate and rediscover tradition through their poetry. And Paul Claudel in French. These are not completely traditional writers but they have certain positive qualities which can be appreciated. In the domain of painting, there are some Mexican painters who try to use American Indian language in a contemporary form, and some Navajo painters bring out certain qualities. The paintings of Frithjof Schuon—he was a painter in addition to being a metaphysician—are a very fine example of this, of a person who paints in a medium that's not totally traditional. So it is possible.

JZ: *Even with the few people you mention, one can see that there is somewhat of a resurgence of interest in traditional art. But, of course, it's miniscule compared to what was available centuries ago. What are the possibilities for traditional art today? And what are the possibilities for most people to respond creatively? These seem to be dark times. Are they?*

SN: They are dark times, but they also have their very profound compensation, in the sense that the more the truth becomes inaccessible to us the more closely does it embrace us from the outside. The very darkness of the times makes possible and easy things which themselves were very difficult in the old days. And therefore there are possibilities even in these dark times. One should never lose hope. But the most important thing, of course, is to be able to live a spiritual life and to have a traditional discipline to live by inwardly, and therefore to be able to respond to God from the depth of our being. Once we do that, whether we happen to be a bookkeeper or a flute player or something in between, there's no lack of creativity. We will not say, "Oh, I wasted my life because I wanted to be creative and I wasn't and I was just putting books on the shelf," when we realize that to have lived in fact according to the Divine

Command, according to the Will of God, is to respond in fact to God at every moment of life. And whether that response comes in the form of going to an office or cutting wood or painting—that really becomes somewhat secondary, because our own inner nature dictates that. Today, for many people what is called creativity is really a substitute for finding their own center. They place their center in that work which is outside of them. That's why oftentimes you have people producing remarkable works who themselves are terrible people to be with, and whose works in a sense are not them, because they have no center within themselves. The most important thing is to discover one's center.

Parabola
Volume: 16.3
Craft

SOME NOTES ON ARAB CALLIGRAPHY

Jean Sulzberger

Plato wrote, "Writing is the geometry of the spirit, and it manifests itself by means of the organs of the body."

And the Arab calligraphers say, "The essence of writing is in the spirit, even though it is manifested by means of the limbs."

The harmony one feels in Arab calligraphy comes from specific rules that are followed, so that knowledge and presence as well as a disciplined hand are required. Calligraphy is a spiritual exercise. The calligraphers teach that when a man is inwardly free, his writing is good. Disciples of master calligraphers have to undergo fasts and a long training to purify themselves before they can write. "Purity of writing is purity of soul," it is said.

Ali, the fourth Caliph, was a calligrapher, and other follows of Muhammad were known as *Sahib as-sayf wa'l-qalam* (masters of the sword and the pen). "God first created the *qalam* [the pen]," Muhammad said.

Everything connected with the calligraphers' art has significance, beginning with the qalam. Several kinds of trimmed reed pens play as important a role in calligraphy as voices do in song. After a sharp knife makes a point in the qalam, the point is then split lengthwise into two parts "so that when it is put to paper it should vibrate and a ringing be heard." The part nearer the thumb, when the pen is held for writing, is called *unsi*, or human, and the other side is called *wahshi*, or wild.

The letters—there are twenty-eight letters in the Arabic alphabet—are said to be various aspects of human beings and animals. Each letter is spoken of as having a head, an eye, a nose, an arm, a leg, a trunk, or a tail. The letters are spoken of as being erect, straight, bent, standing, seated, good-looking, ugly, fat, tall, or short. For example, in the cursive scripts, the first letter, *alif*, is compared to a man standing up and looking down at his feet as if standing in prayer.

Disciples learn how to make the qalam, how to make it a good tool, how to make ink without fuss, the kind of paper to use, the colors to use to write in gold, how to make paste, how to polish the paper so that there are no creases in it, how to trim the qalam and clip its nib. They have to study the letters, to look at the "strengths and weaknesses" of the letters, to watch their "ascents and descents," and they have to prepare themselves before copying so that they can give it full attention. They are told to refrain from mistakes—"through mistakes no one will become someone."

O you who have not yet written one letter,
How can a master give you instruction?
For instruction in good writing
Cannot be given in your absence.
If the elements are hidden from you, and
    you yourself are absent,
Your objection has no sense.
Know that the theory of writing is shrouded,
And no one knows it until he has made an effort.
Until your teacher has told you by word of mouth,
You will not write with ease.
The means to impart some knowledge
Is both by writing and by word of mouth,
But know that the important thing is oral instruction
By which difficulties become easy.
                    —*From an eleventh-century Persian manuscript*

Arab sources say that the first man who wrote in Arabic and used the pen was Adam; after him Seth. Others say Abraham or Enoch invented writing. After the Quranic revelation, Arabic script became the carrier of the revelation to the Muslim world. "The noblest of the visual arts in the world of Islam is calligraphy, and it is the writing of the Quran that is sacred art *par excellence*," Titus Burckhardt wrote. "It plays a part more or less analogous to that of the icon in Christian art, for it represents the visible body of the Divine Word."[1]

God says through His prophets, "Be!" (*kun*), and this command and all that issues from it was first written in the Quran in *jazm*, the earliest Arabic script, and the progenitor of the famous Kufic script. Kufic was followed in the tenth century by six major styles: *thuluth, naskh, muhaqqaq, rayhani, tawqi, and riqa*. These styles are named after certain masters and schools. Kufic was named after the Iraqi city of Kufa where there was a school during the caliphate of Ali. In Kufic writing, one-sixth is circular and the rest is straight. Its horizontal and vertical lines look like squares and rectangles and are usually drawn with such geometric precision that the length and width and the distances separating them are equal. The Dome of the Rock in Jerusalem and the Alhambra Palace in Granada have Kufic inscriptions. Thuluth is the style often used for writing titles of chapters (*surahs*) in the Quran. *Naskhi*, a simpler, more rounded form than thuluth, is generally used in the body of Quranic texts. It is said that thuluth has the face of a grown-up and naskhi the face of an innocent boy.

Scripts that go into the writing of the Quran are also present in Islamic architecture, in tilework and woodwork, in pottery, inlaid bronzes, miniature paintings, and in the "zoomorphic" calligraphy that takes the shape of lions, camels, birds, or men.

The patterns of calligraphy, the distended, arched, or rounded letters endlessly reproducing themselves in a harmonious order that is somehow felt, are symbolic of the order of nature which in always changing is always repeating itself. The meandering horizontal lines are said to represent the continuity of life, and the vertical lines correspond to a permanent inner structure. "The richness of the Arabic script comes from the fact that it has fully developed its two 'dimensions': the vertical, which confers on the letters their hieratic dignity, and the horizontal, which links them together in a continuous flow," writes Burckhardt. "As in the symbolism of weaving, the vertical lines, analogous to the 'warp' of the fabric, correspond to the permanent essence of things—it is by the vertical that the unalterable character of each letter is affirmed—whereas the horizontal, analogous to the 'weft,' expresses becoming or the matter that links one thing to another."[2]

Notes:

1   Titus Burckhardt, *Sacred Art in East and West* (London: Perennial Books, 1967), p. 116.

2   *Ibid.*

Parabola
Volume: 21.3
Peace

Underneath Which Rivers Flow

Emma Clark

It is written in the Quran that the only word spoken in the Gardens of Paradise is "Peace": "There hear they no vain speaking nor recrimination. [Naught] but the saying 'Peace, [and again] Peace'" (56:25-26). These gardens are the archetype on which all Islamic gardens of the *chahar-bagh* (literally, "four-gardens") design are based. One of the principal functions, therefore, of these earthly "Gardens of Paradise" is to provide beautiful and harmonious surroundings—a retreat from the world—where the soul can let go of distracting thoughts and be at peace.

No words except "Peace," *salam.* The search for paradise on earth is, essentially, the search for peace—not just peace from the world but more importantly, peace from our own soul (*nafs*)—not the immortal soul, but the passional soul, the ego and its desires. The greater *jihad* (*al-jihad al-akbar*), according to a saying of the Prophet, is the war with our own souls. The longing, more often unconscious than conscious, for serenity of soul is like a vague memory of our primordial state before the Fall when man was at peace with his Creator and therefore at peace with himself and his neighbor. In order to regain this primordial paradise, those seriously committed to the spiritual path (*at-tariqa*) must reach a state of constant remembrance of God (*dhikr Allah*). The Islamic garden can be an aid in this remembrance; like all sacred art, the chahar-bagh aims to draw the visitor closer to God. Thus the concept of paradise is symbolic of the true peace of heart and soul for which each one of us, "exiled on earth", yearns.

The chahar-bagh is a garden divided into four quarters (sometimes each quarter also divided) by water-channels or pathways, with a fountain or pool at the center. This fourfold design of the Islamic garden developed from a combination of the ancient Persian prototype and the Gardens of Paradise as described in the Quran and the Sayings of the Prophet. Also, inherent within the number four is a universal symbolism based on an understanding of the natural world: it encompasses the four cardinal directions, the four elements and the four seasons—and the cube, the three-dimensional form of the number four, represents solidity, the Earth.[1] The religion of Islam re-confirmed these ancient and universal truths and invested them with a rigorous spiritual vision. In describing his ascent to heaven (*mi'raj*), the Prophet speaks of four rivers: one of water, one of milk, one of honey, and one of wine. These four rivers are also mentioned in the Quran 47:15,[2] and in Genesis it is written, "And a river went out of Eden to water the garden and from thence it was parted into four heads" (Genesis 2:10).

   In the Quran there is also to be found another, more esoteric, reason for the quartered layout of the Islamic garden—in *Surat ar-Rahman* (*sura* 55: The All-Merciful). This is the longest reference to the Gardens of Paradise in the Quran, and in this sura four gardens are described. According to the commentator, al-Qashani, these four gardens are divided into two parts, the lower pair being the Garden of the Soul and the Garden of the Heart (reserved for the Righteous) and the higher pair being the Garden of the Spirit and the Garden of the Essence (reserved for the Foremost). Each of these four gardens contains, respectively, its own fruit—the olive, the date, the fig, and the pomegranate; each also contains its own fountain. There is a complex and profound symbolism contained in the four gardens of *Surat ar-Rahman* which is not appropriate to go into here.[3] However, what is important to emphasize is that the fourfold form of the Islamic garden is not just a whim of design but a reflection of a higher reality.

Thus the chahar-bagh became the principal symbol of the Quranic Gardens of Paradise. It was taken up and developed all over the Islamic world—Iran (in Isfahan, for instance, there is a road called the Avenue of the Chahar-Bagh, which in earlier times was lined with several beautiful gardens), India (for example the gardens of the Taj Mahal), Morocco, and Moorish Spain—notably the courtyard gardens of the Alhambra Palaces and the nearby gardens of the Generalife. One glance at any of these gardens shows that they all have a fundamental element in common: water.[4] Water is the supreme element in the Islamic garden, both on a physical and a metaphysical level.

Since the Arabs were used to a harsh desert climate they already, before the Quran was revealed, considered water and any indication of nature's greenness as sacred. On a purely practical level, life on earth cannot survive without water; water is life-giving and in a hot country it is far more than this—it is a blessing from God. In the Quran, as Martin Lings points out, "the ideas of Mercy and water—in particular rain—are in a sense inseparable."[5] Water was considered a direct symbol of God's mercy: "He ... sendeth down water from the sky, and thereby quickeneth the earth after her death" (30:24). However, water contains within itself far more than physically nourishing properties; as Titus Burckhardt beautifully explains, "the soul resembles water, just as the Spirit resembles wind or air."[6] The concept of water as an image of the soul is a universal symbol appearing in Christian, Hindu, Japanese, and many other cultures as well as Islamic—and this symbolism derives from its very essence. Water is used not just to cleanse ourselves of physical dirt but also to "wash away sins"—in Christian baptism for instance—and in Islam the ablutions before prayer cleanse the soul as well as the body. The fountain in the center of the Islamic garden represents the ever-flowing waters of the Spirit, constantly renewing the soul, like the purity of natural spring water constantly renewing itself. According to Burckhardt, there is an inscription in the Alhambra: "The fountain in my midst is like the soul of a believer, immersed in the remembrance of God."[7]

The concept of the soul recognizing itself "when it beholds water—finding animation in its play, refreshment in its rest, and purity in its clarity"[8] is rarely more in evidence than in the different manifestations of water in an Islamic garden. The water trickles gently, cascades down small waterfalls, sprays from fountains, runs along channels and streams, or remains still in pools, reflecting the sky above. Constant movement and stillness combine to create a harmonious environment which both soothes the soul and reflects its own fluidity, while at the same time remaining pure and "true to its undivided essence."[9]

In the Quran there are over one hundred and twenty references to the Gardens of Paradise, variously described, but the phrase most often repeated is "Gardens underneath which rivers flow." Irrigation in a hot country is often conducted underground to avoid evaporation by the sun; this is true of many Islamic gardens where water is channeled below the earth in order to nourish the plants from beneath.

Nowhere is water more in evidence and more soothing—to the eye and to the ear and, above all, to the soul—than in the courtyard gardens of the Alhambra and in the gardens of the Generalife in Granada, Spain. When the Muslim Arabs first arrived in Granada, with its combination of mountain and Mediterranean climate, they must have believed they had found their earthly Gardens of Paradise. Here there was plenty of water flowing down from the snow-capped Sierra Nevada mountains—it was just a question of harnessing it for their needs, which they soon achieved with an ingenious system of aqueducts and reservoirs. Burckhardt wrote that water is the secret life of the Alhambra[10]—and certainly this is true. From the Cuarto Dorado (or Mexuar), with its perfect central fountain—a low scalloped basin of pale marble with a gently trickling stream of water—to the large still pool of the Court of Myrtles, and then to the Court of Lions where the central fountain is a large basin supported by twelve lions, water is prominent, awakening and inspiring the senses: not just the sense of sight, but the senses of hearing and touch too. The Court of Lions, with its four channels of water streaming from four fountains, one on each side of the courtyard, toward the center, echoes the Quranic four rivers returning to their source, the "reservoir of heavenly waters."[11]

These courtyards echo the courtyard of the typical Arab-Islamic house, which opens inwards, towards the heart, rather than outwards, towards the world, and corresponds to separation of the private and public domains in a traditional Islamic society. It represents the inward, contemplative aspect of man, Rumi writing that "the real gardens and flowers are within, they are in man's heart, not outside."[12] The courtyard is thus itself a kind of miniature garden of paradise, the essential ingredient being not trees, plants, and flowers, but running water.

From the courtyards of the Alhambra palaces it is a short walk to the Generalife gardens. The jewel at the heart of the Generalife is the Patio de la Acequia, meaning literally "of the Aqueduct." This garden is high up on the side of the hill; it is approached through a small courtyard, up some steps and then up some more—covered, dark—steps, and then, altogether unexpectedly, a small arch opens out onto what can only be described as a "vision of Paradise." Here we experience a taste of what the Quran promises to the God-fearing: a "garden underneath which rivers flow." To sit in this garden for any length of time, slowly absorbing the peace contained there, allows the sound of the water gradually to drown out all preoccupations of the soul; an overwhelming sense of peace descends, and the visitor is drawn into a state of contemplation of Divine Unity.

"Exiled on earth as we are, unless we are able to content ourselves with that shadow of Paradise that is Virgin Nature, we must create for ourselves surroundings which, by their truth and their beauty recall our heavenly origin and thereby also awaken our hope."[13]

Notes:

1   The Ka'bah is symbolically the center of the world to Muslims; its shape is almost exactly a cube and the word Ka'bah means "cube." The circle represents Heaven, and so the circumambulation of the Ka'bah is symbolically where a man joins heaven and earth.

2   In the Garden are "rivers of water unpolluted, and rivers of milk whereof the flavor changeth not, and rivers of wine delicious to the drinkers, and rivers of clear-run honey."

3   For a fuller explanation of *Surat ar-Rahman* please refer to Abu Bakr Siraj ad-Din, *The Book of Certainty* (Cambridge, England: The Islamic Texts Society, 1992) and Frithjof Schuon, *Islam and the Perennial Philosophy* (London: World of Islam Festival Publishing Company Ltd., 1976), Chapter 12.

4   In many cases, very sadly, it has proved too expensive to maintain the water, and dried-up channels, pools, and fountains are all too common—literally the life and the soul of the garden are gone.

5   Martin Lings, *Symbol and Archetype, A Study of the Meaning of Existence* (Cambridge, England: Quinta Essentia, 1991), p. 67.

6 Titus Burckhardt, *Mirror of the Intellect* (Cambridge, England: Quinta Essentia, 1987), p. 128.

7 Burckhardt, *Moorish Culture in Spain*, (Munich: George D. W. Calley, 1970; English translation by Alisa Jaffa, London: Geoge Allen and Unwin, 1972), p. 208.

8 Burckhardt, *Mirror of the Intellect*, p. 128.

9 *Ibid.*

10 Burckhardt, *Moorish Culture in Spain*, p. 206.

11 *Ibid.*, p. 209.

12 Jalal al-Din Rumi, *Mathnawi* IV:1357, quoted by Annemarie Schimmel, *The Celestial Garden* (Washington: Dumbarton Oaks, 1976).

13 Frithjof Schuon, *Esoterism as Principle and Way* (London: Perennial Books, 1981), p. 196.

Parabola
Volume: 26.1
The Garden

GRAZE IN THE MEADOWS

Shems Friedlander

For the Sufi, the garden had many meanings. It was a place of repose, a centrally located space that allowed one to enter any number of buildings, a place of beauty and meditation, a horizon where Allah had indicated the signs of life, and a place where one could find the Gardener.

Every *tekke*, or prayer lodge, of the dervishes had a garden that was shielded from the outside by exterior walls. The garden was a heart to the many buildings, which, like the projecting wings of a great bird, would enfold it, making up the whole of the tekke. The *semahane* (for the Mevlevis the place for turning and for other dervish orders the place for their ceremony of the remembrance of God), *majlis* (the room for spiritual conversation), women's quarters, kitchen, library, ablution fountain, sheikh's residence, and mosque could all be accessed from the garden.

The Konya Mevlevi tekke is a conical tower, blue-green tiled, fluted, and with a pointed roof, indicating that the tomb of Rumi is in the interior space below. On special occasions a sema would be performed in the tekke's spacious garden court under a sky dotted with birds and billowing clouds.

Rumi said:

> *I am a bird of the heavenly garden.*
> *I belong not to the earthly sphere.*

They have made for two or three days,
A cage of my body.

During these "two or three days" of his life on earth, the dervish remains hidden, his concealment a protection, like the beautiful rose protected by the thorn. He is disguised by clothing or a mental attitude. Fariduddin Attar, the twelfth-century Sufi poet and author of *The Conference of the Birds*, engaged in the trade of a chemist and had a shop in the bazaar. Others wrote on literary matters, were booksellers, poets, or pursued other callings. Many sheikhs wrote verses about love; like Rumi, they were writing of metaphysical love, that which was beyond the physical, but not everyone understood this. They concealed who they really were so as to avoid the "pestering" of worldly persons. The Prophet Muhammad said: "Allah has hidden the true men of piety."

One day Sirajuddin, a *khalifa* or high initiate of Rumi, went to the garden of Husamuddin and picked a bunch of flowers for Rumi. When he entered the house, he saw that many important and learned people were sitting and listening to Rumi give a spiritual discourse. Sirajuddin was taken by the talk and forgot about the flowers. Rumi turned to him and said that whoever comes from a garden should bring flowers with him, as whoever comes from the shop of the sweet-seller is expected to bring back some sweets.

Rumi once said in such a discourse that God had a collyrium that, when applied to one's eyes, opens the inner vision, allowing one to see the mystery of existence and know the meaning of hidden things. One also can be illuminated by the gaze of a sheikh. Rumi reminds us that when the inward eye is opened one sees that the flowers that grow from plants are living but a moment, while the flowers that grow from reason are ever fresh. The flowers that bloom from earth become faded while the flowers that bloom from the heart produce joy. All the delightful sciences known to us are only two or three bunches of flowers from that Garden. We are devoted to these two or three bouquets because we have shut the Garden-door on ourselves.

"Behold our words!" Rumi said. "They are the fragrance of those roses—we are the rosebush of certainty's rose garden." The fragrance of the rose can lead one to the rose and even the Rose-seller. But sometimes Rumi was anxious that time not be wasted, as he indicates in this poem:

> *My poetry resembles Egyptian bread:*
> *When a night passes over it you cannot eat it anymore.*
> *Eat it at this point when it is fresh,*
> *Before dust settles upon it.*

For Rumi the sema was an emotional relationship between man and God. In his *Divan* he states:

> *Sema is only for the restless spirit—so jump up quickly, why do*
> *you wait?*
> *Do not sit here with your own thoughts—if you are human, go*
> *to the Beloved.*
> *Do not say, "Perhaps He does not want me."*
> *What business has a thirsty man with such words?*
> *Does the moth think about the flames? For Love's spirit, thought*
> *is a disgrace.*
> *When the warrior hears the sound of the drum, at once he is worth*
> *ten thousand men.*

The sema has become a window towards the sacred rose garden.

Several kilometers outside of Konya, sitting peacefully on a hilltop in Meram, was the house of Husamuddin, Rumi's khalifa and confidant. The wooden house was spacious with a generous garden and an orchard. Rumi often came to this garden to meditate, give spiritual discourse, and make a sema in which he was joined by many of his disciples. Rumi turned with his arms close to his body, holding his robe, not like the turn we see today from the Whirling Dervishes, which was created by Rumi's son Sultan Veled. Rumi's nature was filled with kindness and so he allowed his disciples to embrace him gently as he turned and for a short time to turn with him.

A similar movement can be seen in the Bedevi Topu of the Halveti dervishes. The sheikh breaks the turning *dhikr* circle and holds the hands, crossed at the wrists, of one of his dervishes. They slowly turn together repeating the Name of Allah. The other dervishes form concentric circles around them with the blessing of the inner reaching the outmost circle.

It was on such a summer evening in the garden of Husamuddin that Rumi began to speak of the Prophet Muhammad.

> *The Prophet is not called "unlettered" because he was unable to write. He was called that because his "letters," his knowledge and wisdom, were innate, not acquired. Is a person who made inscriptions on the moon unable to write? What is there in the world that such a person does not know, when all learn from him? What can partial intellect have that the Universal Intellect has not? The partial intellect is not capable of inventing anything it has not seen before. Remember the story of the raven: when Cain killed Abel and stood not knowing what to do with the body, one raven killed another, dug out the earth, buried the dead raven and scratched the dirt over the body. From this Cain learned how to make a grave and bury a body. All trades are like this. The possessor of partial intellect needs instruction. Those who have united the partial with the Universal Intellect and become one are prophets and saints.*

There is a story that Charlemagne sent a most perfect rose as a gift to the caliph Harun Rashid. He gave it to his gardener and told him to plant it with great care and to bring the first rose to him. The gardener carefully planted the rose in a beautiful part of the garden.

The next day a crow came and ate the rose. Trembling, the gardener told the news to Harun Rashid. He told the gardener not to worry, for the punishment of the crow would be the same as that of the rose. A few days later a snake came upon the crow and killed him. The gardener told the news to the caliph who again told him that the fate of the snake would be the same as the crow. The next day the gardener was working in the garden when he spotted the snake. He picked up an axe and killed the snake. The caliph told him that his fate would be the same.

As it happened the gardener did something wrong and was thrown in jail. The day he was to be hanged he requested to see Harun Rashid. He reminded the caliph of the rose, the crow, and the snake and said that if the caliph would show forgiveness toward him, then he would save himself from a like fate.

Rumi says:

> *The one who sleeps in the midst of a garden*
> *wants to be awakened.*
> *But the one who sleeps in a prison, to be*
> *awakened is a nuisance.*

A hadith of the Prophet Muhammad states:

> *When you pass by the meadows of the*
> *   Garden, graze!*
> *They asked:*
> *   O messenger of God,*
> *   What are the meadows of the Garden?*
> *And he replied:*
> *   The circles of remembrance.*

For the Muslim the greatest of all gardens is Paradise. Rumi expresses this with a concise verse:

> *The gardens may flow with beauty*
> *But let us go to the Gardener Himself.*

Parabola
Volume: 30.2
Restraint

ADAB: THE SUFI ART OF CONSCIOUS RELATIONSHIP

Kabir Helminski

Etiquette, manners, thoughtfulness – no single expression adequately captures the full meaning of *adab*. Adab is the ability to sense what is appropriate to each moment and to give to each its due – a continuous process of refining one's speech and actions. To have adab is to be cultured.

It has been said that the highest attainment of Sufism is nothing but good character. What is meant, however, is not a rigid moralism but a natural, spontaneous beauty of character that is the result of a long maturing process of transformation. The ripened fruit of this kind of practice is not an abstract and impersonal ideal, but a person with whom you would like to sit down and have a cup of tea. It is an embodied spirituality.

Some years ago, a group of American spiritual teachers, all of whom were representatives of traditional Sufi lineages, were gathered in a home in San Francisco. Someone proposed a question: Of all that this tradition has taught us, what stands out as most important and valuable? We were all trained in different orders, from cultures as different as Turkey, North Africa, Iran, and South Asia, and were startled by how quickly we arrived at a consensus. Adab stood out as the most valuable teaching we had received.

•

Neither our American culture nor the times we lived in had put much emphasis on "manners." We had been a rough-and-tumble generation that had passed through a period of rebellion against what we saw as the hypocrisies of our society: informality was viewed as authentic behavior; manners, or etiquette was at best a quaint and irrelevant concept. What, then, accounted for the magnetic power of adab?

From what I remember of our conversation that day, we seemed to think that adab had enabled a certain quality of relationship among ourselves, across the boundaries of our orders, and in the teaching situation within our own communities. It had softened our egos, and introduced a quality of refinement in our relationships. On the path of Sufism my own idea of spiritual attainment had been transformed from austere enlightenment to an embodied humility. This is not to say that any of us felt we had attained this ideal, but we held an image of it in our hearts, an image that had been formed by contact with certain of our teachers who were living examples of humility, sincerity, sensitivity, respect, courtesy – in short, adab.

Some of the best examples of adab are those I have seen being lived in certain Sufi families. We have known and welcomed as guests into our home three generations of the direct descendants of Rumi. A more cultivated and courteous family I have never known. Adab is reflected in every aspect of life: dressing, eating, serving food, speaking, welcoming guests. I remember one cold winter morning in our farmhouse in Vermont when I came down to the mud room, to find that the dozens of shoes and winter boots had all been aligned in rows with the toes pointing into the house. Jelal Chelebi, the twenty-year-old twenty-third generation descendant of Rumi, had taken it upon himself to put our shoes into order. Instantly, it came back to me that in Turkey I had never seen a chaos of shoes in a Sufi home. When I thanked our young Chelebi, it was clear that his was an act of humble service and not in the least a criticism or reprimand.

Children in Sufi families are lovingly given subtle cues about how to behave and move through the world. Abdulbaki Gölpinarli, perhaps the greatest documentor of Sufi life in the last century, wrote this about his own upbringing:

I remember that, when I was a child, if I walked quickly, or stamped my feet, people would say to me (not out of anger), "What are you doing, Baki? What kind of a way is that to walk? My child, everything has a heart, a life, a soul; wouldn't the wood get hurt? Look, it's laid itself on the floor for us to walk on. Shouldn't we show respect, and not hurt it?"

If I smacked my lips during a meal, all it took to stop me was a look. Except for conversation, a meal was to be silent. If one made a noise by setting one's glass down, for instance, it was considered unmannerly, a sort of minor sin; neither the glass nor the place one put it on should be treated carelessly. What a bad thing it was to drink water without interacting with the glass, without kissing it before drinking from it, or again before putting it back down! "The glass," they would say, "is serving us; we should honor it." While going to sleep every night and again while waking up every morning, I would kiss the pillow; while pulling the sheets up over me or taking them off, I would interact with them as well.

In the Mevlevi tradition this respect was extended to inanimate objects to such an extent that one would never say, "Please put out the candle," but rather, "Put the candle to rest." Nor would one "close" a door, but "cover" it. Fastidious care was taken to convey respect in one's language. And for every object that one used in daily life, one would engage in a reciprocal seeing with it. In other words, as I pick up my coat, I might kiss it lightly, see it, and *be seen by it*. In Turkish there is a phrase which literally means "seeing with it." Gölpinarli continues:

In our household, we wouldn't shout to each other, or interrupt someone while he was speaking, and when in a group, we would speak to the whole group, not just to one or two people. The idea of whispering in someone's ear, or of laughing loudly, was foreign to our household.

The practical outcome of adab was to help create an atmosphere of sharing, of unity, of coherence. Within a Sufi environment, conversation around a table does not quickly break up into several personal discussions with whoever is adjacent, but proceeds as a shared experience. If one has reason to address another person, one doesn't thereby cut oneself off from the conversation of the whole.

Another aspect of adab is being conscious when one uses the words "I" or "me," when one uses them at all. In certain Sufi orders, for instance, it would be customary not to use the word "I" while working or serving in the *tekke*. Some prefer to refer to themselves as "this fakir," meaning one who is destitute and utterly dependent on God for everything.

Adab in practice is subtle and nuanced. To become judgmental because others fail in their adab would be rude and antithetical to adab itself. And for adab to degenerate into rigid formality would also belie its essence, for there is a proper adab for every situation. Among intimate friends, for example, the proper adab may sometimes be utter informality and ease. Adab is best learned by example and in community.

It is said that there is an adab within spiritual circles, with parents and children, with elders, and even with God. Al-Hujwiri, an early (d. 1077) commentator on Sufism, wrote:

> *A person who neglects this discipline cannot ever possibly be a saint, for the Prophet said, "Adab is a mark of those whom God loves." One must keep oneself from disrespect toward God in one's private as well as one's public behavior. We have it from a sound Hadith that once, when God's Messenger was sitting with his legs akimbo, the Angel Gabriel appeared and said: "Muhammad, sit as servants sit before their master."*

There is a story of a Sufi, Muhasibi, who for forty years never stretched out his legs even when alone. (To point the soles of one's feet directly in the direction of others is not considered well-mannered in most cultures outside of America.) When questioned, he answered, "I am ashamed to sit otherwise than as a servant while I remember God."

It should be emphasized, however, that in Sufi understanding substance takes precedence over form, inner intention counts for more than outer behavior. The Prophet Muhammad, peace and blessings upon him, said that to be valid the ritual prayer must be accompanied by presence (*hudur*) – it is not the outer form alone which is obligatory. At the same time, Rumi proposes that the observance of these outer requirements polishes the essence. Properly understood and consciously applied, attention to the details of form is a way of working on our own essence. Ritual prayer gives the body an experience of surrender that would be difficult to achieve in any other way.

The Prophet Muhammad is known to have acted in specific ways – always putting on the right sandal first, or stepping into a house with the right foot, and out of it with the left. His behavior is widely imitated. Some formalists insist on mimicking his behavior as if there was something objectively better about using the right foot first, but could it be that these behaviors are reminders to help us live more attentively? The outer aspect of adab is intended to guide us toward greater consciousness and inner sincerity. The form is not an end in itself but a potential container for various qualities of being.

The spiritual path of Sufism is informed by an awareness of levels of reality, of inner purification, of qualities of consciousness. *Shari'ah* is the level of religious law and external morals, while *tariqah* is the esoteric path, a complete education of the human being under the guidance of a teacher. Among the Sufis, adab practically became their shari'ah. Instead of merely avoiding immoral and destructive behavior, the Sufis attempted to embody the qualities of kindness, thoughtfulness, generosity, and self-sacrifice.

Here is a story as told by Abdulbaki Gölpinarli that shows how he as a young child was taught the significance of adab in relationship to the mystical Path:

> *One day, I went to a tekke with Ahmed Hamdi Tanyeli to ask a question. I knocked on the door of the harem, and we heard a shrill female voice, as if it was scolding us: "Who is it?"*
>
> *Ahmed Hamdi Tanyeli said that it must be the tenants. We asked for the shaikh.*
>
> *The woman shrieked again:*
> *"They are on the other side of the building."*
> *"I told you so," said Ahmed Hamdi.*
> *We went to the selamlik, the part of the building reserved for greeting people outside the immediate family. From the main entrance we*

walked through the garden and knocked on the door. From inside we heard a sweet voice ask us, "Who is it?" We asked for the shaikh.

She replied, "He has traveled to Allah." We asked for his son. The sweet voice said, "He has gone as well." She asked if we needed anything. "Please, sit on the bench in the garden," she said, "and fakir *will soon come to you."*

We sat down. After a couple of minutes, a middle-aged woman came out and served us cups of Turkish coffee. She sat down and greeted us. We told her what we had come for, and she gave us as much information as she could.

We talked a little more, and then we asked for permission to leave. She accompanied us to the door, and as we departed we heard behind us her sweet voice saying, "Goodbye! Be well! You brought good luck. Inshallah, *come back again."*

Ahmed Tanyeli turned to me and said:

"That first place we went to was shari'ah; this place is tariqah."

It will certainly seem unfair in the eyes of some to dismiss, or even condemn the level of shari'ah in this way. Perhaps what the shaikh was pointing to is the need for another level of awareness. Sufis refer to an "adab of service" which is the realization that every moment of our lives can be lived in service to Allah. If such an adab were to permeate one's life, one would know how little belongs to us and how much is owed to God.

From *Mevlevilik Sonra Mevlanadan* by Abdulbaki Gölpinarli, translated by Nilufer Devecigil and Kabir Helminski.

•

CHAPTER FOUR

Signs in the Cosmos

You are the notes, and we are the flute.
We are the mountain, you are the sounds coming down.
We are the pawns and kings and rooks
you set out on a board: we win or we lose.
We are lions rolling and unrolling on flags.
Your invisible wind carries us through the world.[1]

—Rumi

The double movement of apogee and perigee of the stars
resembles the double journey of the pilgrims who approach
and recede from Mecca in their going and returning.
Each pilgrim carries with him his business, money,
masterpieces, gifts, and rings before encountering on the
sacred ground pilgrims coming from all the nations and
belonging to all sects and all doctrines.
The pilgrims make intimate contact among themselves and
exchange during their stay merchandise and ideas.
Once the rite of pilgrimage is accomplished, each returns to his country
provided with the pardon and the satisfaction of God.

Likewise, O Brother, is the propagation by effusion of the forces of the
superior beings from the outermost sphere to the center of the earth.
Their union and provisional stay in matter of particular bodies gives rise
to exchange among individuals belonging to the realm of generation and
corruption—that is, minerals, plants and animals.
Their enthusiastic return, once the end of their journey is reached,
toward their point of departure resembles
term by term the stages of human pilgrimage to Mecca.

*The particular souls who regain—in passing
beyond the outermost sphere—their original source,
return happily to the world of Eternity.*

*Man should thus meditate on his original home
and awaken from his ignorant sleep,
and desire fervently to return to his celestial abode
announcing finally* Labbaika Labbaika,
*"At Thy orders," to the call of God:
"But O thou soul at peace! Return unto thy Lord content in
His good pleasure!" (Quran 89:27–28).*[2]

—The Ikhwan al-Safa

Parabola
Volume: 6.1
Earth and Spirit

IN PRAISE OF THE CREATOR

Fariduddin Attar

Praise to the Holy Creator, who has placed his throne upon the waters, and who has made all terrestrial creatures. To the Heavens he has given dominion and to the Earth dependence; to the Heavens he has given movement, and to the Earth uniform repose.

He raised the firmament above the earth as a tent, without pillars to uphold it. In six days he created the seven planets and with two letters he created the nine cupolas of the Heavens.

In the beginning he gilded the stars, so that at night the heavens might play tric-trac.

With diverse properties he endowed the net of the body, and he has put dust on the tail of the bird of the soul.

He made the Ocean liquid as a sign of bondage, and the mountain tops are capped with ice for fear of him.

He dried up the bed of the sea and from its stones brought forth rubies, and from its blood, musk.

To the mountains he has given peaks for a dagger, and valleys for a belt; so that they lift up their heads in pride.

Sometimes he throws bridges across the face of the waters. ...

Sun and Moon—one the day, the other the night, bow to the dust in adoration; and from their worship comes their movement.

•

It is God who has spread out the day in whiteness, it is he who has folded up the night and blackened it.

To the parrot he gave a collar of gold; and the hoopoe he made a messenger of the Way.

The firmament is like a bird beating its wings along the way God has marked out for him, striking the Door with his head as with a hammer.

God has made the firmament to revolve—night follows day and day the night.

When he breathes on clay man is created; and from a little vapour he forms the world.

Sometimes he causes the dog to go before the traveler; sometimes he uses the cat to show the Way.

Sometimes he gives the power of Solomon to a staff; sometimes he accords eloquence to the ant. ...

In winter he scatters the silver snow; in autumn, the gold of yellow leaves.

He lays a cover on the thorn and tinges it with the color of blood.

To the jasmine he gives four petals and on the head of the tulip he puts a red bonnet.

He places a gold crown on the brow of the narcissus; and drops pearls of dew into her shrine.

At the idea of God the mind is baffled, reasons fail; because of God the heavens turn, the earth reels.

From the back of the fish to the moon every atom is a witness to his Being.

The depths of the earth and the heights of heaven render him each their particular homage.

God produced the wind, the earth, the fire, and blood, and by these he announces his secret.

He took clay and kneaded it with water, and after forty mornings placed therein the spirit which vivified the body.

God gave it intelligence so that it might have discernment of things.

When he saw that intelligence had discernment, he gave it knowledge, so that it might weigh and ponder.

But when man came in possession of his faculties he confessed his impotence, and was overcome with amazement, while his body gave itself up to exterior acts.

Friends or enemies, all bow the head under the yoke which God, in his wisdom, imposes; and, a thing astonishing, he watches over us all …

There is none but Him. But, alas, no one can see Him. The eyes are blind, even though the world be lighted by a brilliant sun. Should you catch even a glimpse of Him you would lose your wits, and if you should see Him completely you would lose your self …

When the soul was joined to the body it was part of the all: never has there been so marvelous a talisman. The soul had a share of that which is high, and the body a share of that which is low; and it was formed of a mixture of heavy clay and pure spirit. By this mixing, man became the most astonishing of mysteries. We do not know nor do we understand so much as a little of our spirit. If you wish to say something about this, it would be better to keep silent. Many know the surface of this ocean, but they understand nothing of the depths; and the visible world is the talisman which protects it. But this talisman of bodily obstacles will be broken at last. You will find the treasure when the talisman disappears; the soul will manifest itself when the body is laid aside. But your soul is another talisman; it is, for this mystery, another substance. Walk then in the way I shall indicate, but do not ask for an explanation.

From *The Conference of the Birds* (Boulder: Shambhala Publications, 1971), rendered into English by C. S. Nott.

Parabola
Volume: 8.4
Sun and Moon

Traditional Cosmology and Modern Science

Interview with Seyyed Hossein Nasr

In recent years, the traditional sciences have begun to reclaim their rightful role as inclusive symbolic descriptions of the cosmos. No scholar has contributed more to this restoration than Dr. Seyyed Hossein Nasr. His lectures, essays, and authoritative books on Islamic science and metaphysics have alerted many to the rich possibilities of a perspective in which, as he writes in Islamic Life and Thought, *"nature and its grand phenomena such as the shining of the sun and the moon, the seasonal cycles, the mountains and streams, are ... means for the contemplation of the spiritual realities."*

Born in Tehran in 1933, Dr. Nasr studied mathematics and physics at M.I.T. before receiving his doctorate in the history of science and philosophy from Harvard University in 1958. For twenty-one years, he was a professor of Islamic philosophy and the history of science at Tehran University. In 1974, Dr. Nasr founded and served as the first president of the Iranian Academy of Philosophy, a position he held until 1979. In 1981, he became the first Muslim invited to deliver the prestigious Gifford Lectures at the University of Edinburgh. His books include Man and Nature, Science and Civilization in Islam, Islamic Sciences: An Illustrated Study, *and most recently (as of 1983),* Knowledge and the Sacred *(Crossroad Publishing Co.), the basic text of his Gifford Lectures.*

Neither sun nor moon was visible on an overcast day early in August when we arrived at Dr. Nasr's home in the low hills of suburban Boston. But our host rapidly replaced the gifts of these absent celestial spheres with his own warm hospitality (tea, a platter of Persian sweets) and a stream of intellectual radiance. He answered each of our questions at length, talking quietly, without verbal embroidery. His responses, drawn from an astonishing store of knowledge, effortlessly embraced centuries and civilizations, linking together al-Biruni's metaphysics, Christian cathedrals, and the sleight of hand of modern quantum physics

—Philip and Carol Zaleski

Parabola: *You have a deep knowledge of both contemporary and traditional sciences. Could you tell us what led you into studying each of these areas?*

Seyyed Hossein Nasr: I have been interested in science ever since I was a young boy. I thought that through sciences I would discover the nature of things; that was really what was at the back of my mind. At the same time I had, both as a child and later as an adolescent, a great deal of contact with my own traditional culture, which was not only religious in the usual sense—dealing with acts of worship, morality, and so forth—but also dealt with the science of the nature of things. Traditional culture, especially as it exists in Islam, to which I belong, as well as in the other great traditions of Asia, and of course Christianity, not only concerns itself with acts, but also with knowledge. And therefore that was also part of my background, training, and world view.

I went to M.I.T. to pursue my scientific studies; I thought that there I could get the best scientific education. When I was a sophomore, as a result of contact with leading physicists, with the late Giorgio De Santillana, the great philosopher and historian of science, and through hearing lectures by such famous people as Bertrand Russell about the nature of modern science, I became aware that the most important proponents of the scientific world view believed that, in fact, it was not the role of modern science to reach the nature of reality at all.

I felt that somehow this was not what I was looking for, that I was not going to understand the why of things, which was outside the domain of modern science, or even the how of things. In modern science, things are presented in terms of parameters without really dealing with the essence of those parameters except by means of mathematical descriptions. If you ask, "What is an electron," you can write out its mathematical function and solve it, but the "whatness" in a philosophical sense is circumvented. And so from that time on, when I was only eighteen years old, I became interested in seeing if there were other ways to study the nature of things and the world of nature. This urge, which was really metaphysical, led me very far afield. I began to study with De Santillana and a few other people at M. I. T. and later on at Harvard, benefiting especially from the great library of traditional sciences of the late Ananda Coomaraswamy. I also began to study various Oriental doctrines. At that time Suzuki was here in Cambridge, and I attended some of his classes. Gradually my interest shifted from the study of modern Western sciences—which I nevertheless wanted to know in depth, so that if I wanted to go beyond or criticize it at least I would know what it was—to other possibilities of studying reality. I became interested in metaphysics. It was at this point that the writings of certain people who were trying to resuscitate Oriental metaphysics—metaphysics in its real sense—in the West, such as René Guénon, Frithjof Schuon, Coomaraswamy, and others drew my attention. After several years of study of Far Eastern, Indian, and medieval Christian thought—Dante was key at this time in my life—my interests centered and came back to my own tradition, to Islamic cosmology. At Harvard, where I was then studying with George Sarton, Harry Wolfson, and Sir Hamilton Gibb, who were great scholars, philosophers, and Islamicists, I decided to concentrate on this subject. I did my Ph.D. thesis in this field, and from that grew the first book written in the English language on Islamic cosmology.

So my own personal contact with the worlds of traditional and modern science came from a fundamental question within myself—what is the nature of reality? That is what I was seeking.

P: *Do you think that it is possible for modern and traditional sciences, cosmology in particular, to work together, or must they conflict? What is the value in the modern world of studying traditional science?*

SHN: As to how these two worlds go or do not go together, I believe that there is no such thing as modern cosmology. Modern cosmology is a generalization of modern physics, whereas cosmology as it is understood traditionally is knowledge of the cosmos—not just knowledge of the material world generalized to include the whole of the astronomical world. The cosmos is not reducible to its physical or even psychological elements. Therefore, I do not even use the term "modern cosmology." We have modern astrophysics, and modern physics, but what we call modern cosmology is a generalization based upon the study of the physical parts of the cosmos. It certainly cannot constitute the whole of the cosmos. And that is why, when it tries to become cosmology, it always vacillates from one view to another. When you consider the question of the origin of the cosmos, you have a kind of fashion that changes more quickly than that of dress; one year it's the Big Bang theory, one year it's a slow accretion of gases, and so on. It's not based upon a scientific foundation, even if you accept the modern definition of science. Modern cosmology is not like modern chemistry or thermodynamics; it doesn't have the same basis.

Traditional cosmology starts from the other end. It is the application of metaphysical principles to the cosmos. That is, you first have to have knowledge which deals with the Supreme Principle, which is metacosmic, above the cosmos. In Christian terms, God, the Divinity, or the Godhead. And cosmic reality, which is created or manifested and sustained and finally reabsorbed into that Principle, is studied in the light of the knowledge of that Principle. That is why you have many cosmologies, even within a single tradition; there are many ways of studying the cosmic reality. Modern science claims to be the only way of studying nature, whereas traditional cosmology—look at Chinese or Indian cosmology—may have several cosmologies which are not inwardly contradictory.

I want to avoid two extremes, one of which is often held by certain people. One is that there is no conflict between modern science and religion, or traditional cosmology. There is a conflict, a very profound conflict. Modern science wants to study the whole of creation while abstracting the Divine Principle from it. Of course, modern science is now breaking up, and we might have another paradigm in the future, but the paradigm that has dominated from the seventeenth century until now is one in which the effect is studied without the supreme Cause. No matter how much you study the cosmos you never run into the supreme Cause because it is excluded by definition from the modern scientific view. Science defines itself in such a way as to be not interested in, and not related to, metaphysics. But what it discovers, to the extent that it corresponds to an aspect of reality, has a metaphysical significance. But that significance cannot be discovered through science itself. It can only be discovered by a person who knows those metaphysical principles. To say that there is no conflict between modern science and religion would reduce religion to faith alone and thus destroy the element of knowledge in religion. You end up with a secularization of knowledge, which leads to the catastrophes which humanity is faced with today.

The other pole is to say that there is complete conflict between science and religion. That I also do not accept. It's theoretically possible to rediscover a metaphysical point of view into which you can absorb all that is positive in the attainments of modern Western science without doing injustice to that science. For example, you can be a perfectly good biologist and yet reject Darwin and evolution. In fact, there are many good biologists who do that and have a completely different metaphysical background to explain the multiplicity of life forms and their relationships, without going against the given data. That is a possibility. During the last two or three decades there has been a great deal of discussion by people who try to relate the most recent developments of modern physics to Oriental doctrines. A whole literature has been created, the most famous book of which is the *Tao of Physics* by Fritjof Capra. Although much of this literature is a little shallow and a bit of a fad, there are profound possibilities in this. Many leading physicists believe that the paradigm that makes possible the practice of physics in the Western sense has to change. A good example of this is David Bohm, who in *Wholeness and the Implicate Order* says you have to have another philosophy of nature, another cosmology, to make it possible to do physics. Now, I'm not precluding this kind of possibility; in fact in my *Knowledge and the Sacred* I've alluded to that. These writers are very different from the flabby, wishy-washy synthesis of pseudo-yogis and bhikkus and Zen masters who say meditation is just like modern physics, and that the space that you meditate upon is just like that of modern science. It is neither this, nor is it that total opposition which would exist if you refuse to go beyond the world view of modern science.

P: *You are carving out a middle position between these two extremes, and you talk about the possibility of absorbing the modern scientific viewpoint within a much wider and more comprehensive metaphysics. I wonder if you can see ways in which scientific discoveries might contribute to and might change a traditional cosmology. For instance, many discoveries about the sun have been made through scientific observation. To what extent can we find religious significance in that, and to what extent might that change a traditional view of solar symbolism?*

SHN: Traditional cosmology will never be changed by any empirical observation or any form of knowledge based on the empirical. However, traditional civilizations studied nature with a different end in view from that of modern science. They left many things undone. It wasn't that they were less intelligent, but their interests were not in those sectors of investigation with which modern man has been concerned. In the last three or four hundred years, many important discoveries from an empirical point of view have been made. This nobody can doubt. But these discoveries will never change traditional cosmologies, because traditional cosmologies are symbolic understandings of nature. Whenever medieval or ancient man tried to do quantitative science—say, Eratosthenes or al-Biruni measuring the size of the earth—now you would get a closer measurement. You have all kinds of cases like that. But that is not cosmology, that is quantitative science, which was of some concern to medieval and ancient man, but not of essential concern. Yet the knowledge which they had of nature was much greater than many people think. For example, the knowledge of zoology possessed by the American Indians was very scientific in many ways; their understanding of the habits of living creatures was immense. And it was always integrated into their world view, which would not be changed if they developed another kind of zoology or learned more about the glands which bring about changes in, say, the habits of the eagle. The symbolism of the eagle, as a solar bird who symbolizes the sun and therefore the Divine Intellect in the cosmos, does not change. Therefore there is no doubt that no matter what modern science does, it cannot by itself change metaphysics or traditional cosmologies, which are based on certain symbols sanctified within each tradition.

However, if there *are* new discoveries about the nature of the sun, what significance can they have? If a science of nature has no significance beyond itself, it cannot correspond to a reality from the metaphysical point of view. If it corresponds to some aspect of reality, by virtue of that it also possesses significance beyond the merely physical. Take, for instance, solar storms, which were not known to Mayans or Zoroastrians, for whom the sun was the central symbol of religion. What does this mean? If it corresponds to some aspect of reality, then you can understand its symbolic significance by virtue of possessing knowledge of the metaphysical order. Without that, no matter how much physical discovery you make, you're not going to make a jump from this empirical, sensory, external knowledge to metaphysical knowledge simply by virtue of a progressive accumulation of empirical knowledge. That is the mistake that is often made. You're in two different dimensions.

P: *You've made the general principle clear, but if asked to state what the symbolic meaning of solar storms might be, I'd be at a loss. Perhaps you could indicate the specific symbolic significance of these storms, and of the sun and the moon in general.*

SHN: What do solar storms mean? They mean that although the sun *is* the supernal sun, it is not the supernal sun in all its aspects. The symbol *is* the symbolized—but through an identity of essence or inner meaning, not through an identity of material substance. I refer to a passage of the Quran (6:76-79) in which Abraham looks upon the stars and thinks, that is the Divinity. But then he sees the stars set and says, "I do not worship that which sets." When he sees the moon, he says, "Ah, that must be the Divinity." And the moon sets, and he says, "I do not love that which sets." Then he sees the sun, and he says, "Ah, but surely that must be the Divinity." Finally that also sets, and Abraham concludes that the Divinity must be transcendent and above all in the universe which symbolizes it. The usual meaning given to this story is that it shows the transcendence of God. But why does it concern the stars, the moon, and the sun? Why is it that Abraham did not look at some creature in the field? Because the celestial, no matter how much we reduce it to intergalactic gas and so forth, is a symbol of the spiritual world. Celestial bodies, which are studied by modern astronomy and physics as an extension of terrestrial physics, are not only that. They possess a relationship as a symbol of the spiritual world. However, this story wants to show that this symbol is not to be mistaken for the symbolized, which was a danger, especially to the Semitic people, both Jews and Arabs. Special care is taken in Judaism and Islam not to create any icons, idols, or symbols of a plastic nature which would be mistaken for the symbolized. And therefore you find this belittling of the sun, you might say, in order to avoid the idolatry of sun worship.

As far as the sun and moon are concerned, in all traditional cosmologies these two play a very important role. Usually the sun represents the divine intellect, because it is the source of light for the world and also its source of life. It is also the source of the measurement of space and time. So the fundamental parameters of our existence are defined by the sun.

As for the moon, usually it represents the feminine aspect, the aspect of receptivity, because it receives its light from the sun. Here I mean femininity on the highest level, in its metaphysical significance. But femininity and masculinity have to manifest themselves on the phenomenal level as two visible bodies in the heavens. Do you ever wonder why we don't have three of these bodies, and how different human existence would have been if we did?

P: *We're the only planet with one moon, isn't that so?*

SHN: Yes. So the polarization of the human state, of the androgynic reality in the male and female, has a profound significance which is not only biological, not only social, but also intellectual and spiritual. It goes all the way to the Divine Presence itself. It's metacosmic. On the cosmic level, it's symbolized by these two bodies which complement each other rhythmically. They complement each other from a temporal point of view. One corresponds to a time when everything is light, the other to a time when everything is dark. They correspond to the two major cycles of the alchemical rhythm of existence, expansion and contraction, which defines life. Our breath expands and contracts, and that's how we keep alive. That is the *solve et coagula* of classical Western alchemy. The day is the period of expansion, the night is the period of contraction. And the sun and the moon also represent the complementarity of activity and passivity, of giving and receiving, the two of which create together the whole, the totality.

There's an even more profound aspect to this. There's a Persian poem by the great poet Shabistari, one of the greatest Sufi poets, that says that when you have an experience of God, it is like an illuminated night in the middle of a dark day. I could spend the whole of my life explaining the symbolism of that. The day in that sense is also the external, the manifested, the profane; the night is the eternal, the inward, the sacred. This is also one of the symbolisms of the male and the female which is very much emphasized in Islam. The male symbolizes external activity; the female is seen as the perfect embodiment of this interiority, inwardness, and sacredness which the night symbolizes. Of course, man and woman combine both elements within themselves, but in each, one element predominates. In a civilization like that of Islam, the spiritual quality of each sex is seen as a perfection of its particular genius and not as a kind of least common denominator. And so this poem by Shabistari means that the realization of God corresponds to the illumination of a night which is otherwise dark for the blind man. Once it is illuminated, it is the real illumination in comparison with the day, which seems adequately illuminated, but which in fact is the period of scattering, externalization, forgetfulness, and dissipation of our energies and thoughts, and therefore marks a loss of center, a loss of the sacred. If you look at it like that, you have a kind of yin-yang between the sun and the moon, a complementarity in which you have something of one element in the other. There is something of the solar cycle in the lunar cycle, and something of the lunar cycle in the solar cycle.

So you find a universal complementarity between the sun and the moon in all traditions by the nature of these two celestial bodies and their symbolism. In addition to that, these bodies have a special significance in each religious tradition, because there are two types of symbols, those which are natural to things and those which are sanctified by a particular tradition. For example, the symbol of wine as that which inebriates and is therefore a knowledge which delivers and frees, is universal. Even in Islam, where wine is banned, it is used in Sufi poetry. But the symbol of wine as the blood of the founder of a religion is particular to Christianity. It's the coming of Christ which sanctified that symbol in that particular way. A Moslem or a Jew does not take Mass and drink wine in the name of the blood of Christ. So there are two types of symbols.

In Islam, as I said, there is in the Quran a kind of belittling of the sun as the central symbol of the Divinity. Natural phenomena, the grand promenade of nature as theophanies, as manifestations by which God takes witness, appear in the Quran very often. But at the same time great care is taken not to open the possibility of idolatry. However, precisely because of the innate symbolism of the sun, in the Islamic tradition the name of Shams, which is the Arabic word for sun, comes up again and again. The name Shamsuddin, the sun of religion, is a very common name. Ali, the cousin and son-in-law of the Prophet, who represents, more than any of the companions of the Prophet, the inner, esoteric teachings of Islam, was often compared to the sun. And also to the lion, which is a solar animal. The sun and the lion go together; the classical Persian flag has the sun and the lion, and many other Muslim emblems combine the two. It's an astrological combination, of course, but it also has cosmological significance. You have a wonderful example in the incomparable Sufi poet Rumi, whose very mysterious spiritual teacher was named Shamsuddin Tabrizi. Now, Shamsuddin is a common name, like John or Peter in English. But Rumi uses it in two ways, both as the name of the mysterious figure who called forth this tidal wave of poetry from him, and at the same time as the sun of religion, God himself in the esoteric understanding of the divine reality.

So the sun, despite this limitation put upon it by the Quran, nevertheless is in Islam a symbol of life and illumination. There is a whole school of illumination, *Ishraq*, in Persia and other eastern lands of Islam, which integrates the ancient Persian cult of the sun—the Mazdean religion, which saw the sun as a center of light and a direct symbol of the divinity—into Islamic esoteric and metaphysical teachings.

As for the moon, it plays a much more important role in Islam than in many other traditions. Think of the crescent which appears on so many Muslim flags. In fact, whenever Western people think of the Islamic world they think of the crescent. Now the crescent, which is the moon, has a belly which receives and two tips which symbolize activity. Like the horn of the bull, which is also crescent-shaped, it is the symbol of the perfection of activity and passivity together. It is essentially another symbol of the archetype of the Seal of Solomon, which has two triangles, one upward and one downwards, one with the base toward heaven and the other with the base toward earth. In one case you have the receptive pole toward heaven and the active pole toward earth, and in the other case the receptive pole toward earth and the active pole toward heaven. This is really the juxtaposition of the saint and the fallen man. The two together represent the totality of human nature. The saint receives from heaven and is active toward the earth; the profane man is the other way around, he rebels and is active against heaven and passive toward the earth; he receives from the lower nature of himself and the world around him. The crescent is a symbol of the origin of Islam, in the sense that the Prophet of Islam embodies the universal man, the perfection of the active and passive states.

But there's another reason for the importance of the moon, and for the many *hadiths* (sayings) of the Prophet in reference to the moon. If you look at it astronomically, of course, the moon is the last planet. But if you look at traditional cosmologies, the moon is seen not only as the moon of the earth—because people knew the moon went around the earth—but, with a stationary earth, it is the first of the planets.

P: *So it's the lowest level in the cosmic hierarchy.*

SHN: Exactly. It's the boundary between the heavens and the world of generation and corruption, to use the Aristotelian subdivision of the cosmos.

The moon, by virtue of that, in a sense receives all of the higher levels of influence. Therefore, it is the recapitulation of all the cosmic forces as well as being the cosmic memory. Each planet symbolizes one of the heavenly worlds; God himself is beyond the cosmos, beyond the cosmic level. All influences that come through to the earth are summarized, recapitulated, and synthesized on the level of the moon. And the Prophet of Islam, as the last prophet in the prophetic cycle, synthesizes and recapitulates the whole prophetic message. In that sense he corresponds to the moon. The word for moon, and especially the word for the full moon, is very important in Arabic and Persian poetry. The beauty of the full moon is often compared to the beauty of the face of the Prophet of Islam. He was often in fact called Badruddin, the full moon of religion. Ali was called Shamsuddin, the sun of religion. Their relationships are reversed in a very interesting way; the moon receives its light from the sun, but Ali receives all that he has from the Prophet. Nevertheless, because of the complex symbolism that I mentioned, the roles in this case are reversed. It is also interesting to note here that in Arabic, the word for the sun is feminine and for the moon masculine, referring to the same symbolism.

P: *Would it be correct, then, to think of the moon not just as a symbolic recapitulation of everything above it but also as a transmitter to that which lies below it?*

SHN: Yes, definitely. It both synthesizes and transmits to the earth.

P: *If the human being is a microcosm, is it correct in any sense to think that we have a sun or a moon within us which corresponds in some way to the external sun and moon. Is there a connection between these internal and external suns? Is that a legitimate idea in traditional thought?*

SHN: The first part is certainly legitimate. As far as the connection is concerned, there are certain astrological texts which have alluded to that, but it's a lot more problematic. Traditional cosmologies are not only concerned with the cosmos. There's also a microcosmology—a cosmology of the microcosm—which is anthropology, in the traditional sense of the word. I think the word "anthropology" has to be resuscitated in English, as a science of man dealing not only with measurements of the cranium and the feet, but with the microcosm. Otherwise, you have no word in English for the science of man. I use the word "anthropology" as the science of the *anthropos*, as *anthropos* is understood in classical Greek. Traditionally, anthropology and cosmology complement each other. Always, in all traditions. Look at the sacrifice of Purusha in Hinduism, the doctrine of the universal man in Islam and Taoism, and so on. There is within man a reality which is itself the archetype of the cosmos. In every tradition which has preserved its inner, esoteric teachings, there is an allusion to this. In Islam, for example, there are several hadiths of the Prophet in which God speaks in the first person to the Prophet; these are called the sacred, prophetic sayings. And in one of them, God says to the Prophet of Islam, "If thou wert not, I would not have created the heavens." That is a direct reference to the causal relationship between that "thou," which means the universal man, that is, the archetypal man, the primordial anthropos, and the heavens, which are created on the model of that archetypal reality—which in turn is our primal and fundamental reality. So obviously the sun, the moon, the solar system, and the traditional cosmology identified with them must have some kind of correspondence with the inner state of man. Now, some traditions have expanded this and others have not. For example, in the Western tradition it's only in Kabbalistic sources that we get some reference to this, but in another light. There the Sephiroths played the role of both the principles of the cosmos and the principles of the microcosm. But in both Islam and Hinduism there's a very elaborate literature in which the human microcosm is seen not only as body and soul—which is a modern usurpation, and in fact a deviation from the norm—and not only as the more simple traditional tripartite division into body, soul, and spirit, but as comprised of seven inner bodies. You find this in Tantric Buddhism and also in Tantrism within Hinduism.

P: *And this corresponds to the seven planets.*

SHN: And to the seven chakras, which are well known now after the work of Arthur Avalon and others. This idea was developed very elaborately in the so-called Central Asiatic school of Sufism; it was developed by the Persian Sufi, Simnani, whose teachings spread to Kashmir and from there to India and present-day Pakistan. Simnani said that within thy being not only is there thy known, everyday consciousness, but there are seven prophets of thy being. Each human being has the Moses of his being, the Christ of his being, the Muhammad of his being, the David of his being, and so on. These figures, in traditional cosmology, are related to the seven planets, going back to the *mi'raj*, the nocturnal ascent of the Prophet. When the Prophet ascended all the scales of being—and the mi'raj is the prototype of all spiritual wayfaring in Islam, and also obviously of all posthumous experiences of the higher cosmic states—he encountered, according to traditional sources, one of the great prophets on each of the planets. A whole cosmology in Islam developed from this, which is related to prophetology. That is, each planet corresponds to one of the prophets. This is very interesting for comparative religion; as I said, the Prophet himself corresponds to the moon, but who corresponds to the sun? It is Christ. This is because in the Abrahamic tradition, Christ is the one who gave out the inner meaning; it is he who rent the veil asunder. He thus corresponds to the direct shining of the sun. Within Islam, Ali plays the same role. That is why in the Islamic tradition Ali is called the Shams of religion, but within the Abrahamic family it is Christ who occupies the level of the sun.

As man journeys inwardly, according to the Sufis, it is like the mi'raj. Man has seven subtle bodies through which he journeys until he gets to the heart, where the Divinity resides. This is the very center of the microcosm, which according to the Quran is the seat of God; the Quran says that the heart of the faithful is the seat of the Divine Mercy, and God *is* the Merciful. So as man journeys inwardly, in a sense he is also journeying cosmologically outwardly. There is a correspondence between the two, and at each level there is an encounter with one of the prophets who rules over a particular planetary orbit, symbolically speaking of course, which corresponds to one of the levels of existence. There is a very elaborate cosmology in Islam. It is not a necessary development for every tradition. As I said, in traditional civilizations, cosmologies are keys to open doors. They are not necessary for every person, but they have to be there because a tradition has to integrate different types of mentalities and psyches and provide for different needs.

As far as the relationship between the two journeys is concerned, that is, as I said, a bit more problematic. The idea that the outer sun directly influences the inner orbit of the sun exists in certain astrological treatises. But in the Abrahamic religions of Islam, Judaism, and Christianity, this idea is too astrological, in the sense of cutting off the hands of God from what goes on within the soul of man. So usually the vertical ascent toward the Divine and the ascent toward the Divine by penetrating to the center of one's being are emphasized without one causing the other.

P: *Perhaps that's why in Christianity and Judaism there's a suppression of cosmological expressions. There's this fear that it would cut off the sense of direct relationship to God.*

SHN: It's a cutting off only on the juridical and theological levels. Cosmology can only be integrated on a metaphysical level. That is why all Islamic cosmology is developed either by Sufis or by Islamic philosophers who are closely related to Sufism, despite all the Western scholars who say that Islamic philosophy is just Aristotelian rationalism that Muslims took over and then gave back to the West. That is not the case at all. Look at Avicennan cosmology, with which I've dealt so extensively, and we see how close it is in fact to Islamic metaphysics.

In the West you see something similar in the cosmologies of such figures as Nicholas of Cusa or Dante. Dante is incredible. You can't say there's no such thing as traditional Christian cosmology. If there were no Christian cosmology, there would be no Christian cathedrals. There is no sacred architecture without sacred cosmology. That's why you can't create sacred architecture today; the best you can do is to emulate. If an architect tries to create a cathedral on his own, he cannot do so, because there's no correspondence with the higher states of being. You might say he doesn't have a map of the cosmos. The fact that you have Chartres Cathedral means that you have Christian cosmology. But neither Chartres Cathedral nor the *Divine Comedy* issue from the juridical or the usually understood theological dimensions of religion.

P: *So within some traditions there's ambivalence toward cosmology.*

SHN: There are different dimensions to a tradition. Judaism is close to Islam in the sense that the dimensions are very specific and clearly marked. In Christianity there's more of bringing the two together, and therefore more ambivalence; you don't know who belongs exactly where. That is one of the reasons why, after the Middle Ages, this type of thought caused so much difficulty.

P: *In* An Introduction to Islamic Cosmological Doctrines, *you write about the Ikhwan as-Safa, the Brethren of Purity, and you mention their belief that "the intellect gives life to the sun and the moon." That raises the question of whether human consciousness is somehow essential to the activity of these higher spheres. Do they only work on us, or do we also have an effect on them?*

SHN: The Divine Intellect has an effect on both. If you try to answer this question à la Cartesian dualism, which is the background of all modern thought unless you consciously get out of it, you have a world out there and a subject here which has consciousness. Somehow this subject comes to know the world out there. We don't know how; ever since Descartes posited his dualism, nobody has known how this takes place, and so you find many forms of materialism and idealism, which are two sides of the same coin. This is one of the interesting points in contemporary physics. Physicists say now that there is no physics without consciousness. Consciousness is part of the structure of physical reality. With that in mind, if we can get rid of this three-hundred-year heritage of Cartesian dualism, we can answer your question in a much more profound way. When the Brethren of Purity say that the Divine Intellect is the life of the sun and moon, they're speaking from within a universe in which there is no absolute division between what we call physical light and the divine light. They are grades of the same reality, which goes from the physical to the psychological to the spiritual to the divine. Since these two bodies reflect light upon the world, they must receive their light from the Divine Intellect, the source of all light according to the tradition of Islamic cosmology.

According to this perspective, our consciousness is also derived from the same light. Human consciousness is an incredible thing, and the most direct proof of the non-physical nature of our existence. We don't need any other proof for the existence of God than to understand human subjectivity. Our consciousness also comes from that Divine Intellect; if there were no Divine Consciousness, there would be no human consciousness. Seen in this light, if our consciousness did not exist, the Divine Consciousness would still exist, but the polarization of reality into the microcosm and the macrocosm would not. The metacosmic reality is refracted and polarized in the world of creation into the macrocosm and the microcosm, so they are in a sense the complements of each other. It is impossible to understand, in terms of modern science, that there would be no universe if there were no man. This sounds absurd. We are talking about a little speck of dust in cosmic space which is called the earth, itself just an accident, and on that earth there are even smaller specks which are called human beings. That it is these very small specks who are saying these things is forgotten, as well as the fact that these "specks" can hold the knowledge of these galaxies.

P: *Consciousness seems to be the essential glue.*

SHN: Exactly. There is no knowledge without adequation. There must be a correspondence between the knower and the known in order for the knower to know the known. If we can know the whole of the vast galactic space, that means that something in our consciousness corresponds to that reality to make that knowledge possible. You cannot have one half of a syzygy, something which is comprised of two complementary parts, and remove one part without the other part being removed. It's like holding something before a mirror and having a mirror image on the other side; once you remove the object, the image is also gone. If you really understand that, you can say that if there were no human consciousness, there would be no sun and moon.

Parabola
Volume: 8.3
Words of Power

THE WORDS OF THE ALL-MERCIFUL

William C. Chittick

The Quran is the Word made Book, just as Christ is the Word made flesh. The images of the Quranic revelation are the pen and the tablet, ink, paper, letters, words, and verses. The first verses of the Holy Book revealed to the Prophet set the tone:

> *Read: "In the Name of thy Lord who created, created man of a blood-clot."*
> *Read: "And thy Lord is the Most Generous, who taught by the pen, taught man what he knew not." (96:1-5)*

Imagery connected with the word and the book suffuses Islamic thought and colors the everyday life of Islamic society. Ritual centers on the recitation of the Quran, architecture is shaped by the needs of listeners and decorated with written verse, calligraphy is regarded as the supreme art, music is preeminently Quranic recitation, and literature, especially poetry—known by literate and illiterate alike—rings with the resonance of the Scripture.

All the words of the Quran are God's words, but the most fundamental are His names. Islamic theology, both scholastic and mystical, is a great commentary upon the names of God, which reveal His nature to mankind. God's primary utterance, whereby His Books were revealed and man and the universe created, was His own name. Alluded to in the Old Testament as "I AM THAT I AM," it is rendered in the Quran as "Verily I am God [Allah]: There is no god but I" (20:14). God—Allah—is the "supreme" or "all-comprehensive" name, since it refers to God's very Self. The other names mentioned in the Quran and in the Hadith (prophetic sayings) are subordinate to it. It is God who is the Hearing, the Wise, the Vengeful, the Powerful, the Forgiving, the Life-Giver, the Exalter: "The Most Beautiful Names [i.e., the "ninety-nine names"] belong to God, so call Him by them" (Quran 7:180). According to the Sufis, these very names demand and bring about the existence of the cosmos. For what meaning has the name "Creator" without creatures, "Light" without illuminating rays, "Forgiver" without sinners, "Life-Giver" without death?

In one of his sayings, the Prophet alludes to the "Breath of the All-Merciful"; and in the Quran God says, "My Mercy embraces all things" (7:156). As the All-Merciful, God exhales His Breath, and the universe is born. The Breath is also referred to as the "Cloud" (*al-ama*) that envelops the Divine Essence. When the Prophet was asked, "Where was God before He created the creatures?" he replied, "In a Cloud, neither above which nor below which was any space." Thus the famous Sufi Ibn al-Arabi (d. 1240) writes that "in its state of existence the cosmos consists of the forms assumed by the Cloud. ... So the Cloud, which is none other than the Breath of the All-Merciful, is the substance, while the world and all the forms manifest within it are the accidents."[1]

But the Breath or Cloud is not a simple exhalation; it is the articulated speech of God. "Our only word to a thing, when We desire it, is to say to it 'Be!' and it is" (Quran 16:40). Elsewhere, in place of "Our only word," the Quran has "His only command" (36:82). These terms are joined in the verse, "Our Command is but One Word, like the twinkling of an eye" (54:50). Through the Command the One Word issues from its source like a ray of light, refracting itself into the ontological words that are the creatures. Thus Ibn al-Arabi writes, "The Cloud derives from His exhalation, while the forms that take shape within it, which are called the 'cosmos,' derive from the word 'Be!' So we are His words that are never exhausted."[2] Here he alludes to the Quranic verse, "Though all the trees in the earth were pens, and the sea were ink—seven seas after it to replenish it—yet would the words of God not be exhausted" (31:27).

The Quran repeatedly refers to God's "signs" (*ayat*), which are the creatures on the one hand and the verses of the revealed Book on the other:

> *Surely in the creation of the heavens and the earth and in the alternation of night and day are signs for men possessed of minds. (3:190)*
> *It is He who made the sun a radiance and the moon a light. ... [God created that not save with the Truth;] He deploys the signs for a people who know. (10:5)*
> *A book We have sent down to thee, blessed, that men possessed of minds may ponder its signs and so remember. (38:29)*

These signs, whether revealed in the cosmos or the Book, are the theophanies of God's names and attributes:

> *Know that the creatures are pure and limpid water,*
> *shining within them the attributes of Almighty God.*
> *Their knowledge, their justice, their kindness*
> *are stars of heaven reflected in flowing water.*
> *Kings manifest God's Kingship,*
> *the learned display His Knowledge.*
> *Generations have passed, and we are a new generation—*
> *the moon is the same, but the water has undergone change. ...*
> *All pictured forms are reflections in the river's water—*
> *when you rub your eyes, you see that all are He!*
> *   —Rumi*[3]

Because all creatures are signs displaying God's names and manifesting His creative Word, all are constantly speaking: "There is nothing that does not proclaim His glory, but you do not understand their glorification" (Quran 17:44). Ibn al-Arabi comments: "There is no form in the world—and the world is nothing but forms—that is not glorifying its Creator with a special praise with which He has inspired it." Rumi writes:

> *The speech of water, the speech of earth,*
> *the speech of clay—*
> *The Possessors of the Heart perceive*
> *each one with their outward senses.*
> —*Mathnawi*[4]

Man plays a unique role among the world's creatures since he was created to be the vicegerent (*khalifah*) of God. According to the Prophet, man was created "upon God's Form"; he manifests the all-comprehensive name and thus reflects all other names as well. This is one meaning of the Quranic declaration that God "taught Adam all the names" (2:31). Another meaning is that Adam was taught the names of all created things, which are the signs and "effects" (*athar*) of the names.

Certain hadiths add that Adam was taught not only the names but also "100,000" languages. Here there is an allusion to the all-comprehensiveness—at least potentially—of human knowledge. In a similar vein, the expression "man is a rational animal" was translated into Arabic as "man is a speaking animal," since it is speech—his knowledge of the names—that sets man apart from all other animate things.

Man, then, is the integral and summary reflection of the divine name— or divine Word—"God." Opposed to him stands the cosmos (*al-alam*), which also reflects the Word, but deployed in its infinite possibilities of outward manifestation. Thus the microcosm corresponds to the macrocosm, a fact often referred to as the "collation of the two transcripts" (*taqabul al-nuskhatayn*)—again an image drawn from writing. Because of his knowledge of the names of all things, man is active, while the cosmos is the passive object of his perception. This is why some Sufis have said that man is the macrocosm, while the universe is the microcosm.

Though man is the servant (*abd*) of God, he is also His vicegerent; because he has knowledge of all creatures, they are his servants: "Do you not see that God has subjected to you everything in the heavens and the earth?" (Quran 31:20). This power over other creatures helps explain the grave responsibility of the human state, the "Trust" (*amanah*) man accepted to bear even before his physical creation (cf. Quran

7:172, 33:72). The responsibility for the corruption of the earth—or the destruction of its natural environment—lies squarely on his shoulders.

Man's superiority over all creatures extends even to the angels. They are "partial" or "peripheral" creatures, while the Perfect Man is known as the "Point at the Center of the Circle." According to the Quran, the angels were commanded to prostrate themselves before Adam because they had knowledge of only some of the names: "We know not save what Thou hast taught us" (2:32).

Ibn al-Arabi summarizes the relationship between man and the divine names as follows:

Man is the utmost limit of the Breath. ... The potentiality [or "power," *quwwah*] of every existent thing in the cosmos lies within him. So he possesses all ontological levels; that is why he alone was singled out for the Divine Form. He comprehends the divine realities—which are the names—and the realities of the cosmos. Thus the Breath of the All-Merciful did not reach its farthest extension within his existence until it gave to him the potentiality of all the ontological levels of the cosmos. In man becomes manifest that which does not become manifest in the separate parts of the world, nor in the individual divine names.[5]

To become the "vicegerent of God" (*khalifat Allah*) is to act as a conscious locus of manifestation for all of God's names and at the same time to encompass the myriad perfections of the macrocosm. When Sufis hear the Prophet's words, "Assume the moral traits (*akhlaq*) of God!" they understand this to mean that man must attain to a state of perfection wherein all of the divine names display themselves within him. Ibn al-Arabi writes:

God did not create the heavens and the earth and what is between them "for vanity" (Quran 38:27), nor did He create man "for sport" (23:115). He created him so that he alone might be "upon His Form." So everyone in the cosmos is ignorant of the whole and knowledgeable only of a part, with the sole exception of the Perfect Man. For God "taught him all the names" (2:31) and [according to a prophetic saying] gave him the "all-comprehensive words." Hence he combines the Form of God with the form of the cosmos.[6]

The Breath of the All-Merciful acts as a vehicle for the Creative Word "Be!" which appears outwardly as the ontological letters that make up the cosmos: "In the same way, the human breath encompasses all letters."[7] Ibn al-Arabi and his followers develop the symbolism of the letters and words transmitted through the Breath into a complicated cosmology. For example, his stepson and chief disciple, Sadraddin al-Qunawi (d. 1274), writes that the things of this world exist in God's knowledge before their creation as "non-manifest letters," though if we consider them in relation to their properties, attributes, and concomitants, they are called "non-manifest words." Then these letters and words become outwardly manifest within the Breath.[8] Elsewhere he deals in similar fashion with phrases, verses, chapters, and books. He compares each universal level of existence, from God down to the physical universe, with a Scripture, and he declares that the Perfect Man is like the Quran, the Scripture that encompasses all other Scriptures:

> *The Perfect Man is a book that comprehends all the divine and created books ... for he comprehends all things, both in the manner of summated unity and in that of particularized deployment. The Prophet said, "Whoso knows his own self knows his Lord" and all things. It follows, my son, that your meditation upon yourself is enough for you, since nothing is outside of you. ... Have you not heard the words of God? "Read your book! Your self suffices you this day as a reckoner against you!" (Quran 17:14), for whoso reads his book has come to know what has been, what is, and what shall be. So, if you cannot read all of your book, read of it what you can. Have you not seen God's words? "And in your selves: What, do you not look?" (51:21). And have you not seen His words? "We shall show them Our signs in the horizons and in their selves, till it is clear to them that it is the truth. Suffices it not as to thy Lord, that He is witness over everything?" (41:53). ...*
>
> *When the army of Ali gained the upper hand over the army of A'isha—peace be upon them both—in the battle that took place after the murder of Uthman, A'isha's party held the Divine Book aloft with a spear so that Ali's followers would not slaughter and rout them. ... Then Ali said, "O people! I am the speaking Book of God, and that is the silent Book of God! Attack them and leave them not!"*

In the same way God says, "Say: 'God suffices as a witness between me and you, and whosoever possesses knowledge of the Book'" (13:43). So this, my son, is the Book and the knowledge of the Book. And you are the Book, as we said. Your knowledge of yourself is your knowledge of the Book. "And there is not a thing, neither wet," which is the world of the visible creation, "nor dry," which is the world of the Spirit and everything beyond it, "but in an Elucidating Book" (6:59), which is you.[9]

Unless man "carries the Trust," the names—or "moral traits"—encompassed by the supreme name remain as so many potentialities within him. He is a book, the manifestation of the Divine Word, but he is shut off from himself without the guidance referred to again and again in the Quran: "These are the signs of the Quran and a Manifest Book, a guidance, and good tiding unto the believers" (27:1-2). Without the light of heaven, his book cannot be read, nor can the two transcripts be collated. Man is in need of God's guidance in order to regain his primordial nature (*fitrah*) according to which he was created, i.e., his Divine Form. Since man is a theophany of the Word, he must return to the Word. The Quran provides the means, for it is the One Word of God revealed to creatures in the form of a multitude of words; thus creatures, mired in multiplicity and dispersion, may be drawn back to Unity. All of Islamic ritual revolves around the assimilation of the Quran, the Word made Book, just as Christian ritual centers on the assimilation of the body and the blood of the Word made flesh.

One of the names of the Quran is "Reminder" or "Remembrance" (*dhikr, dhikra*), while one of the Prophet's titles is "Remembrance of God" (Dhikr Allah). As a result of the fall, man has forgotten the Trust and turned away from his primordial nature. The Quran is a Reminder, and the Prophet is the living exemplar of God's remembrance: "You have a good example in God's Messenger for whosoever hopes for God and the Last Day and remembers God often" (33:21).

To recite the Quran and to imitate the Prophet are both means of remembering God. But there is another act of remembrance, taught explicitly by the Prophet to some of his companions and mentioned in numerous Quranic verses, and that is the "remembrance" or "invocation" (dhikr) of God's Name. All believers remember God through recitation of the Quran and certain divine names at least five times a day, during the ritual prayer. But God has placed special power in the remembrance of His All-Comprehensive Name: "Recite what has been revealed to you of the Book, and perform the ritual prayer. The ritual prayer prevents indecency and dishonor—but verily, the remembrance of God (Allah) is greater!" (29:45)

The relationship between the revelatory Book and the microcosmic Book is prefigured in the "Night of Power," during which the Quran descended upon the Prophet, and the "Night of the Ascension," during which the Prophet was taken through the heavens to God's Presence. The descent of the written Book results in the ascent of the human Book. Muslims were not commanded to perform the ritual prayer until after the Prophet's ascent to heaven, during which it was taught to him. Thus the prayer is known as the "ascension of the believer" (al-salat mi'raj al-mu'min), and its physical movements retrace the Prophet's experiences during his journey. The peculiarly physical nature of the Islamic prayer corresponds to the absolute necessity of reciting the Quran in Arabic for ritual purposes, since Arabic is the physical form of the descent, or the "body" of the Word made Book. The physical body of the human word is as much a manifestation of the Divine Word as his soul; therefore both prayer and resurrection are bodily.

But the greatest power of the recited word is found in the remembrance of God, which is greater than the ritual prayer (though invalid without it). The remembrance of many different divine names is practiced by the Sufi orders. Often the spiritual master or "shaikh" will choose a name on the basis of a disciple's particular need. Once a character trait is developed through constant concentration upon that name, another name will be given. Other masters prefer to turn all of their disciples' attention to the Supreme Name, upon whose Form man was created. Through constant perseverance in the remembrance of God, the adept gradually turns his attention away from all other things. His own attributes are annihilated (fana) and only those of God subsist (baqa).

This then is the ultimate power of the word: just as it creates man in the first place upon the Form of God, so in the end it reintegrates him into his prototype. He thus becomes what he ever was, the Logos, God's

Word, the intermediary between God and creatures, the Vicegerent, the bearer of the Trust. "The All-Merciful taught the Quran. He created man, and He taught him the Explication" (Quran 55:1-4).

Notes:

1   *al-Futuhat al-makkiyya* (Cairo: 1911), vol. 3, p. 443.

2   *Futuhat,* 2:331.

3   *Mathnawi* (Nicholson edition), Book VI, verses 3172 ff.

4   *Mathnawi,* I 3279.

5   *Futuhat,* 2:369.

6   *Futuhat,* 3:398.

7   *Futuhat,* 2:468.

8   Al-Qunawi, *Miftah al-ghayb,* edited by Muhammad Khwajawi (Tehran: Mawla, 1995), pp. 93-94.

9   Qunawi, *Mir'at al-arifin,* edited by Sayyid Hasan Askari in *Reflection of the Awakened* (London: Zahra Trust, 1983), pp. 20-23 of the Arabic text.

Parabola
Volume: 22.2
The Shadow

Extending the Shade

Ibn al-Arabi

Know that what is "other than the Reality," which is called the Cosmos, is, in relation to the Reality, as a shadow is to that which casts the shadow, for it is the shadow of God, this being the same as the relation between Being and the Cosmos, since the shadow is, without doubt, something sensible. What is provided there is that on which the shadow may appear, since if it were possible that that whereon it appears should cease to be, the shadow would be an intelligible and not something sensible, and would exist potentially in the very thing that casts the shadow.

The thing on which this divine shadow, called the Cosmos, appears is the [eternally latent] essences of contingent beings. The shadow is spread out over them, and the [identity of] the shadow is known to the extent that the Being of the [original] Essence is extended upon it. It is by His Name, the Light, that it is perceived. This shadow extends over the essences of contingent beings in the form of the unknown Unseen. Have you not observed that shadows tend to be black, which indicates their imperceptibility [as regards content] by reason of the remote relationship between them and their origins? If the source of the shadow is white, the shadow itself is still so [i.e., black].

Do you not observe that mountains distant from the observer appear to be black, while being in themselves other than the color seen? The cause is only the distance.

The same is the case with the blueness of the sky, which is also the effect of distance on the senses with respect to nonluminous bodies. In the same way the essences of contingent beings are not luminous, being nonexistent, albeit latent. They may not be described as existing because existence is light. Furthermore, even luminous bodies are rendered, by distance, small to the senses, which is another effect of distance. Such bodies are perceived by the senses as small, while being in themselves large. For example, the evidence is that the sun is 160 times the size of the Earth, while, to the eye, it is no larger than a shield. This is also the effect of distance.

No more is known of the Cosmos than is known from a shadow, and no more is known of the Reality than one knows of the origin of a shadow. Insofar as He has a shadow, He is known, but insofar as the form of the one casting the shadow is not perceived in the shadow, the Reality is not known. For this reason we say that the Reality is known to us in one sense and unknown in another.

"Have you not seen how your Lord extends the shade; if He so willed He would make it stay" (Quran 25:45), that is, it would be in Him potentially, which is to say that the Reality does not reveal Himself to the contingent beings before He manifests His shadow, the shadow being [as yet] as those beings that have not been manifested in existence. "Then We made the sun as an indication of it" (25:45), which is His Name, the Light of which we have already spoken and by which the senses perceive; for shadows have no [separate] existence without light.

"Then We take it back to Ourselves easily" (25:46), only because it is His shadow, since from him it is manifest and to Him the whole manifestation returns, for the shadow is none other than He. All we perceive is nothing other than the being of the Reality in the essences of contingent beings. With reference to the Identity of the Reality, it is Its Being, whereas, with reference to the variety of its forms, it is the essences of contingent beings. Just as it is always called a shadow by reason of the variety of forms, so is it always called the Cosmos and "other than the Reality." In respect of its unity as the shadow [of God], it is the Reality, being the One, the Unique, but in respect of the multiplicity of its forms it is the Cosmos; therefore understand and realize what I have elucidated for you.

The Bezels of Wisdom, translated by R. W. J. Austin (Mahwah, N. J.: Paulist Press, 1980), pp. 123-24.

Parabola
Volume: 20.1
Earth, Air, Fire, Water

TRAVELS OF THE SOUL

Sheikh Tosun Bayrak al Jerrahi

What is the origin of the human being? Most of us attribute our existence to the biological formation of the two cells in the mother's womb and the chromosomes in them. We explain the events of our life in terms of luck or, worse still, we attribute them to our own doing. Yet deep inside we know this is not the meaning of life. We are dissatisfied.

In order to be created, it is first necessary to have the One who creates, and that is the Essence of God. Each human being is a manifestation of the Essence of God. Secondly, the One who creates us must have the will to create us. Thirdly, He has to have the power to create.

The three divine elements of creation correspond to the three divine elements in the oneness of God that are responsible for the act of creation. The first is that the existence of a thing prior to its creation depends on an original existence, an existence within which are contained its shape, its character, its actions, its birth and death, and its destiny. That creative existence is God's Essence, the Causal Mind. The thing to be created must have the potential to receive all of this, and the acknowledgment of this is Divine Wisdom. The second is the acceptance of the created to be created, which is faith. The third is the ability of the created to be receptive to the will of God, which is submission. Thus the trinity in created things is linked with the trinity within the Unity of God, like the relationship between a mirror and the one who is reflected in the mirror.

God said in a divine tradition: "I was a hidden treasure, I loved to be known, so I created the creation." When He was a hidden treasure, He was in a state of Pure Essence which cannot be described, because this state has no words, names, attributes, or likenesses. Before creation, all was a total void, a limitless ocean of darkness which moved when God said: "I loved to be known." When the ocean of Essence moved, from its waves arose the first creation, the first manifestation of God, the light of the Causal Mind, the realm of the word, Pure Essence manifested in its divine attributes. …This realm contained the Total Soul, the soul of all the creation yet to come.

Then the ocean of the attributes of God containing all the souls yet to be created moved, by the power of the Pen and the Word, and from its waves were created the realm of spiritual beings, paradise, hell, death, angels, and the rewards and punishments of God. With the wind of God's wish to see Himself, the ocean of the spirits moved and the world of matter was created—the world of suns and stars, minerals and vegetables, animals and human beings. God, in His love, dressed the souls of His creation in the most beautiful shape and form, made out of fire, water, earth, and air.

The four stages of creation were not separate from each other, nor were they created at different times. They were created all at once. When God said "Be," they all became. Neither were they created from nothing, as nothing can be created from nothing, nor can a thing which exists become nothing. All existences, all incidences, come from God and return to God.

God created the human being last as His most perfect creation, in His own image. The perfect human contains all these realms. He is the microcosm, a jewel, pressed from the essence of the eighteen thousand universes. But the human being was created in two parts. God created the human soul from the light of His own Essence, and He created his body from the coarse matter of fire, water, earth, and air, and He blew his soul into him. The soul was meant to be the master, to ride the body, which was meant to serve as an animal of burden. The body yearns for the world because it is made of the same material and eventually will return to it. The soul yearns for God and will return to Him.

The soul traveled through the realm of the Causal Mind and through the realm of spirits and angels and the seven heavens down to the material realm, where it passed through the element of fire, bursting into fire, then passed through the realm of water, which put out the fire, then through earth, turning into mud, and finally exposed to air, turning into dried clay. Then, it grew into a vegetable, then it became an animal, and then it turned into the form and shape of a human being. The jewel of the soul was darkened when burnt by fire, it gathered rust when it hit the water, it was covered with mud passing through earth, and it became heavy and coarse when it came into contact with air. This is the descent, the fall of the human being; when the body dominates the soul, the horse rides the master.

Ascension is possible only when we can reach the soul imprisoned in the body of coarse matter. It cannot be seen with worldly eyes. Truth can be seen only by true eyes, perfection can be recognized only by the perfect. We must shed the weight of the flesh and its desires, attached as it is to this world which pulls us down. Our mind and senses cannot be relied on; with their associations and their imagination, they alter and hide the Truth.

That is why we have different opinions, likes and dislikes. We discuss, we get angry with the ones who do not agree with us. We fight, wage wars, condemn, kill … sometimes even in the name of truth.

There is but one Truth, one God, one soul. The character of the soul is to love its origin, whom it yearns to meet. The eye of the heart, which can see the soul, may only be opened by love. The eye of the head sees the beautiful and the ugly; the eye of the heart sees only the beautiful. It sees the Truth. If we knew this, everybody else who opposes the Truth, who curses it, who fights against it, would be a part of the Truth. Then we would embrace those people and not condemn them. Love is the only force which can rid us of the crust hiding the jewel and weighing us down. Only it can permit our essence to rise to our original state as the best of creation, as the deputy of God, whom He created in the image of His own attributes, to whom He taught all His divine names, whom He addresses by saying: "I have created all and everything for you and you for Myself."

Parabola
Volume: 12.4
The Sense of Humor

The Safeguard of the Mystic

Henry Corbin

What is the connection between humor and mysticism? To begin with, I agree with the general opinion that there is no possible definition of humor. Even our British friends, despite their familiarity with the subject, have long ago given up trying to find a truly accurate definition. I shall therefore not make yet another vain attempt. But even though there is no satisfactory definition of humor, it may be possible to ascertain some of its effects. So I will suggest that humor implies the ability to establish a certain remoteness, a certain distance towards oneself and the world. That distance enables one to appear not to be taking quite seriously that which one's inner self takes, cannot but take, terribly seriously, yet without betraying the secret. Without that distance towards the object, one is in danger of becoming its captive and prey. Conversely, if the necessary distance is maintained, all the tension in features and gestures, the defensive and aggressive attitudes, may give way to a smile.

This brief indication may already suffice, or so I hope, to point out that the connection between mysticism and humor resides in the fact that humor may be the safeguard of the mystic insofar as it protects him or her from the double hazard which I have described as "subjective peril" and "objective peril." And we may appeal to Suhrawardi himself to illustrate this statement.

•

Rather, I shall propose both the testimony of Avicenna (Ibn Sina) and of Suhrawardi, since this first example comes from the "Recital of the Bird," written in Arabic by the philosopher Avicenna and translated into Persian by Suhrawardi. This "Recital of the Bird," as a mystical narrative, is one of Suhrawardi's small masterpieces. Its translation is in a book on Avicenna[1] in which I tried to show its place within the cycle of Avicennian stories—that is, situated in the context of what Avicenna's *Oriental Philosophy* would have been had its manuscript not been destroyed during the sack of Isfahan, and had Avicenna had the time to write it over again. Better still, this tale finds its place in the cycle that developed around the symbol of the Bird from Ghazali down to the great mystical epic of Attar. Its origin is remote. The first reference that comes to mind is Plato's *Phaedrus* where the soul is imagined in the likeness of an Energy whose nature would be incarnated by winged horses driven by a charioteer who too is winged. Also, we find there the splendid image of the celestial procession of souls following the Gods, and of the fall of some of these souls. "The natural property of a wing," writes Plato, "is to raise that which is heavy and carry it aloft to the region where the gods dwell, and more than any other bodily part it shares in the divine nature."[2] So much for the symbol of the bird, other magnificent examples of which are to be found, for instance, in certain Manichean psalms.

Let us now turn to Avicenna's story, translated by Suhrawardi. Its prologue is full of pathos. "Is there none among my brothers who will lend me ear for a time, that I may confide some part of my sorrows to him?" asks the author. ... "Brothers of Truth! Strip yourselves of your skins as the snake casts his. ... Love death, that you may still live. Be ever in flight; choose no settled nest, for it is in the nest that all birds are captured ..."[3] There are two splendid pages in this same style. Then the narrator tells his story: a party of hunters spread their nets and caught him together with the troop of birds to which he belonged. During his captivity, he forgot everything—his origin, his relation to another world—and he eventually lost consciousness of the very shackles that bound him and of the narrowness of his cage. Then one day he noticed other birds who had managed to free themselves; he eventually joined them; they flew away together, cleared the highest peaks and traveled through the high valleys of Mount Qaf, the psycho-cosmic mountain, at the cost of exhausting efforts. They met their brothers near the City of the King, and in that very city the King, whose beauty amazed them, received them; they made their way back escorted by the King's messenger, who was bearing an order for those who had tied the bond and who alone could unbind it. I cannot insist on any detail, only on the sudden change in tone that occurs at the end of the story.

The reader is enraptured by his vision of "He who is all a Face that thou contemplatest: all a Hand that bestows,"[4] when all of a sudden the narrator, anticipating the gentle irony that will greet his story, takes the place of the skeptics and writes the following lines:

> *How many of my brothers will there not be who, my recital having struck upon their ears, will say to me: "I see that thou art somewhat out of thy wits, unless sheer madness hath fallen upon thee. Come now! It is not thou who didst take flight; it is thy reason that has taken flight. No hunter ever made thee his prey; it is thy reason and naught else that has been hunted down. How should a man fly? And how should a bird fall to speaking? ...'Twere well to diet: drink a decoction of thyme dodder, take frequent hot baths, take inhalations of oil of water lily. Then go on a light diet, avoid sitting up late; and, above all, no over-exertion of mind. For in the past we have always known thee as a reasonable man, of sound and penetrating judgment. God knows how greatly we are concerned over thy state. Seeing thee thus deranged, we feel utterly sick ourselves!"[5]*

I believe that these lines in which Avicenna lets the physician's humor run free have an exemplary quality; the mystic has spoken; he has tried to relate his adventure. But he knows beforehand how "rational" people will accept it; they will accept it in the same way many historians of philosophy received the teachings of the Neoplatonists—Proclus, Iamblichus, and their disciples. If he tries to confront them, meeting argument with argument, he will become infinitely vulnerable; he will convince none of the skeptics but he may increasingly convince himself of the excellence of his case. And then he will be lost, frustrated, ready for schizophrenia. On the other hand, if he is capable of taking that distance, of clearly and consciously formulating the objections that the skeptics and the agnostics will raise, then what would have been negative, aggressive criticism is transformed into an achievement of humor that permits him to slip through their fingers. Humor is his double safeguard, for while it protects him from ego-inflation and excessive exhilaration, it also obliterates the effects of what might have been an infringement of the discipline of the arcanum. Only he who is worthy and able will comprehend; the others will perceive nothing. But despite all and everything *his message will have been transmitted*. It is thus simultaneously that the mystic finds his protection against both the subjective peril and the objective peril that threaten him. This protection is offered by the language of *symbols*. And it may occur, as in the case of Avicenna and of Suhrawardi, that this language is inspired by a superior humor.

But then, what exactly is a symbol? In order to explain it strictly, it would be best to return to the meaning of the Greek word *symbolon*. In Greek, the verb *symballein* means to agglomerate, to join together. For instance, two men, quite by chance, happen to be fellow-guests. Before taking leave of each other, they break a ring of potsherd in two; as each man takes his half, each of the two pieces becomes the symbolon of the other. Years may go by with all the changes they bring, but it will suffice that the owner of one symbolon joins it to the other in order to be recognized as the fellow-guest of old, or at least his deputy or friend. In the case of our mystical metaphysicians each symbolon belongs to its respective universe: the invisible world of *Malakut* on the one hand, the visible world of sensible perception on the other. The symbolon of one world joined to the symbolon of another forms a superior unity, an integral unity. Because the fact, in this context, that one symbolon conjoins the other proclaims that the visible world *symbolizes with* the invisible one—if we use the language that Leibnitz still knew how to speak. Here is the very source of Goethe's famous phrase at the end of Part Two of *Faust*: "All things ephemeral are but a symbol."[6] (We might even say: *nothing less than* a symbol.) The difference between "symbol" and what nowadays is commonly called "allegory" is simple to grasp. An allegory remains at the same level of evidence and of perception, whereas a symbol guarantees the correspondence between two universes belonging to different onto-logical levels: it is the means, and the only one, of penetrating into the invisible, into the world of mystery, into the esoteric dimension.

When I speak of the importance for a culture of having a philosophy that guarantees the function of symbols, it is the ontological, "objective" validity of the intermediary world, between the intelligible and the sensible, that I am referring to. The idea of this intermediary region implies the triple articulation of reality with the world of the Intelligible (*Jabarut*), with the World of the Soul (*Malakut*), and with the Material World. The anthropological triad—mind, soul, body—corresponds to this triad. The day that philosophical anthropology is reduced to a dyad, be it soul and body or mind and body, that day signifies the end of the noetic, cognitive function of symbols. That triad, which has been suppressed in the West since the ninth century, has only survived in philosophical and theosophical schools mistakenly considered to be "marginal." Cartesianism recognizes nothing but thinking and extension. Sensible perceptions and abstract concepts of understanding alone remain. Then the vast world of Imagination, the world of the Soul proper, falls into disgrace; it is identified with the imaginary, with the unreal.

It is very striking to note how carefully Suhrawardi and the *Ishraqiyyun* (the philosophers and spiritual masters belonging to his school) applied themselves to a metaphysics of Imagination. Because they realized its ambiguous role, they maintained it firmly centered between the intelligible and the sensible worlds. Its function in serving the intelligible, that is to say, the Intelligence—*nous* in Greek—is to present the *Veiled Idea* in the form of the Image, that is, of the symbol. The characters and events in a parable are all symbols, and that is why a parable is also the only story that is true. In return, when Imagination allows itself to be entirely caught by sensible perceptions, fluttering from one to the other, it is literally "off center" and loses itself in unreality. In the first case active Imagination is the organ of penetration into a real world which we must call by its proper name, to wit: the *imaginal*; in the second case, Imagination merely secretes the *imaginary*. For Suhrawardi, Imagination in the first case is the celestial tree at the top of Mount Sinai, from which the Sages pick the high knowledge that is the "bread of Angels." In the second case, it is the accursed tree mentioned in the Quran. There is a great deal of talk at present of a civilization of the "image"; in this respect, I believe that we have much to learn from our philosophers, the *Ishraqiyyun* and other masters. It is certainly a most complex subject, which makes me fear to appear obscure where I would only be concise.

For time obliges me to stick to essentials only. We have here reached the source of Suhrawardi's genius, the source of an inspiration that enabled him to move from one register to another as if playing upon a grand organ; that is to say, to present through the media of the symbols and parables of initiatory tales what he expounded elsewhere, in his major works, in a theoretical and systematic form.

I shall restrict my choice to three examples only, culled from a treatise of Suhrawardi's. Its form is not that of a continuous narrative, but rather that of a *rhapsody* linking together several symbolic stories. In it appear the Tortoise People, the Fairy People, and the Bat People. The subject is obviously not zoology—these are symbols of humans spiritually ignorant, the blind men of the soul. They are recognizable in their symbolic form because their hidden inner form, therefore their true form, *symbolizes with* these manifestations. And therein resides the whole difference from their daily life, which reveals only their apparent form. In displaying themselves in symbolic forms, they appear to us as they really are in the *imaginal* world, in which their ignorance or their blindness fixes them in a wholly *negative* relation with the Malakut, with the world of the Soul. It is their truth, or rather, their inner falseness which bursts forth when projected against the background of superior evidence, and here precisely a great mystic like Suhrawardi gives full vent to his humor.

A first example: what is at stake is *Na-Koja-Abad*, "the country of nowhere," removed from the dimensions of sensible space. One could write a scholarly metaphysical dissertation on hyper-space. But the doctrine may also be experienced, no longer a theory, but instead a real *event* of the soul. We see the mystic at grips with the Tortoise People.

One day the Tortoise People were watching from the shore the wheeling round of a many-colored bird at the surface of the sea: sometimes it dived underwater, sometimes it surfaced. One of the tortoises asked: "Is the nature of that bird aquatic or aerial?" Another replied: "If it were not aquatic, what would it be doing in the water?" But a third one said: "If it were aquatic, it could not live out of the water." Among the tortoises lived a wise judge whom they questioned. He answered: "Study that bird carefully. If it can live out of the water, that means that it does not need it. For proof, take the fish who cannot live out of the water." Just then a strong wind arose; the lovely colored bird soared and vanished into the clouds.

Did the tortoises understand? Far from it. They began to ask the Sage to explain himself. He answered them allusively by quoting a few of the great spiritual masters' sentences, culminating with the declaration of the mystic al-Hallaj concerning the Prophet: "He blinked his eye outside of the *where*," meaning that his inner vision removed him from the dimensions and orientations of sensible space. The tortoises became enraged: "How," they asked, "could a being who is localized in space go out of *place*? How could he remove himself from the directions and coordinates of space?" (We may recall the end of the "Recital of the Bird.") The Sage replied: "But that is precisely why I told you all I have been saying." Whereupon the indignant tortoises threw dirt and rocks at him: "Be gone! We remove you from office; we no longer acknowledge you as our judge."

Here is a second example. The issue this time is the connection between night and day. What appears as daylight to the blind men of the soul is nothing but darkness for him who possesses spiritual vision; and conversely, what is full daylight for him seems like dangerous and threatening obscurity to those who do not have spiritual vision.

Thus a hoopoe (wise Solomon's bird), in the course of one of its journeys, stopped off with the Fairy People. And, as everyone knows, the hoopoe is endowed with remarkably sharp vision whereas fairies are totally myopic. The hoopoe spent the night chatting with the fairies, and at dawn he wanted to set off again, but the fairies violently opposed this plan: "You poor wretch! What kind of new-fangled idea is this? Since when does one travel by day?" The hoopoe replied that the time had come to leave precisely because it was light. The fairies answered: "But you're quite mad! How can one see anything during the day since the day is dark while the sun is passing through the regions of gloom?" "But it is exactly the opposite," said the hoopoe. The discussion turned vicious and the fairies demanded an explanation, provoking the hoopoe to a formulation in which we hear the profession of faith of a great mystic: "Whosoever sees during the day can only testify as to what he sees. Here am I, myself, I see! I am in the world of presence, in the world of direct vision. The veil has been lifted. I perceive the radiant surfaces like so many revelations; doubt does not encroach upon me." Whereupon the fairies, exasperated by the behavior of this bird who claimed he could see in broad daylight, fell upon his eyes with their nails and teeth, screeching at him derisively: "Hey, you who-see-clearly-during-the-day!"

The hoopoe finally understood that there was no way out—what he knew to be the broad daylight of supra-sensible universes was nothing but darkness, bewildering those who see no further than their carnal eyes can perceive. He realized that the fairies would kill him since they were attacking his eyes, in other words, his inner vision, and that a mystic could not survive in this world without the power of his inner vision. The hoopoe knew that he must revert to the discipline of the arcanum, following the wise rule: "Address people only according to what they are able to under-stand." So, in order to free himself from his enemies, he told them: "Of course I am like you. Just as everyone else, I see nothing during the day. How could I see in broad daylight?" Whereupon the fairies were soothed and stopped torturing him. The hoopoe pretended blindness until he man-aged to escape, although this caused his soul to suffer a thousand torments. For it is hard not to be able to communicate to others the wonders one beholds. But the author reminds us of a divine law that admits no breach: "To reveal the divine secret to the unworthy is a crime of impiety (*kufr*)." The necessity for esotericism is founded on that very law.

The theme of the last example accentuates the story we have just read. This time Suhrawardi's parable introduces an innocent chameleon and the Bat People. How their quarrel began is left to our speculation. But the bats' hatred for the chameleon grew such that they plotted to imprison him under cover of darkness and to seek revenge by putting him to death in one way or another. They set off on their expedition and managed to drag their unfortunate enemy into their house of woe. They kept him imprisoned all night and consulted him in the morning. "How shall we punish this chameleon? What will be its death?" The worst torture for a bat would be to have to endure the sight of the sun, so they decided to punish the chameleon in this way. But what their bat minds could not even begin to apprehend was that this was exactly the kind of death the poor chameleon had hoped that God would send him. And here the author interrupts the bats' discussion with two of the mystic al-Hallaj's most famous distichs: "Do kill me, O my friends. In killing me you shall make me live, since for me dying is to live and living is to die." At sunrise the bats threw the chameleon out of their house of woe so that he should be chastised by the radiance of the sun. What they could not know was that the very thing that seemed like a torture to them was precisely the chameleon's resurrection.

Here are three mystical parables, at once very similar and very different. They draw upon the wealth of humor specific to Suhrawardi, a humor that conceals in its depths a profound sadness. It is the sadness of "he-who-has-understood" in the face of his impotence to overcome most men's incapacity to comprehend, because this incapacity is the "secret of destiny" and no human being can resolve that particular secret. I had been careful to warn you that there is no possible definition of humor. In trying to analyze Suhrawardi's humor too minutely, we would be sure of losing its presence.

But what we can do before ending is to follow our shaikh along the path of symbols. He was able to create marvelous ones, because he was endowed with the interior vision of the figures with which they symbolized. Perhaps a man must reach the summit of spiritual maturity—which bears no relation to his actual age—in order to create his own symbols. This summit is the self-knowledge which, as we noted, pervades Shaikh al-Ishraq's spirituality from beginning to end. The attainment of this self-knowledge blossoms in a visionary experience whose memory recurs throughout his tales. And this visionary experience gives shape to the most beautiful symbol of the Self that the philosopher goes in quest of, the Self of his transcending Ego, the celestial Ego that symbolizes with his terrestrial Ego. That symbol is the Figure of light, dazzlingly beautiful, with whose vision several of Suhrawardi's mystical tales open or close. It is the figure of the Angel who, in Avicennian philosophy, is the Angel of Humanity, Tenth in the Hierarchy of Intelligences, and whom theologians call the Holy Spirit. The remarkable thing is that this same Figure in the Western world also polarized the interior vision of those known as "*fedele d'amore*," chiefly Dante's companions who had read Avicenna and Averroes; they named that Figure of the Angel *Madonna Intelligenza*.

Suhrawardi always calls the Figure of the Angel encountered in initiatory recitals a shaikh. "Why a shaikh?" asks Musannifak, one of the commentators of these mystical recitals. The term has no bearing on years or old age, since the youthful features of the apparition are almost always underlined. The commentator goes on to explain that *shaikh* means *murshid*, spiritual guide, and that the Ishraqiyyun have no murshid other than this Angel of knowledge. That is precisely where they differ, he says, from the Sufis who proclaim the need for a shaikh or a human master. In any case, for the *Ishraqiyyun* this master could never be more than a temporarily necessary intermediary because their shaikh, their murshid or spiritual guide, is the Angel himself, the Angel of their vision and their nostalgia. Thus, we may say that this experience of the Angel for the *Ishraqiyyun* is very close to the experience of the personal interior guide, the invisible master called *shaikh al-ghayb, ustad-i ghaybi* in the school of Najmuddin Kubra. And this is also why this Figure of light, who rules the mystic's inner horizon, is the symbolon par excellence, the figure with whom one's most intimate personal being symbolizes; it is the Self reached through self-knowledge by the subject who is its mere earthly counterpart. Here we touch on a fundamental inner experience that could be illustrated with a great number of texts; the entire Valentinian gnosis could be cited in confirmation.

By the same token, one may catch a glimpse of Suhrawardi's "actuality." I apologize for using the word "actuality" in this context, as it is really too full of unpleasant associations. I would prefer "presence, urgency"... In saying this, I am thinking of a man who died in 1965, a playwright and a novelist, who at first sight might seem as far removed from Suhrawardi as possible, but a particular page of his suggests the comparison. I am thinking of Jacques Audiberti, whose extremely diverse works are admired by an equally diverse public. But any reader of a book such as *Les tombeaux ferment mal*[7] will agree that he was a mystic and something of a visionary. Yet I am referring to an episode from another book, a book called *Dimanche m'attend*.[8] This episode is set in one of Paris's many churches, the Eglise Saint-Sulpice. The architecture of this monument may not be altogether admirable, but it contains two treasures: its great organs and, in the first lateral chapel to the right of the entrance, Eugène Delacroix's huge painting of Jacob's struggle with the Angel. That is doubtless what suggested the comparison to my unconscious, although Suhrawardi's experience of the Angel is a struggle *for* the Angel rather than *with* the Angel. Nevertheless, without having read Suhrawardi, whenever Audiberti happened to be in the neighborhood of the church, he was wont to go meditate before Delacroix's picture for a few minutes, and his meditation readily turned into a visualizing experience. This is how he ends the account of one of his visits:

Jacob and the Angel, after bending sarcastically over my confusion, regain their attitude ... I begin to feel the cold, the church grows empty. Outside, rain glazes the square. Between the stopped cars (stopped but not arrested) walks a young girl in boots, wearing a toque and a grey coat whose sleeves are replaced by wing-shaped cloth. Her eyes are very slanting and her hair blonde. I gaze at her in wonder. But, come to think of it ... believe me if you will, I rushed into the church.
The Angel was still there...

Well then! Here again is an example of the *sui generis* humor that belongs to a somewhat visionary mystic. How could he tell us what he *saw*, not merely what he *thought he saw*, without admitting that he went back into the church to check if Delacroix's Angel was still there?

Here all philosophical reflection must stop, for it would destroy precisely what gives value to this humor. There is only one last thing we must do before parting, and that is to recall this verse of Rimbaud: "J'ai vu parfois ce que l'homme a cru voir" (I have sometimes seen what man believed he saw).

Notes:

1 Henry Corbin, *Avicenna and the Visionary Recital*, trans. Willard R. Trask, (Bollingen Series, LXVI) New York and London, 1960.

2 Plato, *Phaedrus*, 246e.

3 Corbin, *Avicenna*, pp. 186-87.

4 *Ibid.*, p. 192.

5 *Ibid.*

6 Goethe, *Faust*, Part II, Act V.

7 Jacques Audiberti, *Les ferment mal*, Paris: Gallimard, 1963.

8 Jacques Audiberti, *Dimanche m'attend*, Paris: Gallimard, 1965.

From *Spring: An Annual of Archetypal Psychology and Jungian Thought,* 1973. Translated from the French by Cornelia Embiricos Schroeder.

Parabola
Volume: 11.2
Mirrors

BODILY RESURRECTION

Henry Corbin

The hierarchy of being is ranged in a series of universes,
all of which end finally in our terrestrial Earth, this
Earth which is like the "tomb" to which they have been
entrusted; it is from this tomb that they must emerge
and be resurrected. But this resurrection is conceiv-
able only if the "descent" of the eternal Forms onto this
Earth is understood in its true sense. Just as the astral-
ness of the Sun does not "descend" from its Heaven, so
there is no question of an inherence or an "infusion" nor
of a material incarnation, an idea which an "Oriental"
philosophy definitely rejects. On the contrary, the idea
of *epiphany* dominates its mode of perception and that is
why the comparison with a "mirror" is always suggested
to us. Human souls, being eternal, do not themselves
mix "in person," so to speak, with the world of material
and accidental things, which are temporal. It is their
silhouette, their Image, their shadow, which is projected
onto it. Each of them has its own particular activity and
perfection, which are an effect and an influx of the universal and absolute activity of the Soul of the World.[1]

Know that when God had created Intelligence (*Ennoia*)
on the first of the Days, he said to it: "Now go down."
And Intelligence went down until it reached our world.

The final stage of its descent coincided with the time of Adam. Then the call resounded in the world through the mouth of Hadrat Adam and through the mouths of all those who summon men to God: "Now turn around and go up again." At the time of the Descent, those who spoke for God were cosmic expressions in the language of cosmogenesis. At the time of the Ascent they were inspired expressions in the language of prophecy. The world undertakes its ascent, its gradual return, thanks to the prophetic language of the Messengers. If it should happen that past times are revealed to you, you will see them under your feet, vertically, not beside you, horizontally.

The adventure of our world is the adventure of someone who has to be brought up from the bottom of a well. Moment by moment he reaches a certain level in the well: from level to level he comes to the upper level. At each moment the level he has passed is under his feet. Whoever knows how to look with the organ of inner sight will thus see past times beneath his feet more and more opaque and dense, and dark; whereas, day after day, he continues to ascend time, drawing nearer to the primordial Will and becoming more luminous, more subtle.[2]

—Muhammad Karim Khan Kirmani

The paradise of the faithful believer is his own body. His virtuous works (after the manner previously described) are its trees, fresh running water, castles, and houris. The Gehenna of the unbeliever is likewise nothing but his own body; his hateful works are its fiery furnaces, monsters, serpents, dogs, dragons.[3]

—Muhammad Karim Khan Kirmani

A number of symbols need to be pondered here. Glass, for example; it is produced from silica and potash, both of these, dense and opaque, are homologous to the elemental material body, the body of perishable flesh with which we are all familiar. When subjected to fusion, their impurity and dirt go away; we are left with clear glass; the interior is visible through the exterior, the exterior is visible through the interior. This, then, is homologous to the spiritual body, the *caro spiritualis*; the body which survives "in the tomb," that is, in Hurqalya, and to which "respite and sojourn in Paradise" are given, whereas the opaque density of the silica and potash was homologous to the material elemental body.

Consider how, from silica and potash, dense and opaque, there issued a body in a transparent subtle state. The latter is unquestionably the same mineral substance, and yet it is not. It is something other.

Now, supposing this glass in its turn is subjected to fusion: let a certain appropriate chemical be projected onto it and thoroughly penetrate the whole mass; the glass becomes very fine and brilliant glass. If the Elixir of whiteness, the "philosopher's chemical," be projected onto this fine glass, it then becomes a crystal which flames in sunlight (lens glass), because it causes the sun's rays on striking its surface, to converge. It is certainly still glass, and yet it is something other than glass; while remaining glass, it is, however, glass to which something has happened, something which has so completely purified it that now it ranks much higher than the first glass. This incandescent glass is homologous to the astral body which accompanied the Spirit at the time of the *exitus*, when the latter departs from its elemental material body. It is the body with which the Spirit enters the Western Paradise, the Paradise of Adam. Well then! if this sparkling crystal is melted once again and the white Elixir is again projected onto it, lo and behold! it becomes diamond. It is still glass, and yet no—it is something other—but not so, it is certainly itself but itself after undergoing all these trials.[4]

—Shaikh Ahmad Ahsa'i

Notes:

1 Henry Corbin, *Spiritual Body and Celestial Earth* (Princeton: Princeton University Press, 1977), p. 80.

2 *Ibid.*, p. 237.

3 *Ibid.*, p. 224.

4 *Ibid.*, pp. 200-1.

Parabola
Volume: 6.2
The Dream of
Progress

Progress and Evolution
A Reappraisal from the Traditional Perspective

Seyyed Hossein Nasr

There is little doubt that the idea of human progress, as it has come to be understood since the eighteenth century in Europe, is one that is confined to Western philosophy, especially in the form of the wedding of the idea of progress with material evolution. Moreover, this idea is a latecomer upon the scene of Western civilization, although some have tried to find its roots among the Greeks. Traditional Western man, like his fellow human beings in various Eastern civilizations, saw the flow of time in a downward rather than an upward direction—whether this was conceived of as cycles, as among the ancient Greeks and Romans, or in linear fashion, as in the Judaeo-Christian traditions. Nor was the moving force of history seen in purely materialistic terms except in rare instances, such as in remote antiquity. But even in such cases the concepts involved were very different from those held today, since the ancients did not have the conception or even use the word for matter as this term is used today. For most pre-modern peoples of the West, the moving forces which governed human existence and its history were in any case non-material, whether these forces were seen as *moira* or *dyké* by the Greeks, or the Will of God and various angelic hierarchies in Judaism and Christianity.

As for the non-Western world, among all of the civilizations which this world embraces, the perfection of the human state has always been seen as being at the beginning or the origin, which is of course also reflected perpetually in the ever-present now. The perfect state of things, for both individual and collective man, has been envisaged as being at the time of the first Emperor in the Far East, or at the beginning of the last Golden Age or Kritayuga in Hinduism, and the like. Likewise in Islam, which is closer to the Judaeo-Christian traditions, perfection is associated with the Origin. The most perfect man is the Prophet of Islam and the most perfect society that of Medina. Even in cases where perfection has been described as belonging to the future, it has always been associated with another Divine intervention in human history: with the coming of the Saoshyant in Zorastrianism, or the Kalki Avatara in Hinduism, or the Mahdi in Islam. The traditional East joined the traditional West in distinguishing clearly between a messianic vision based on Divine Agencies and a messianism which is reduced to purely human proportions.

To discuss the idea of human progress through material evolution in Western philosophy is therefore to deal with a recent phenomenon in Western intellectual history. It is also to deal with an idea which is confined to modern civilization as it developed in the West, although it has spread during the past century beyond this geographical area. The ideas and concepts which served as the background for the rise of the typically modern idea of human progress through material evolution are, however, somewhat older. Some reach back to the origins of the Western tradition, although these ideas were in every case distorted and even subverted to make it possible for the idea of progress based on material factors to be created from them.

Perhaps the most basic factor which gave rise to the modern idea of human progress through material evolution was that reduction of man to the purely human which took place in the Renaissance. Traditional Christianity saw man as being born for immortality, born to go beyond himself; for, as St. Augustine had stated, to be human is to be more than merely human. This also means that to seek to be purely human is to fall below the human level to the subhuman level, as the history of the modern world has demonstrated so clearly. The Renaissance humanism, which is still spoken of in glowing terms in certain quarters, bound man to the earthly level, and in doing so imprisoned his aspirations for perfection by limiting them to this world.[1]

Until that time, and of course for a short period afterwards (since no major change of this order can come about so abruptly) progress had been associated with the perfection of the human soul and the perfection of society, with the kingdom of God to be established on earth, with the coming of the Messiah and the new Jerusalem. Renaissance and post-Renaissance humanism and secularism made the traditional idea of the progress of the human soul towards its perfection (which resulted in its ultimate wedding with the Spirit) and the actual reality of the eschatological events associated with the descent of the Celestial Jerusalem and the coming of the Messiah, even more "far-fetched" and inaccessible, until both were reduced to the category of illusion, superstition, or some form of psychological subjectivism. But the imprint of the idea of progress and perfection in human nature was too profound to be obliterated so easily. Man still had lived and breathed with these ideas in his heart and soul.

Meanwhile, the conquest of the New World, Africa, and Asia was bringing great wealth into Europe and creating a new mercantile society which saw, in its power to manipulate the world, the possibility of perfecting it in a material and economic sense. Certain forms of Protestant theology in fact saw moral virtue in economic activity and were associated with the rise of capitalism and its well-known link, until very recent times, with the idea of material progress.

With this new confidence gained by European man in his ability to conquer the world and to remold it, the human background was prepared for the transfer of the idea of perfection and the progress of the soul from its upward, vertical dimension towards God to a purely this-worldly and temporal one. These ideas, thus suppressed, had to find an outlet in the world view of modern man, since they were so deeply ingrained in the human soul. The natural outlet was provided by this exceptional chapter of European history during which, despite incessant wars between Catholics and Protestants, Spain and England, England and France, etc., European man as a whole found himself mastering the earth rapidly and being able to mold the destiny of humanity. It took but a single step to see, in this very process of the expansion of European civilization and the amassing of wealth which accrued from it, the road to human progress and the confirmation of the secularized conception of man which had made such a domination possible in the first place. Had not Europe rejected its own traditional civilization, it would not have been able to develop all the means and techniques which made the conquest of non-European civilizations possible. This success was due to the secularization of man, and in turn hastened the process of secularization and this-worldliness by encouraging human beings to devote all their energies to worldly activities, as the hereafter became more and more a distant concept or belief rather than an immediate reality. Moreover, the belief in human progress in history provided a goal which aroused men's fervor and faith and even sought to satisfy their religious needs. Perhaps there is no modern ideology which has played as great a role in replacing religion and, as a pseudo-religion, attracting the ultimate adherence of human beings as the idea of progress, which later became wed to evolutionism.

Another element of great importance, whose secularization and distortion contributed a great deal to the rise of the idea of human progress through material evolution, was the Christian doctrine of incarnation and the linear conception of history associated with it, and especially with the type of Christology adopted by the Western Church. For Christianity, the Truth entered into history, into the stream of time and, through this event, time and change gained significance beyond the domain of time itself. In other religions also, time is of course of significance. What human beings do affects their immortal souls and the state of their being in the worlds which lie beyond time. Whether the world is seen as *maya* as in Hinduism, or as mirrors reflecting God's Names and Qualities as in Islam, there is not the concern in these religions with the "historicity" of the incarnation of the Truth in the same way that one finds it in Christianity. This statement would also include Zoroastrianism, although it sees time itself as an angel; and it would hold true even in later developments of the religion in the form of Zurvanism, where Zurvan or "boundless time" is seen as the principle of the Universe.

As long as the integral Christian tradition was alive, in which Christ was seen as the eternally present Logos and not only as an "historical personality," the doctrine of incarnation was preserved from desecration, distortion, and perversion, but as suprasensible levels of being began to lose their reality for Western man and Christianity became bound solely to an historic event, history itself became impregnated with ultimate significance affecting the Truth as such. The Aristotelian Averroism of the Latin Scholastics, as well as the Enlightenment view of European man and his position in human history, were also to play a crucial role in this process. From this position there was but a single step to take to arrive at nineteenth-century European philosophy, which with Hegel converted the philosophy of history practically into theology itself. The secularization of the Christian concept of incarnation removed Christ in one degree or another from the center of the arena of the historical and cosmic drama, but preserved the idea of the ultimate significance of temporal change for human existence. Belief in progress through temporal and historical change replaced to a large extent the central role occupied by the doctrine of incarnation in traditional Christian theology. One cannot imagine a philosophy which makes changes in human history the ultimate determining factor of human destiny, and even of the Truth Itself, arising anywhere but in a world in which the historical flux had been impregnated with theological significance to an extraordinary degree. In a way Hegelianism and Marxism could have arisen only in a world whose background was Christian, and Marxism could only be a Christian heresy as far as its philosophical aspect is concerned; although its concern with every aspect of life makes it in a sense a parody of Judaism, with its all-embracing notion of Divine Law as incorporated in the Talmud.

As for the linear conception of time which is to be found in traditional Christian sources such as St. Augustine, it saw history as a single line or movement punctuated by that one great event which was the descent of the Logos or the Son into time. Time had three points of reference: the creation of Adam, the coming of Christ, and the end of the world associated with his second coming. History had a direction and moved like an arrow towards that target which is described so powerfully in the *Revelation of John*. There was no cyclic conception of rejuvenation, gradual decay, and decomposition, followed by a new period of rejuvenation resulting from a new intervention by Heaven upon the human plane, as one finds in so many Oriental religions. Nor was there an emphasis upon the cycles of prophecy, as we see in Islam, although the more metaphysical and esoteric forms of Christianity were certainly aware of the everlasting and ever-present nature of the Logos.

But as these more profound teachings became less accessible and theology more rationalistic, it became easier for the secularistic thinkers to take the one step needed to convert the Christian conception of linear time to the idea of continuous and linear human progress, and the popular idea that things simply *must* become better every day simply because time moves on. As the Celestial Jerusalem became replaced by a vaguely defined perfect society in the future, the Christian conception of linear time became replaced by the secular one, which kept the idea of the linear character of time moving towards the goal of perfection in some undefined future, but rejected the trans-historical significance of historical events as envisaged by Christianity. In a sense historicism, and the idea of progress associated with it in many philosophical schools, is the result of the secularization and perversion of a particular type of Christology adopted by the mainstream of Western Christianity.

It is in this context that one must understand the rise of the idea of utopianism, which is another important element among the array of factors and forces that gave rise to the idea of progress in the modern West. Traditional teachings had always been aware of the ideal and perfect society, whether it was the *Civitas dei* of St. Augustine or the *al-madinat al-fadila* of al-Farabi, not to speak of Plato's well-known description of the perfect state in the *Republic*, which antedates both. But in a profound sense these "cities" were not of this world, at least not in the ordinary sense of the term "world." The word *utopia* itself, used by Sir Thomas More as the title of his famous work, reveals the metaphysical origin of this concept. Utopia means literally nowhere (*u* which implies negation and *topos*, space, in Greek). It is the land that is beyond physical space, in the eighth clime as the Muslim philosophers would say. It belonged to the spiritual world, and was not realizable on earth unless it were to be the descent of this celestial city upon the earthly plane.

The secularization which took place in the West after the Middle Ages gradually transformed the idea of utopia to create utopianism in its modern sense. In this transformation, messianic ideas emanating from Judaism, and to a certain extent Christianity, were also to play an important role. Through this religious zeal to establish a perfect order on earth, the already secularized notion of utopianism gained much momentum and became a major force in Western society. It is not accidental that the most dogmatic ideology based on the idea of inevitable human progress to issue from the West, namely Marxism, was to combine a pseudo-religious fervor deriving in many ways from a subversion of messianic ideas with utopianism. The role of the messiah in establishing the kingdom of God on earth became converted into that of the revolutionary in bringing about the perfect social order through revolutionary and violent means. In this way also religious eschatology was converted, or rather perverted, into the secular vision of the perfect order established by means of human progress through material evolution or revolution, for both views existed among the Western philosophers of the eighteenth and nineteenth centuries.

As far as material evolution is concerned, it too is the result of transformations which began during the Renaissance and reached their peak in the seventeenth-century scientific revolution, although the evolutionary idea itself was not to appear until two centuries later. The science of the Renaissance was still medieval science based on symbolism, correspondence between various levels of being, concern with the totality and the whole rather than parts, and other features associated with the traditional sciences. The scientists of the age were concerned with Hermeticism and Kabbalistic sciences, and sciences associated with names such as Marciglio Ficino, Pico della Mirandola, Nicolas Flamel, and even Leonardo da Vinci and Giordano Bruno recall more holistic sciences of nature than the mechanism which came to the fore in the seventeeth century.

Yet, it was during this period that the cosmos was becoming gradually desacralized, following upon the nominalistic perspective of the late Middle Ages which was depleting the cosmos of its sacred presence. This was also the period of the eclipse of a serious philosophy based on certainty and the vision of Being. The result was the quest after a new science and a new philosophy, the science based on a mechanistic conception of the Universe as developed by Galileo, Kepler, and Newton, and the philosophy upon the certainty of one's individual consciousness divorced from the world of extension or "matter," as developed by Descartes. The two went hand in hand in creating a view of things in which the knowing subject, or the mind, was totally other than the known object or "matter," which then became reduced to a pure "it" or "thing" in a mechanistic world where quantitative laws were to explain the functioning of all things.

This new transformation of the European mentality was itself responsible for the birth of the very concept of "matter" as it is known to modern man today. Neither the ancients nor the medieval people had the conception of matter which is taken for granted now, nor in fact do those sections of the human race even today who have not been affected by the influence of modernism. Neither the Greek *hylé*, the Sanskrit *Prakriti*, the Arabic *maddah*, nor even the Latin *materia* means matter in the modern sense. It was the seventeenth-century scientific revolution, combined with the philosophical changes associated with Cartesianism, which made possible the very idea of something being "material" and materialism in its current sense. Even the so-called materialistic philosophers of the Hellenistic period or the Hindu atomists cannot be considered, strictly speaking, as materialists, since the modern concept of matter had no meaning for them.

Although the birth of mechanistic science and a purely material conception of the world is associated with the seventeenth century, the world view of this period, including the eighteenth century, was still a static one. Even radically materialistic philosophers such as La Mettrie envisaged the material world as a static order, with change occurring within it, but not with the directed movement which would be associated later with the idea of evolution. This latter idea was to come not from the domain of physics but the temporalization of the ancient philosophical idea of the "great chain of being," which was applied to the world of living things, and was the paradigm through which natural historians since Aristotle had explained the chain of life relating the creatures of the three kingdoms to each other and to the whole of creation.

Traditional man saw a scale of perfection in existence ranging from the angels to the dust beneath the feet of earthly creatures. As long as there remained alive, on the one hand, the intuition of the world of Platonic Ideas, and on the other, the living faith in a Divine Being who created and ordained all things, man had no problem in envisaging this "chain of being" in a "spatial" manner so that the hierarchy of the planes of being was a living reality for him here and now. This static vision of the cosmos did not of course preclude the possibility of cosmic rhythms as stated explicitly by the Greek philosophers and alluded to by certain Jewish and Christian sages; but such a vision did definitely preclude the possibility of a gradual growth in time from one state of being to another. Such a growth was possible inwardly in the life of man, but not for the species as a whole.

The eclipse of faith, the spread of secularism, the loss of intellectual intuition, and the mechanization of the cosmos combined to make the hierarchy of universal existence appear as unreal. Having lost the vision of the Immutable, Western man could not but turn to the parody of the concept of the chain of being in time. The vertical "great chain of being" was made into something horizontal and temporal, resulting in the birth of the idea of evolution. Wallace and Darwin did not induce the theory of evolution from their observations. Rather, in a world in which the Divinity had been either denied or relegated to the role of the maker of the clock, and where sapiential wisdom based on the contemplation of the higher states of being had become practically inaccessible in the West, the theory of evolution seemed the best way of providing a background for the study of the amazing diversity of life forms without having to turn to the creative power of God. The theory of evolution soon turned into a dogma, precisely because it rapidly replaced religious faith and provided what appeared to be a "scientific" crutch for the soul to enable it to forget God. It has therefore survived to this day, not as a theory but as a dogma, among many scientists whose world view would crumble if they were but to take evolution for what it is—namely, a convenient philosophical and rationalistic scheme to enable man to create the illusion of a purely closed Universe around himself. That is also why logical and scientific arguments against it have been treated not at all rationally and scientifically, but with a violence and passion that reveals the pseudo-religious role played by the theory of evolution among its exponents.

This loss of the vision of the Immutable was to generalize the idea of evolution and extend it far beyond the domain of biology. At the same time, Hegelian dialectic was introducing change and becoming into the heart of reality as it was conceived by nineteenth-century European man. It did not take much to transform Hegel's idealism into material-ism, considering how prevalent were the various materialistic schools at that time. The new form of materialism announced by Marx, however, differed from its predecessors in its insistence upon the dialectical pro-cess to which was grafted the idea of progress whose development has been already mentioned. In the crucible of nineteenth-century European thought, the strands of the ideas of human progress, materialism, and evolution became welded together under the general banner of human progress through material evolution. Of course there were major differences of view among Marx and his followers, the French exponents of progress, the English evolutionists—not all of whom were "materialists" strictly speaking—and others. But these were all variations upon the same themes of central concern which had grown out of the experience and thought of postmedieval European civilization, and which had reached a point of view that was totally different from that of other civilizations in either East or West.

During the nineteenth century, Christian theology remained in general opposed to this amalgamation of ideas and forces outlined above, especially the theory of evolution and materialism. But as it was not able to marshal evidence of a truly intellectual—rather than simply rational or sentimental—order, it fought a continuously defensive battle. The opposition to these forces and ideas usually remained on the emotional level often associated with various fundamentalist positions bereft of intellectual substance. Nevertheless evolutionary concepts remained for the most part outside the citadel of Christianity.

One had to wait for the twentieth century to witness a fusion—which can also be called a perversion—of these ideas with Christian theology itself, of which perhaps the most radical and extreme example is Teilhardism. This phenomenon is particularly strange in that the idea of progress itself has ceased to attract the attention of the most perceptive of Western thinkers for several decades, and many people in the West seek to rediscover the nature of man beyond the image of the evolving mammal, striving through evolution to higher states of consciousness or a more perfect society as presented in the nineteenth century. It is a paradox that at the moment when the idea of progress through material evolution is itself becoming a victim of historic change and going out of vogue, the force of religion, which had for so long resisted this idea, is becoming influenced by its theses. The direction of life of contemporary man itself will be determined by the degree to which he is able to distinguish once again between the immutable and the changing, the permanent and the transient, and the apparent in contrast to the real progress available and possible for man as a being who, no matter how much he changes, remains in the depth of his being the same creature he has always been and will always be, a being born for the immortal empyrean of the Spirit.

Note:

1 On the significance of this event which, from the traditional point of view, implied a new "fall" for man, see F. Schuon, *Light on the Ancient Worlds*, trans. by Lord North-bourne (London: Perennial Books, 1965), especially pp. 28ff.

CHAPTER FIVE

•

SIGNS IN THE SOUL

Do not occupy your precious time except with the most precious of things, and the most precious of human things is that state of being occupied between the past and the future.[1]

—Ahmad ibn Isa al-Kharraz

It is pain that guides a man in every enterprise.
Until there is an ache within him, a passion and a yearning for that thing
arising within him, he will never strive to attain it.
Without pain that thing remains for him unprocurable,
whether it be success in this world or salvation in the next,
whether he aims at being a merchant or a king, a scientist or
an astronomer. It was not until the pains of parturition
manifested in her that Mary made for the tree:

And the birthpangs surprised her by
the trunk of the palm-tree. [Quran 19:23]

Those pangs brought her to the tree,
and the tree which was withered became fruitful.
The body is like Mary. Every one of us has a Jesus within him,
but until the pangs manifest in us our Jesus is not born.
If the pangs never come, then Jesus rejoins
his origin by the same secret path by which he came,
leaving us bereft and without portion of him.[2]

—Rumi

Parabola
Volume: 30.3
Body and Soul

Spirit, Body, and In-Between

William C. Chittick

Before God blew of his own spirit into clay, there was no soul—only spirit and body. The soul is neither spirit nor body, but rather an ambiguous something that wavers in between. It is alive and dead, awake and asleep, luminous and dark, one and many, wise and ignorant. Each soul is a unique image of the unity of God and the multiplicity of his attributes. The exact manner in which a soul is configured depends upon the relative predominance of oneness and manyness, and this changes constantly throughout its life. When it falls into forgetfulness and ignorance, multiplicity and dispersion predominate. When it lives in wakefulness and awareness, unity and integration increase.

The Quran tells us, however, that when God created heaven and earth, he also created "what is between the two." The ambiguity of this intermediate realm helps establish a more subtle understanding of the relationship between spirit and body. God created human beings as he created the universe, with both unseen and visible dimensions. He shaped Adam's clay "with his own two hands" (Quran 38:75) and then blew into him of his own spirit. His two hands can be understood as unity and multiplicity, mercy and wrath, light and darkness. The divine inblowing is often associated with the creation of

Adam in the divine image and God's teaching him "all the names" (Quran 2:31).

The universe is a single, multi-layered reality. Its unseen dimensions are home to spiritual beings like angels, and its visible dimensions to minerals, plants, and animals. Its in-between realms are the dwelling place of beings that are neither fully spiritual nor fully corporeal, such as demons. The human microcosm is structured in the same way: spirit, body, and in-between. The last is commonly called "the soul" and is nothing other than the locus of our awareness and selfhood.

Islam has no concept of original sin; in Quranic terms, Adam's problem was that "He forgot" (20:115). The Quran calls the cure of forgetfulness *dhikr*, "remembrance," and it also calls the prophetic messages by this same word dhikr, though here it is usually translated as "reminder." Dhikr, then, comes from the side of God to awaken the soul to the spirit's realm, and dhikr is also the soul's response to the divine initiative and its means to achieve awakening.

The final outcome of the soul's becoming is determined by the creative tension between spirit and body, light and darkness, remembrance and forgetfulness, understanding and ignorance. Rumi puts it this way:

> *The states of human beings are as if an angel's wing were brought and stuck on a donkey's tail so that perhaps the donkey, through the radiance and companionship of the angel, may itself become an angel.*[1]

The genesis, becoming, and destiny of the soul are frequently discussed under the rubric "origin and return," which are understood as the descending and ascending arcs of the circle of created existence. The descending arc traces out the movement of existence from the initial unity of the divine breath to the multiplicity of its reverberations in the material realm. The ascending arc, that of eschatology, describes the stages by which existent things return to their origin. In the case of human souls, the return is divided into two sorts: compulsory and voluntary.

The compulsory return is followed by each human being in the ascending arc that is the natural course of corporeal and spiritual development. The major stages are birth, death, the isthmus (separating this world from the next), resurrection, judgment, and paradise or hell. Those who return by choice do so by undertaking the various sorts of praxis and remembrance necessary to reintegrate themselves into the realm from which they descended. Those who refuse to go back freely pass through the same stages of development but are likely to end up in a different realm. "Paradise" designates the fruit of successfully completing the voluntary return, and "hell" the fruit of rebelling against the natural course of events.

Suhrawardi (d. 1191), founder of the Ishraqi School of philosophy, and Ibn Arabi (d. 1240), "the greatest master" of the Sufis, both engaged in comprehensive analysis of the in-between realm of the soul, which they often called *khayal*, image, or imagination. In Ibn Arabi's view, spirit and body are the heaven and earth of the human microcosm. The soul is the intermediary realm in which everything is an imperfect image of what lies beyond and beneath. What lies beyond is the spirit, and what lies beneath is the body. The in-between is neither heaven nor earth, neither invisible nor visible, neither spirit nor body, but an imaginal (not imaginary) isthmus. In order to take advantage of human embodiment, people need to delve fully into this mysterious realm, which is, as Ibn Arabi puts it, "an ocean without shore." Within the soul the divine breath lies in wait for the seekers. There alone do the lovers find the Beloved. Rumi makes the point in his own typical fashion:

> *Have you heard about the king's edict?*
> *He wants all the beauties to come out from their veils.*
> *This is the command he gave: "This year*
> *I want sugar very cheap."*
> *What a year! What a blessed day!*
> *What a king! What laughing good fortune!*
> *Now it's forbidden to sit in the house—*
> *the king is strolling in the square!*
> *Come with us to the square and see*
> *a joyful banquet, manifest and hidden.*
> *Tables have been set with plenty—*
> *all sorts of sweetmeats, barbecued chicken,*
> *Serving boys standing like moons before the cup-bearer,*
> *minstrels playing music sweeter than life.*
> *But the souls of the lovers have been freed*

from cup and table by their love for the king.
You say, "Where is this?" Right there
where the thought of "where" arose.[2]

The fullness of human possibility pertains much more to the unseen realms of the king's banquet than to the visible realm of activity. Even the most mundane of our goals is driven by the desire for invisible qualities, such as pleasure and happiness, or prestige and power. Philosophers and Sufis offered extensive analyses of the manner in which the invisible, spiritual side of the soul gradually comes to predominate over the visible, corporeal side during the compulsory return, when attributes and powers gradually display their signs in the developing embryo and then in the infant. Vegetal life appears through growth and differentiation, animal powers through volitional movement. The specifically human characteristics make their appearance somewhat later in intelligence, discernment, and speech.

Islamic law becomes incumbent only at puberty, when the compulsory return needs to be augmented by the voluntary return. The soul has now achieved sufficient independence to shape its own becoming: despite constraints placed upon it by physical embodiment, vegetal and animal characteristics, genetic predispositions, the law of karma—and whatever else you want to name—these are not absolute. The spirit, deeply buried though it may be, has no essential connection with the bodily realm. To the extent that its light shines in people's awareness, they have a say in what they do.

The soul is an imaginal realm from the beginning, which is to say that it is born of spirit's light and matter's darkness. Though it is dependent on the body's clay for the initial manifestation of spirit within itself, it gradually increases in substantiality to the point where it no longer needs a body to make its qualities manifest. Premonitions of its independence are experienced in dreams, which give us clear insight into imaginal reality.

The unity of dreams stems from the oneness of the spirit's light, and their multiplicity from the external, sensory realm, whose representations have been stored by memory. In dreams bodily and spiritual attributes are thoroughly mixed. The five senses truly function, but what we observe does not exist in the external, visible world, only in the invisible and multitudinous unity of our own selfhoods.

Mulla Sadra (d. 1640) epitomizes the soul's nature in a famous dictum: "The soul is bodily in origination and spiritual in subsistence." The multiplicity that we experience stems from the external world, but the singularity of the conscious self derives from the divine breath. The soul is both one and many, and everything it knows and experiences is located within itself, which is to say that its perception and understanding are essentially imaginal, a merging of the body and spirit.

The creative activities of the human species externalize the soul's imaginal realm, giving rise to culture and civilization. It is the soul's destiny, however, to be released from its connection to the outside world. According to Sadra, natural death takes place when the soul discards what it no longer needs. Bodily attributes continue to play a significant role in the soul's posthumous becoming because, by definition, it combines spirit and body in a unified whole. The fact of its having discarded its physical shell has no effect on its essential nature.

According to Ibn Arabi and others, the next world turns the soul inside out. What is spiritual and invisible here—the selfhood constructed from beliefs, thoughts, character traits, and memories—becomes bodily there. What is bodily here—the external characteristics that make us human—becomes invisible there. In the posthumous realm we experience our own selfhoods in corporeal and psychic forms that accord with our own soulish nature. This helps explain why, says Sadra, we will cease being human after the resurrection. Instead, we will be divided into four broad genera, each with many species: angels, demons, predatory beasts, and dumb brutes. These four correlate with the basic tendencies of the human soul: ascending, descending, active, and passive.

Let me end with another quote from Rumi, who sums up this dimension of Islamic thought with his usual magic:

> There are thousands of wolves and pigs in our existence,
> godly and ungodly, beauty and bastard.
> The ruling property belongs to the predominant:
> If gold is more than copper, then you are gold.
> The character that predominates in your existence
> will of necessity give you form at the resurrection.[3]

Notes:

1   *Fihi ma fihi* (Furuzanfar edition), p. 107.

2   *Diwan* (Furuzanfar edition), ghazal no. 1903.

3   *Mathnawi*, Book 2, 1416-19.

Parabola
Volume: 17.3
Oral Tradition

To the Ones Who Would Listen

Kaygusuz Abdal

Translated by Sheikh Tosun Bayrak al Jerrahi

The following text is extracted from Budalaname, *"a letter from one who gave himself up to receive his Lord," written by the fifteenth-century* ashik *(wandering lover-poet) Kaygusuz Abdal. The original manuscript is located in the Nuruosmaniye Library in Istanbul.*

In the beginning He is beyond the lowest and the highest, further than the front and behind the back, more to the right than right and more to the left than left.

He has no name or attribute at a place called Void, hidden in the mother of all words, where there is neither word, nor name, nor light, nor weight, nor form, nor place.

At that timeless time when there is no before or after, in that void where there is nothing evident or hidden, in eternity before the beginning and the end, was a pure He, the divine identity.

When He wished to be known, He said "Be."

He struck the sound of the first letter upon the sound of the second, and a single dot formed within the endless void. The dot moved down, became a line, like one [the letter A in Arabic]. And He picked up the end of the line and moved it upwards, a concave curve. He put a dot under it and made the letter B.

Well before all that happened, I was with Him.

Before I wore the clothes of Adam, I was alive within the being of the divine unseen, until He wished to show Himself to Himself.

Then He moved the dot from right to left; some things He dotted, some not. He set the twenty-eight letters in Adam's face. He built the seven worlds below his waist, the seven heavens above, placed His footstool upon his chest and His throne upon his head, and taught him His names. And with His beautiful names He showed Himself to Himself.

In the eighteen thousand universes that He set between the B and the E, He made His creatures two by two. Then He put a dot from a man's loins in a mother's belly and dressed it in Adam's clothes and His mercy—for He made me for Himself, and everything else for me.

O you who seek truth and reality, come, have pity on yourself. Find a cure for the sickness of ignorance by which you take your imagination to be reality and from which you suffer all your life. While you can, search for a cure day and night, until you feel secure from all that you fear.

You do see some people at peace, saved from the disease of ambition, though they have less than you do—while you are in pain and oppressed by all that you have.

A day will certainly come when you will regret all this, but it may be too late. Seek wisdom now, start to learn and leave this ignorance which you take for knowledge. Seek the company of those who have come to know the truth and learn their language so that you understand what they say. Salvation is in a perfect man.

After you find the perfect teacher for you, let your love for him be your guide. It is from him that you will learn to find yourself and find the truth in your own being.

Imam Ali, may Allah be pleased with him, asked the Messenger of Allah, "What action can I take that is not totally lost and worthless?"

The Messenger of Allah answered, "Seek truth. You will find it in yourself: therefore know yourself. Seek the company of the wise, who know. Agree with what they say, for one understands only that with which one agrees. Be sincere in what you say—a single tongue should not speak two different words. No deceit or fraud should enter into your thoughts. Do not belittle anyone or anything, for everyone and every-thing, in its beginning, wishes for the same thing.

"Do not touch anything that is not yours. Avoid crowded places; even in such places, try to be with yourself, for that is the place where truth is manifested. That is where the truth is.

"If you do all this, your sight will reach to the end of the worlds and to the end of the heavens and you will be one and complete. Then your life will not be spent for naught and you will be safe from temptation and pain."

O seeker of truth, the path to truth is very short. It is closer to you than your jugular vein, yet there are seventy thousand barriers, all created by you.

> *The one who already knows, understands.*
> *What have I told the one who is heedless?*
> *He is not here.*
> *And what does the animal hear*
> *but noise?*
> *It either runs away or comes here.*
> *If you did not understand you are not here.*

Let me tell you so that you can judge yourself. If you knew, you would be with Man, not with animals shaped like men.

One day the inhabitants will leave this place. Your every cell will return to dust, and you will be left by yourself. Woe to the one who does not know himself! Then you will walk alone.

If you are made of gem, wherever you go they will come to your door. If you are made of rubbish, no one will want it.

Time as you know it will pass into timelessness. The cycles will be completed, the oceans will evaporate. The one who owns your soul will not look at your face, neither have compassion on you, if you are not a part of those who know Him.

O you who wish to understand, wake up from heedlessness, look at reality, admit that now you are drunk and that all you know is your imagination. If you honestly seek truth, if you really wish to wake up, you must first attain the truth of dying before dying. You must die before dying in order to be alive. You must leave the imagination of this world so that you can arrive.

To learn constancy and love you have to suffer the beloved's hiding from you, and only if you are patient in suffering will you find faith. But if you claim you are faithful already, and exhibit yourself worshipping the one to whom you claim to be faithful, hoping to receive His reward … suddenly one day you may find yourself face to face with the truth that should have been worshipped. Only it will be too late. You will be dead. You will regret it, but to no avail.

I have gone there and come back and am giving you the news. Only when your soul is in human shape can you gain or lose. Take lessons from all you see, but never say, "Why is it not another way?"

They are but bits and pieces and they seem disconnected. Try to gather them together; your reason is the means. Be in the now, but contemplate your end.

Know that this realm has an owner and the sultan lives in the palace of your being. Know yourself so that you will not be ashamed when you meet Him. Don't look down on anything, don't try to take someone else's share, know right from wrong, just from unjust—for the human being is built from the brick of lawful sustenance and the mortar of the advice of the wise. The human being is destroyed by that which is unlawful, by the chatter of the ignorant.

Be conscious, take advice from what you see. Listen to your conscience and talk with reason. Behave correctly even when you are by yourself. Know your place and be humble. Kneel and sit low in the presence of the wise. Do not speak before being asked. If asked, be brief and say only that which you know. Do not be selfish. Know that the truth is with you always and everywhere. Be loyal to your friends and trustworthy to all.

Speak gently to the ignorant. Be polite and quiet in the presence of the wise. If you ask of a teacher, ask with respect. Never ask a question with an intent to test, and accept the answer and agree with it, even if it is not what you expected. If you reject, you will be rejecting yourself.

In this palace of your being there are many chambers with His secret treasures, but the palace is His. There is none other than He. If you accept yourself as His servant, behave as a servant, but if you have become the perfect man, then you are the sultan; all is yours—and you have to keep it safe and secure.

If you do not know yourself, you are neither sultan nor slave. Be prepared, then, to be put to shame and never to see the sultan of the domain. Then you are only the dust thrown hither and thither with each breath. Hold on to the one who knows so that you know also. Otherwise, you will be disconcerted and confused.

The purpose of your coming to this world is to know yourself and to know the truth. At this stage of your eternal life you must learn to differentiate truth from falsehood. Do not spend your one and only lifetime in vain.

If you call yourself a human being, then climb to the summit of your being, where you will find reason, and seek. Look at the flat lands, the climbs, and the falls—for there are many fearful chasms—so that you will be secure from fear.

Those who are unable to discern truth from falsehood walk through this life blindly. They still run in circles today.

Each man is responsible for his own soul. For many, what they think they know is a veil preventing them from finding the secret. They ask each other, What is this place? Who built it?—bewildered, the blind leading the blind.

The one who feels he is high peers down and looks for it below. The one who is low looks up and seeks it above.

From the time He gathered the souls and asked them, "Am I not your Lord?" (Quran 7:172) until the coming of the perfect human being, one hundred and twenty four thousand blessed messengers came and passed.

Each said one thing, and not many took heed.

Then the last blessed one came and saw the builder within what He built, showed Him to us manifest in what He created. The one who sees, sees. What is it to the blind? If you are blind, find a guide who sees. But how do the blind know if someone else sees?

The truth you seek has neither before nor after, is not in the past nor in the future. It is in the now. It has no above nor below. It is where you stand, it has neither right nor left. It is the center. It is an ocean that fits into every existence, for everything that exists is from one existence.

The ones who see anything ugly in it are rejected, because the light comes from the flame as in a crystal chandelier, where each crystal reflects the light of the same candle. All creation is but one being. Alas, they speak different tongues.

It was not my intention to give you any advice, for often the truth is told and all who hear depart. Only the ones who are destined to hear, hear.

I do not speak of myself. It is the truth that speaks, out of compassion. The truth wills none to burn. Someone destitute with pockets full of gems, someone who refuses to put his hands in his pockets, cannot call tyrant the one who gave him the treasures, and the hands to hold them, and the mind to use them. He is the justest of the just who said:

The one who does an atom's worth of
good, will receive good.
The one who does an atom's worth of
harm, will meet with harm.
—*Quran 99:7–8*

Parabola
Volume: 30.3
Body and Soul

THE FRAGRANCE OF THE FRIEND

Interview with Iraj Anvar

"I have known Rumi all my life," Iraj Anvar says. "When I was a baby my father would sing me to sleep with the Math-nawi. *It was part of my household." Born in Iran, Anvar's first career as a theater director in Tehran brought him to America, where he soon found himself estranged from his country by the Iranian Revolution. He found another career as a professor of Persian Literature at NYU and eventually worked with Elizabeth Grey on* The Green Sea of Heaven, *her book of translations of Hafiz. But despite his dismay at the translations of Rumi available in English, he was reluctant to attempt his own until a friend insisted, telling him, "America wants to know what Rumi really says!" Now Iraj completes the cycle that began when he was a child, singing and reciting Rumi in the Persian language and reciting his inspiring transla-tions, some of which have been published in a bilingual edition entitled* Divan-i Shams-i Tabrizi, *excerpts from which are included here. He is also teaching a course in Rumi at Sufi Books, where his intimate experience of Sufism enhances the appreciation of this most inexhaustible of mystical poets.*

— Anne Twitty

Parabola: *Rumi is now known worldwide, and it seems that the effect of his words – even in translation – awakens a deep response within his readers. According to Seyyed Hossein Nasr, the beauty of Persian poetry attracts the soul, melting "the hardness of the soul and the heart." He also refers to an Arabic and Persian word* husn *that means both "virtue" and "beauty." In Western culture, we often think of virtue in terms of the soul, but not necessarily of virtue and beauty being together. In fact, we sometimes think of them as antithetical.*

Iraj Anvar: No, in Islam, they are almost the same. Beauty is virtue and virtue is beautiful. Love is the highest and most beautiful virtue. There is a saying of the Prophet: "If Love had a material face, it would be the most beautiful creature."

The face of God is the most beautiful of all, and in the mystical poetry of Rumi and other poets, there are many lines about the beauty of Joseph, which is actually representative of the beauty of God. They refer to it so often!

This beauty is also represented by the *saqi* who appears in many Persian poems. The cupbearer is beautiful, must be beautiful.

P: *He brings the wine of spiritual love.*

IA: There is another story: When God created Adam, he made this body which was soulless, and he wanted to send the soul into the body, but the soul said, "No, I'm not a fool, I'm not going to get trapped in there." So God cheated it. He sent some angels into the body, with musical instruments, to play beautiful music, and that's how they lured the soul into the body.

P: *Rumi speaks of two kinds of soul in his* Discourses. *He cautions us that you can't really know the soul unless you have some experience of the other world; otherwise you will confuse that soul with the lower self.*

But it seems that there is more than one word in Arabic and Persian that is translated into English as "soul" or occasionally, "spirit." We can easily become confused by them. In one of Rumi's poems, he says that in dreams the soul travels and experiences another world. Is that the ruh, *the soul, or spirit, that God originally breathes into the human being?*

IA: We have the word ruh in Persian and in Arabic, and we also have a Persian word, *jan*. Jan is the soul, but it means "life," as well, and *jan-i jan* is the soul of the soul. Sometimes jan is ruh, used in the same way.

There is another word, *nafs*. When we say nafs in general, we always mean the lower self. Actually, there are five, and you have to have the adjective to distinguish them.

Once Ali was asked, "What is the nafs? Which one are you talking about?" In Arabic, the *nafs al-ammara* is the imperious self, the one that commands. Then you have *nafs al-lawwama*. That is the one that scolds you, tells you that this is not right. And then there's the *nafs al-mulhima*, the one that inspires you. The *nafs al-mutma'inna* gives you certainty and peace. The highest, *nafs an-natiqa*, means the divine soul, the breath of God.

P: *That way of distinguishing them sometimes gives the impression of a ladder that has to be climbed, rung by rung, but perhaps they can also be perceived as different states or qualities of the human being.*

It sounds very much as though this description of the soul includes a warning conscience and aspects that assist, enable, help, inspire. These soul-selves show you the way. So the higher educate the lower ones? And then all of them become unified under the command of the highest?

IA: In reality, the three higher work together under the nafs an-natiqa to tame the lowest one.

P: *I have read that al-Ghazali calls that struggle* jihad an-nafs, *which has been translated as "Fighting the Ego." That nafs is sometimes referred to as the animal nature, but at one point you said in your Rumi class that the lowest nafs is more like what we mean by the ego, in the spiritual sense.*

IA: Yes, I think it is. In the old way, you had to kill it. Even Rumi says that we should kill that nafs. Now we understand that we need it, otherwise we cannot survive. But when it goes out of balance, it causes problems. Therefore, it must be tamed and controlled. It is our vehicle to perfection.

P: *One of the images of the soul that you have talked about in Rumi and in other Persian poets is the imprisoned bird in the cage, which longs to return to its home.*

In your translations, for example, Rumi says: "I was a divine bird, I became an earthly one. I did not see the trap and was suddenly captured in it."

IA: And Hafiz's way of saying it is: "The dust of my body veils the face of the soul. How can I fly if I am imprisoned in the body?"

In fact, we descend and become one with this body in order to evolve, and by reaching a certain level of consciousness we can actually free ourselves from the material body in this life, even if it is only temporary. At that point, Rumi says, "The heavy soul became weightless and took flight."

P: *This great poet and teacher also told his listeners that our souls are originally like fish, utterly at ease in the Ocean of Life, and when they come to earth they are like fish thrown onto dry land, yearning to return to their element.*

IA: Here he emphasizes the suffering of the soul in a very harsh way. The agony of a fish out of water is quite visible. The difference is that eventually the fish dies, but the soul continues to exist in a state of constant agony. However, the word most often used for the desire to return to the source is "longing," which is a milder way of describing it.

P: *How does he speak about this longing?*

IA: In the beginning of the *Mathnawi* he talks about the reed cut from the reed bed, which becomes a flute and sings the song of separation. It says: You have to have felt the pain that I have felt to understand what I am saying. Those who look at Rumi only from the material point of view say: "Well, he's really talking about the fact that he was cut off from his homeland; he had to leave Balkh with his father before the Mongols attacked Persia, and he had to stay somewhere else, very far away, and always longed for 'back there'." But from the spiritual point of view, everyone agrees that he's talking about the soul. This material body, made of matter and mud, becomes a prison for the pure soul, and the soul longs to go back to its origin, to the reed bed.

P: *Rumi offers us so many ways to see the body: as dust, as a donkey, a staff, a serpent, a mountain, a nutshell, a seed pod. He even describes God as a tailor, tenderly fashioning the human body as a robe for the soul. In that view, the body becomes a gift. And while it may be only an outer husk or a pod, the seed can't be planted without it. Then life becomes a matter of growing back in some way.*

IA: The soul is created pure – pure and ignorant. It is sent down to be mixed in with this material world, so that it can evolve and reach perfection. The metaphor for the soul is gold, and when gold is pure, although it is very precious, you can't make things with it. It has to be mixed with some other metal as an alloy so it can be worked into something useful.

According to Nour Ali Elahi, there is evidence in the Quran that in fact the soul, when it descends to earth, has 50,000 years to perfect itself in different successive lives, but the Islamic theologians and most of the Sufis don't talk about it. In some of Rumi's ghazals, you see that he hints about it, about coming back.

In one of the ghazals I have translated, he refers to it in this way:

> *The one who appeared like a moon*
> *in a crimson cloak last year,*
> *this year he came in a brown robe.*
> *The Turk you saw plundering that year*
> *is the same one who appeared as an Arab*
> *this year.*
> *Even though the garment is changed, the*
> *beloved is the same.*
> *He changed the garment and reappeared.*

In another poem Rumi says, "I died as mineral and became a plant," which is pretty close to the doctrine of Ahl-i Haqq which talks about the collective force of the mineral that reaches perfection and goes into plant life, and is then transferred into the animal and the human. Not the soul, not that essence, not the higher self, but the jan or life force that is formed from a group of animals. When finally the human soul is formed in a body, the divine soul joins in. It comes from the breath of God, and by descending into the body it begins the process of perfection.

P: *Another image Rumi offers us is of the body as Mary, pregnant with the soul, who is Jesus. But he adds that sometimes the birth pangs never come, and the soul is never born. Presumably, then, the person dies without ever having realized the soul?*

IA: Yes. That is when we do not struggle toward perfection. Without struggle, there is no improvement, so the soul remains undeveloped.

Whenever Jesus is mentioned, he is given the title of *Ruh Allah* after his name. Ruh Allah means the Soul of God. So when Rumi says that the body is like Mary and the soul is Jesus, it makes perfect sense because of this attribute. He is the symbol of purity. Nevertheless, Muslims believe that he is not the son of God. God doesn't give birth, but Jesus is considered the most perfect Sufi.

P: *Although the body exists as an outer form, it seems that it, too, is capable of transformation. In one poem Rumi addresses his soul as Moses, in reference to the story of Moses among the Egyptian sorcerers. What does he mean when he says that for Moses, the body is a staff when held and a serpent when thrown?*

IA: While the body is held by the spirit, by the soul, it is controlled. Like the staff, it is good and useful. When it is separated from the soul, it becomes wild and violent. The nafs that escapes from control is sometimes pictured as a snake.

P: *Our issue is called "Body and Soul," but are these one or two? Is the body separate from the soul? It sounds in a way when you're talking about Rumi, that it's one. Once it's been lured into the body and becomes entangled with matter, it becomes inseparable.*

IA: Well, it's more like the shell and the fruit inside. They are one, but they are not one. The soul definitely needs the body to develop and evolve, but they are two different things that couple for the short span of earthly life.

You can compare the appearance, the outside, to a shell, that you can touch and see, but the shell without an inside is just a shell. It has no life, no reality.

P: *One is perishable and one is imperishable?*

IA: Exactly. When a soul leaves the body, the body is nothing, you just give it time and it becomes part of nature. "Let our fragile spirit have eternal life. / The soul lives, the body wears out like a cloak."

P: *The celebration of the night of Rumi's death, in Konya, is called the Wedding Night, isn't it? And in the beautiful lines from one of your translations, he speaks of rejoicing at the moment of death: "Tripping on a stone he finds a pearl. / His soul leaves his lips to kiss lips sweeter."*

IA: Yes. And there is this other line from Rumi: "When you are left behind, when you cannot walk anymore, travel anymore, your soul continues the journey."

P: *Though the body is an instrument for the journey, there's a stage in the journey when it is no longer necessary. But the journey continues. ...*
  "The day the soul flies in the rapture of your scent / the soul and only the soul will know the fragrance of the friend."

IA: There is a temporary link between soul and body, yet there is also a division. At the beginning of the *Mathnawi*, we are told: "The body is not hidden from the soul, nor the soul from body. Yet no one, no body, has permission to see the soul."

P: *Rumi often reminds us that the form is the outward part, and the essence or soul is the inward. "Soul" and "body" become ways of looking at the world. At one point, before retelling an old story, he declares that the traditional story is the husk and by reinventing it, he is giving his listeners the kernel, its soul. In the* Discourses, *he refers to the word as the body, and its meaning as the soul. And he describes the outer form of ritual prayer as its body, while its soul is absorption and unconsciousness, which are beyond the scope of the outer form and even exclude it.*

IA: Yes, you're talking about *surat* and *ma'na*; surat is the appearance or the face and ma'na is the essence. There are other words that also refer to this concept: *zahir*, what is apparent, and *batin*, what is hidden.

P: *So the soul is concealed from us … ?*

IA: Well, in a way, when we don't develop properly and we don't have the ability to see our true nature, we can't see it. An undeveloped person is like a child. Originally, the soul is like a child, and it has to grow.

P: *In that process there are "temptations," and at first they are very obvious; the blaming self identifies them right away—whether or not we choose to listen to it. But it seems that as the soul's evolution progresses, temptations become more subtle and harder to detect. That means that we have to become more and more sensitive to the inner meaning of a situation.*

IA: Yes, my teacher said that sometimes the nafs may appear as a very wise man, somebody very respectable, and it gives you advice that is ultimately not very good for you, but it is so camouflaged in a cloak of religiosity and spirituality that if you are not careful, you will do what it suggests.

P: *In another sense, according to Rumi, the soul is infinite. In its essential nature, it has no boundaries, no limits, and yet as we experience it, going through life, it has stages and limitations.*

IA: Time, and space, and that other dimension. We say that, but we don't understand it. We don't know what we are saying when we say there is no time and space. We cannot conceive it with this mind and this rationality.

P: *While Rumi sometimes speaks of the body as a sheath or support for the soul, at one point he calls the soul itself a cup. We keep moving into more and more subtle realms, where even the soul, which seems so ethereal, so immaterial, serves as a vessel for the wine of love.*

IA: The soul is a cup that can hold the wine of love, which can be interpreted as the essence of God, but this cup is still immaterial.

P: *This wine is often associated with the subtle heart, but sometimes Rumi seems to be using "soul" and "heart" almost interchangeably.*

IA: The image is that you have to empty your heart. Your heart can be considered a cup full of other things. You throw out everything, you clean it, and then it will be filled with the wine of love. And yes, sometimes heart and soul are interchangeable.

P: *One thing that has come through this talk with you is the idea of evolution, that the soul comes down and doesn't return in the same state.*

IA: No, if it succeeds in doing what it is here to do, it returns fully aware.

P: *Ideally. Or less aware? Is there also a downward movement, a devolution rather than an evolution? You don't go up every time?*

IA: While we can regress by creating immense pain and suffering for others and ourselves and even hinder the general evolution of mankind, I think we are forced toward this evolution. All we can do is to slow it down.

P: *We're drawn. That's wonderful, that we find our way through an evolution on another scale.*

IA: These are the actions of God's love. It is felt in, echoed in, the human being. Rumi says: "The voice of this reed flute is fire, it is not air / and whoever does not have this fire is lost..."

P: *The fire, then, is the fire of love, and that is the only thing that carries you. ... You were saying that God is love, and the soul is drawn like the moth to the flame. ...*

IA: That is used very often in Persian: the moth that is drawn to the light. And it comes so close that it is burned and becomes part of the flame.

P: *In that moment all of the concepts we have been alluding to are annihilated: "Why even think of heart or mind, when the soul itself has fled."*

IA: *Khamush*, meaning Silent, is one of Rumi's pen names. It is ironic that the poet who composed such an immense quantity of poetry calls himself that. But he uses the imperative Khamush! Silence! at the end of many of his ghazals. For him, there is a point past which language cannot go. We are left in silence.

Parabola
Volume: 26.4
The Heart

The Hidden and the Most Hidden

Interview with Shaikh Ali Jum'a

Every Friday thousands of Muslims in Cairo hear the call to prayer and make their way to Sultan Hasan, a four-teenth-century mosque located in the heart of the old city, to pray and listen to the khutba *(the Friday talk) of Shaikh Ali Jum'a. As one enters the courtyard of the mosque, framed by four enormous vaulted halls, one is struck by the simplicity, beauty, and scale of the structure. It arouses the feeling of man and his Creator.*

Shaikh Ali climbs the stairs to the minbar, *faces the congregation, and begins his talk. He invokes the Name of God with such intensity that men weep, for it has been said that when you hear the Name of God you should weep, and if you do not weep, you should weep because you do not. After the prayer almost the entire congregation remains to hear the lesson that Shaikh Ali presents. As he speaks, his soft eyes penetrate, his voice rings with strength and quivers with emotion. He is the embodiment of intelligence and light.*

It was after Friday prayer on a hot Cairo evening that we

spoke of the heart. This is the first time Shaikh Ali's words have been translated into English.

Shaikh Ali Jum'a is a professor of Islamic Jurisprudence at the Faculty of Islamic and Arabic Studies, University of al-Azhar, Cairo, Egypt. He is the Director of Hadith Scholarship of the Thesaurus Islamicus Foundation and Imam of the Sultan Hasan Mosque in Cairo.
—*Shems Friedlander*

Shems Friedlander: *What is the heart? Where is it located? Is it the pump that physicians call a heart which remains with man between birth and death? Is it physical or metaphysical?*

Shaikh Ali Jum'a: There are words, expressions in the Arabic language that speak about this level: the heart (*al-qalb*), the sensitive heart (*al-fu'ad*), the essence (*al-lubb*), and the intellect (*al-aql*). The word qalb also refers to the physical entity, the pump that pumps blood, the cessation of which separates life and death. But as to this other heart—meaning the inside of a thing, its truth, its central core, and its essence—there are five levels that Sufis speak about regarding this matter. They have spoken of the heart, the spirit, the secret, the hidden, and the most hidden.

These five levels are like circles within circles, each circle higher and narrower than the one before. Meaning that if there are one thousand human beings at the level of the heart, at the level of the spirit there are eight hundred, at the level of the secret six hundred, at hidden two hundred, at the level of the most hidden one hundred—and what is beyond this fewer than one hundred. These levels form a pyramidal shape.

The heart is a level among the levels, and not a piece of flesh. But there is a relation of sorts between the heart as a piece of flesh and the heart as a level. This relation is not perceived or sensed. It is not possible to touch, see, or experience it through the five senses. And yet, we feel the level of the heart near the breast, below it and to the left. We feel it in a place lower than or under the part of the body that is the physical heart.

SF: *How does one enter this heart?*

SAJ: The way leading to the heart is remembrance, repetition of the Names of God (*dhikr*) and contemplation (*fikr*). Just as a human being feels that thinking takes place in the head [Shaikh Ali places his hand on his head] and does not feel that his hand is thinking, so he feels near the heart the unveiling of the secrets and lights in the five realms.

There are five realms which the human being experiences. The world of *mulk*, this is the visible world experienced by the five senses; the world of *malakut*, this comprises the creatures and creation that man cannot see and cannot arrive at through his five senses, like the angels, *jinn*, hell, and heaven. Together, mulk and malakut are the world, which is what is other than God.

Beyond this are three worlds at the divine level; the world of beauty, the world of majesty, and that of completeness. They are also referred to as "what is above the throne" and are what is meant by His saying, "*Ar-Rahman ala'l-arsh istawa*"—"The Merciful sat upon the throne" (Quran 20:5). What is above the throne is God in His Beauty, Completeness, and Splendor. What is beneath the throne is what is referred to as the carpet. There is a throne and there is a carpet.

The aforementioned five levels—heart, spirit, secret, hidden, and most hidden—are levels among the levels of lights and secrets in the world of mulk and malakut, the world beneath the throne, and through which man ascends to the positions of the throne.

Above the throne there are five other levels—heart, spirit, secret, hidden, and most hidden—resembling these five, reflected like a mirror, five facing this way and five that way [Shaikh Ali demonstrates with his open palms, one palm towards the listener, one palm towards himself].

Beyond this are three other worlds which are totally obscure, meaning that we absolutely cannot comprehend them, whether with our thought, our minds, our practice of dhikr, or our sensory perception. For God in His Glory is beyond comprehension.

SF: *And so what is the heart?*

SAJ: The heart is a level among the levels of piety on the way to God, the lights and secrets of which are manifested in a part of the body, the form of which is a pump that pumps blood in the body. In this area, not in the part of the body itself but around it, man feels something of the revelation of secrets, disclosures, and lights.

SF: *Where is the heart?*

SAJ: It is in man. It is a level among levels of the spirit, meaning a circle of the circles of the spirit. Above it is also the spirit; it is a level in which the spirit finds and comprehends itself.

And then there is what is secret. At this level man understands that he is nothing and that God is the foundation of all things. In this stage man might lose his way and believe himself to be God, and believe himself to be nothing because God has totally taken him over and therefore is he.

After this he ascends to the hidden and knows that he is one thing and God is another. That he is mortal and God is permanent and that there is a difference between the creature and the Creator. Then he is elevated beyond this and knows that he is a manifestation among the manifestations of the Beneficent, and that the attributes of God are all reflected in him through ability, will, and knowledge. This is the station of the most hidden.

The first of all these endless levels is the heart, the instrument of contemplation (fikr) and dhikr (remembrance by repetition).

God is eternal, but I perish. I have a beginning and He has no beginning. I need Him but He does not need me, and so a feeling comes from my heart. This is the station of the hidden.

SF: *Does the heart have thoughts? Does it have emotions, feelings? Is the spirit, as the philosopher and mystic al-Ghazali says, a subtle body originating in the cavity of the physical heart, which spreads through the body via the arteries, just as a light from a lantern fills a room?*

SAJ: The hidden which we have talked about is a level of the levels that reside in the heart. This heart is a container, a vessel, and these levels of which the first is also called the heart are another thing. Then there is the spirit, the secret, the hidden, and the most hidden—all reside in the heart as a vessel. For the spiritual world has a connection to the physical world, but in reality this material which includes heart, spirit, secret, hidden, and most hidden is comprised of gradations of the spirit. It is not the pump, but its locus is the pump, just as water is contained in a glass. The pump is the locus of the spiritual of which al-Ghazali speaks. So the question is: Does this spiritual entity which is inside the pump have emotions, feelings? Yes, it has emotions.

These emotions have been the subject of Sufi thinking and are seen as ten levels. These emotions include a feeling called repentance, which is when man feels the need to turn away from what is not God, as if his preoccupation with the universe is a sin on his part from which he wants to turn away, an ugly feeling.

There are ten stations and a section called states. A station is an unchangeable emotion and the states are passing emotions that come and go. Man ascends from one station to the next and does not return to a lower station. If a man does return to a lower station it is a major catastrophe, like returning from faith to unbelief.

The states come and go. The Sufis have given them names such as depressed, happy, union, and separation.

The reply then to this question is: The spiritual heart does have emotions and these emotions are of two kinds, unmovable and passing.

SF: *What closes the heart?*

SAJ: According to the Sufis the heart has two doors: a door to creation, and a door to Truth, therefore to God. There is also what is earned, and what is given. By his nature man's heart is open to creation. He needs food, drink, clothing, a dwelling place, a companion, company, and he needs to live in the world according to its laws. This is the door of creation. It is in the nature of man that this door be open.

When dhikr is achieved, it opens the other door, the door of Truth, and this happens in three stages. In the first, the door of Truth is closed. In the second, it opens, but the door of creation closes from the intensity of dhikr, as if dhikr is a wind closing the door of creation and opening the door of Truth. In the third, the door of creation also opens, and the heart has two open doors. The fourth case is when both doors are closed and this is what is called madness. This is someone who is neither into worship nor into the world—that is, he knows nothing at all. He has exited from the circle of responsibility.

As to the first case—wherein the door of creation is opened, blocking the door to Truth—that is from lack of dhikr, and from man's nature.

So what opens and what closes? This is the answer. The door of creation opens naturally, and the door of Truth is opened by dhikr and fikr. The door of Truth opens little by little until it is wide open.

An important issue to bring up here is that of what is earned and what is given. We can open the door through dhikr, but the door can also be opened by God without dhikr. The Sufis speak of a person who is a seeker and another who is sought. There is one who is on the way and one who is attracted. All these terms lead to the same meaning, namely that there is something man can do that leads to his heart being opened, and there is also a gift from God that opens the heart and has nothing to do with the person's effort.

The Prophet used to say: "O God, let there be in my heart light, and in my hearing light, and in my seeing light, in my hands light, to my right light, to my left light, and let me be light."

SF: *Moses threw the staff and it became a snake. He was commanded to pick up the snake. He did and it again became a staff. Then he was told to place his hand on his heart. When he removed it the Name of God was written in light on the palm of his hand. Can metaphysical light be transformed into light perceived by the senses?*

SAJ: All spiritual things can be transformed into things of a sensory nature. On the Day of Judgment death comes in the form of a ram. Death here is a concept but it becomes materialized.

There are two kinds of secrets and two kinds of lights. We spoke of the realm of mulk and the realm of malakut, circles of the creation. In each there are secrets and lights. The secrets of mulk are of the senses. Meaning the benefits of medicinal plants, the laws of building and engineering, of mathematics, and hydrology—all these are secrets that man discovers every day in the realm of mulk. There are also sensory lights: electricity, the sun, moon, stars, lasers and so on.

There are also lights and secrets of malakut—lights and secrets that are non-sensory. But anything from the realm of malakut can enter the realm of mulk, can be transformed into something perceived by the senses.

Creation is comprised of two sections: mulk, which is perceived by the five senses, and malakut. That realm which may be sensed by the five senses is what we are in now. In malakut it is the spirit ascending the circles which is the perceiver and not the senses.

SF: *There is a saying of the Prophet Muhammad: "All things have a polish. The polish of the heart is the Remembrance of God." What rusts the heart?*

SAJ: In the Quran there are descriptions of what ails the heart. There is the layer of scum on stagnant water, the cover, the locks, veils, pride, and so on, many qualities. These qualities can be removed through faith, others by repetition of the Names of God, and others by contemplation. The Sufis link this to the seven levels of the self (*nafs*): domineering, censorious, inspiring, tranquil, contented, pleasing, and pure. They have linked these to the Beautiful Names of God and to the gradations of man's attempt to remove rust or scum. Seven Names are used: *la illah illa Allah, Allah, Hu, al-Hayy, al-Qayyum, al-Haqq,* and *al-Qahhar.*

There is some disagreement about this as some Sufis choose *al-Aziz, al-Wahid, al-Wadud, al-Wahhab, al-Basit,* and *al-Muhaymin.*

There are various formulas given by a sheikh as to the manner and frequency of the repetition of the Names. The invocation of the Names of God satisfies the heart and opens the door of Truth.

Parabola
Volume: 10.3
The Body

Perfecting the Mirror

Gai Eaton

Traditional symbolism represents a mode of thought and of understanding which is so alien to the modern mind that it can seldom be left to stand on its own. The people of earlier times did not have the same need for explanation and elucidation; they possessed a capacity for sensing the meaning of a symbol (existentially rather than in terms of mental concepts) that has been lost. The assumptions of the modern mind must be questioned and, in many cases, reversed before traditional symbolism can be seen as something more than "superstition."

So far as the symbolism of the human body is concerned, the contemporary Westerner's understanding is blocked twice over. In the first place his "scientific" culture blinds him. Secondly his Christian background introduces certain unconscious prejudices. Each of the great world religions is in some measure colored by the environment into which it was initially projected, and the early environment of Christianity was shaped by the decadent naturalism of the Roman world. An entirely profane glorification of the human body (and of the natural world) obliged Christianity to react by considering the body chiefly in its aspect of corruptibility and its association with "the sins of the flesh." This attitude was balanced—perhaps fully compensated—on the one hand by devotion to the body of Christ and, on the other, by the doctrine of the resurrection. Had the physical body been regarded as inherently (rather than accidentally) "vile," the dogma of incarnation would have been unthinkable as would the notion of the body "raised incorruptible."

The heirs of Christianity, completely secularized, have to a large extent returned to Roman "naturalism," and the "body beautiful" has become a cult object, but without a symbolic element. The modern mind finds the notion of bodily resurrection particularly incomprehensible and the clue to this incomprehension is to be found in one of its most fundamental assumptions. Whether consciously or not—whether as a scientific "fact" or as a "superstition"— the apparent massive solidity of the material world mesmerizes us and we are convinced that the outward produces the inward. The body is the real person; mind, personality, and so on are a kind of by-product of this tangible physical reality. In the light (or darkness) of this conviction, not only the resurrection of the body but also the posthumous survival of the soul become untenable concepts. If mind and personality are shadows cast by the body which, in its solid actuality, is the one thing that cannot be doubted as all else is doubted, then it follows that the shadows disappear when the object that cast them is annihilated.

We shall never understand any traditional doctrine unless we are pre-pared to turn the contemporary view of the human entity upside down, just as we have to turn the dogma of "progress" upside down before we can consider the traditional doctrine of human decline over the course of time. What is this body, this little parcel of flesh and bone, in terms of prescientific beliefs? It is an outer layer of clothing. A geometrical image may be useful in this context, the image of a vertical ray striking a horizontal plane and provoking a process of crystallization at the point where vertical and horizontal intersect. To realize its potentialities—and this may be seen as the whole purpose of its issuing from the unseen "sun" which is the source of its being—this ray requires instruments con-structed from the material of the plane which it has penetrated, and its act of self-expression is necessarily circumscribed by the limitations of this material.

In the world known to us, not only the body but also the mind and personality express what is inherent in the being as such—in the "ray"—but they can do so only in terms of this locality and within the boundaries of what is possible here. The quality of vision, for example, is universal (in Islam one of the Names of God is "He who Sees") as is the quality of audition (God is "He who Hears"), but these universal faculties are particularized in our world by means of the physical structure of the eyes and the ears. It is not difficult to imagine that, if the ray of which we spoke had penetrated a different horizontal plane composed of quite different elements, there would necessarily be "seeing" and "hearing" but the limits set to their range would be of another kind. It follows that there would also be a "crystallization" comparable to the body.

It is in terms of this imagery that we can best understand Rumi's saying that "the body is the shadow of the shadow of the shadow of the Heart" or the Hindu doctrine of the *koshas*, the "envelopes" which clothe the nakedness of the spirit (or, quite simply, of the being's nucleus), "envelopes" which are both psychic and physical.

This imagery would however be misleading if it were thought to be entirely adequate to the reality it illustrates. If the outward were no more than clothing for the inward, then it would follow that the inward is unaffected by outward actions just as shadows do not affect the object which casts them. Images of this kind are helpful to analytical understanding, but they must be transcended in the light of the doctrine of unity, the doctrine of *tawhid* (in Islamic terms). The outward does indeed express the inward, but the inward is— at least in a certain sense—shaped by the outward. It is not by chance that the "nucleus"—the Heart—has taken on this particular clothing and no other, and the theater it has chosen for its manifestation fits it as a glove fits the hand.

What might be described as the interdependence of "nucleus" and "envelopes" is brought out very clearly in the argument used by the Muslim mystic and philosopher, al-Ghazali, concerning the obligation to follow the example of the Prophet Muhammad even in his recorded bodily movements, that is to say in his manner of walking, eating, putting on his sandals, and so on. Every Muslim acknowledges the obligation to follow the prophetic example, the *sunna* in the moral sphere, in worship, and in social life, but al-Ghazali insisted upon an even more total and meticulous practice, and he based his case on the intimate relationship between the phenomenal or "worldly" level of existence and the divine level and therefore between the movements of the bodily members and the state of the Heart, the "nucleus."

The condition of the Heart, he said, is profoundly influenced by the outward actions of the body. This may at first seem an untenable argument, since it is axiomatic that the Heart as such is inviolable and can no more be affected by the actions of its "envelopes" than can God Himself by events in this world. What al-Ghazali means is that the Heart which has clothed itself in soul and body is obscured—"covered" as Islam expresses it—by inappropriate actions. This recalls a major theme found both in the Quran and in the sayings of the Prophet according to which the Heart is comparable to a mirror over which a coating of rust forms when soul and body fall into sin (ancient mirrors were, of course, made of metal). Al-Ghazali points out that this mirror can reflect the true nature of things only if it is "polished, illuminated and maintained in proper balance." Regarding this state of balance, he says that the movements of the different parts of the body are themselves governed by a general law of balance and harmony. There is in consequence an appropriate pattern of movement for each bodily member, and this pattern conforms to what is, in the highest sense, natural and therefore in accordance with the will of God. The balanced and harmonious movement of the members thus has an effect upon the most inward dimension of the being. When this movement obeys the law of balance, then—he says—there occurs in the Heart a state of "natural disposition" which is capable of "absorbing Reality" in the same way that a mirror in proper balance reflects the true form of objects without any distortion. It is not only wrong actions in the moral sphere that produce a veil of rust over the inward mirror; disordered movements of the body may have the same effect. This could be said to follow logically from the Islamic doctrine of tawhid, "oneness": The human creature is a being of many levels, many aspects, but he is nonetheless a unified whole in which all the parts are interdependent.

Even in our everyday experience we are aware of this and may find confirmation of al-Ghazali's argument. An ugly man scarcely seems ugly if all his movements and gestures are coordinated and harmonious; a beautiful girl seems less beautiful if all her bodily movements are clumsy and her outward behavior is uncouth. We tend, whether consciously or not, to judge people or "know" them by their bodies, and physical contact is a form of knowledge (hence the Biblical term for sexual intercourse, "he knew her"). This is true of all touching between human beings, and it is significant that in the Islamic context Satan is said to lament whenever two Muslims shake hands. This simple physical contact between two human creatures is a token of the unity which Satan—the force of evil and disharmony—wishes to shatter. It is in accordance with the very nature of all symbolism that the most outward should reflect or express what is most profoundly inward and hidden. In Islam the principal objective of the spiritual techniques of Sufism is to make awareness of spiritual realities (initially abstract), and ultimately of God Himself, as simple, immediate, and concrete as are our sense impressions. Physical experience has a certain quality of wholeness. Spiritual experience is—almost by definition—the encounter of the total being with Totality. From this point of view, "extremes meet."

Among so-called primitive peoples this point is sometimes underlined by the practice of painting symbolic images on the body; that which is most inward is made visible on the surface of the skin, the most outward "envelope" of the Self. Such practices are alien to Islam, but the body is nonetheless adorned by clothing which expresses the innermost nature of man, or was so adorned before the impact of the West shattered this image. Clothing may indeed be considered as an additional "envelope" both veiling and expressing the "nucleus," the Heart, and men or women dress in accordance with what they believe to be their identity, their meaning, and their role. Those who regard themselves as a species of ant, as was the case in Mao's China, must necessarily dress identically in boiler-suits which confirm their ant-like function, indistinguishable one from another. Those who believe that this world is the only reality, the beginning and the end of our experience, will dress either in terms of sexual enticement or of physical vanity.

A perceptive French traveler in North Africa earlier in this century remarked with some surprise that the ordinary merchants, tradesmen, and craftsmen in the cities of Islam had "the demeanor of our ecclesiastics," in other words they might have been taken for priests, an impression created partly by their physical bearing and partly by their traditional costumes. Since there is no priesthood as such in Islam and each individual Muslim is potentially a "vicegerent of God on earth," his clothing as well as his manner of walking, standing, or sitting might be expected to conform to this role (as they did until fairly recently).

Whatever the arguments for or against the imitation of the Prophet's example in bodily actions, there is one aspect of life in which every Muslim imitates his movements with meticulous precision and this is in the ritual prayer (as also in preparing for it). The prayer is preceded by full or partial ablution, according to the circumstances, and the purification of the body by means of water—God "created all things from water" according to the Quran (21:30)—is a constantly repeated act of renewal, the body's purification implying that of the soul also. Through this virtual rebirth the worshipper is made fit to stand in all simplicity before his Creator and engage in intimate talk with Him. In order to do so effectively he orientates his body, facing the Ka'bah in Mecca, and here again a physical action represents a movement of the total being at all levels. All men seek a direction and an identifiable goal. For the Muslim the Ka'bah symbolizes the center of the universe and therefore, by transposition, his own innermost center—the Heart. In the Pilgrimage he traces by bodily movement the route from his peripheral home to the center, his eternal home, but this is already prefigured in the positioning of his body in prayer.

In the ritual prayer itself the spiritual and intellectual element is represented by the recitation from the Quran and the emotional element by the feelings of fear and of hope with which he is commanded to call upon God, but what might be called the existential element is acted out in physical movements which utilize the body as a vehicle for the spirit. In the first part of each unit of prayer the worshipper stands upright while he recites certain passages from the Quran, and this uprightness, this verticality, is an image of the "straight" (or "vertical") path upon which he asks God to lead him. The body has itself become a symbol of the ray which connects heaven and earth, the divine and the human.

But the Muslim prays not only on his own behalf and on behalf of his fellow men and women but also in the name of creation as a whole; this is an aspect of his function as the "vicegerent of God on earth." The standing is followed by a bowing in which the worshipper is instructed to keep the upper part of his body, from head to hips, parallel with the ground, and it is sometimes said that all the creatures which move upon four legs, their bodies horizontal, are represented by this posture. This bowing is followed by the prostration in which the worshipper places his forehead on the ground, his body folded up as though in the foetal position, and although this is primarily an acknowledgement of the power and glory of the Transcendent, it is also, according to certain sages, a representation of the inanimate realm, the mineral order in particular. Upright, he had prayed as God's vicegerent. While bowing he had glorified God as the infinite, the all-embracing on the horizontal level. Now— in the prostration—he is, as it were, reduced to the dimensions of his own innermost "nucleus." In this way the worshipper's physical body has acted out the variety of relationships between Creator and creation.

There is a further aspect of the body's natural activity which is of great—though complex—significance in Islam. This has to do with articulate speech and the breath which is its vehicle. The Quran itself is to be recited aloud rather than merely read. The Arabic word for "breath," *nafas*, comes from the same root as the word for "self" or "soul," *nafs*. It is said that God created everything that exists by means of *nafas ar-rahman*, "the breath of the Merciful." He "breathed out" creation and, at the end of time, He will breathe it in again, absorbing it once more into Himself, for He is the Origin and the End, the First and the Last. Moreover Islam, according to the Quran, "expands the breast"; the Faith is, in a sense, inhaled so that it fills the lungs and thereby penetrates the body.

We ourselves draw into our lungs a parcel of the universal atmosphere which may be likened to infinity, vivifying and maintaining the body in physical existence by what we take from beyond ourselves, and the gift of oxygen is intimately combined with our blood to circulate through every crevice of our physical being. By expelling this same breath, we speak. The breath is shaped into meaningful words by the vibration of the vocal cords and the air we were given is given back to express our glorification of God, our identity as his vicegerents, and our function as "bearers of the Message."

The Quran tells us that: "The Merciful taught the Quran (that is to say, sacred knowledge), created man, taught him articulate speech" (55:1-4). Here man is the central figure, receiving sacred knowledge and disseminating it, a channel between what is hidden in God and what is to be made actual and immediate on the periphery of the great circle of being. The Word has taken the form of a recitation just as, for Christians, it took the form of Christ's body.

In Sufi practices the summit of speech is the name *Allah*, sanctifying the breath which is its vehicle and ultimately sanctifying the soul. In the final stage of the Sufi "Dance," after the chanting of the Confession of Faith (*la ilaha illa'Llah*) has given way to the single word *Allah*, this word itself fades away leaving only the final 'h'-sound carried by rhythmical breathing, a *ha* deep in the throat accompanied by the beating of a drum. The Mevlevi Dance (that of the "Whirling Dervishes") is a special case but has the same qualities of rhythm and balance. When disordered, fragmented time is ordered and unified by rhythm, then time as we know it in our everyday lives is already transcended; moreover this fast, shallow breathing at the conclusion of the "Dance," when the soul gives itself up utterly to God, is not unlike the breathing of a dying man when, in the most immediate physical sense, he is about to "give up the ghost."

Islam, as the religion of balance, reflecting the "coincidence of opposites," both divides and unites. The Quran itself is sometimes called *al-Furqan*, "the Discrimination," and discrimination divides, putting each thing in its proper place. But Islam is above all the religion of unity and unification, and balance as such reflects in dynamic tension the unity which is, by definition, peace. First there is analysis. Then there is synthesis. In the order of creation the physical body is at the opposite extreme to the "nucleus" of our existence, the Heart, yet the outermost reflects the innermost, and the human creature, composite and multidimensional, is a unity reflecting his Creator, who is supremely One.

Parabola
Volume: 26.4
The Heart

A Subtile Organ

Henry Corbin

In Ibn Arabi as in Sufism in general, the heart is the organ which produces true knowledge, comprehensive intuition, the gnosis of God and the divine mysteries, in short, the organ of everything connoted by the term "esoteric science." It is the organ of a perception which is both experience and intimate taste, and although love is also related to the heart, the specific center of love is in Sufism generally held to be at the *ruh*, *pneuma*, spirit. Of course, and of this we are reminded at every turn, this "heart" is not the conical organ of flesh, situated on the left side of the chest, although there is a certain connection, the modality of which, however, is essentially unknown. It is a notion to which the utmost importance has been attached by the mystics of all times and countries, of Oriental Christianity (the Prayer of the Heart, the charisma of cardiognosis) as well as India. Here we have to do with a "subtile physiology" elaborated "on the basis of ascetic, ecstatic, and contemplative experience" and expressing itself in symbolic language. This, as Mircea Eliade has pertinently remarked, does not mean "that such experiences were not real; they were perfectly *real*, but not in the sense in which a physical phenomenon is real."

In short, this "mystic physiology" operates with a "subtile body" composed of psycho-spiritual organs (the centers, or Chakras, "lotus blossoms") which must be

●

distinguished from the bodily organs. For Sufism the *heart* is one of the centers of mystic physiology. Here we might also speak of its "theandric" function, since its supreme vision is of the Form of God—this because the gnostic's heart is the "eye," the organ by which God knows Himself, reveals Himself to Himself in the forms of his epiphanies (not as He inwardly knows Himself, for in the quest of the Divine Essence even the highest science can go no further than the *Nafas ar-Rahman*). It is also true to say that the gnostic, as Perfect Man, is the *seat* of God's divine consciousness and that God is the seat and essence of the gnostic's consciousness (if it were necessary to draw a diagram, the situation would be far better represented by the two focuses of an ellipse than by the center of a circle). To sum up, the power of the heart is a secret force or energy, which perceives divine realities by a pure hierophanic knowledge without mixture of any kind, because the heart contains even the Divine *Rahma*. In its unveiled state, the heart of the gnostic is like a mirror in which the microcosmic form of the Divine Being is reflected.

From Henry Corbin, *Creative Imagination in the Sufism of Ibn 'Arabi*, translated by Ralph Manheim, Bollingen Series XCI (Princeton: Princeton University Press, 1969), pp. 221-222. Copyright by Princeton University Press. Reprinted by permission.

Parabola
Volume: 26.4
The Heart

A Six-Faced Mirror

Rumi

Translated by Kabir and Camille Helminski

Only the Heart

If a wealthy person brings a hundred sacks of gold,
God will only say,
"Bring the Heart, you who are bent double.
If the Heart is pleased with you, I am pleased;
and if the Heart is opposed to you, I am opposed.
I don't pay attention to 'you'; I look to the heart:
bring it, poor soul, as a gift to My door!
Its relation to you is also mine:
Paradise is at the feet of mothers."
The heart is the mother and father and origin
    of all creatures:
the one who knows the heart from the skin is blessed.
You will say, "Look, I have brought a heart to You."
God will respond, "The world is full of these hearts.
Bring the heart that is the axis of the world
and the soul of the soul of the soul of Adam."
The Ruler of all hearts is waiting
for a heart filled with light and goodness.

—*Mathnawi* V 881-88

The Six-Faced Mirror

The Prophet said, "God doesn't pay attention to your outer form:
so in your improvising, seek the owner of the Heart."
God says, "I regard you through the owner of the Heart,
not because of prostrations in prayer
or the giving of wealth in charity."
The owner of the Heart becomes a six-faced mirror;
through him God looks out upon all the six directions.

—Mathnawi V 869-70, 874

When your heart becomes the grave of your secret,
that desire of yours will be gained more quickly.
The Prophet said that anyone
who keeps secret his inmost thought
will soon attain the object of his desire.
When seeds are buried in the earth,
their inward secrets become the flourishing garden.

—Mathnawi I 175-77

Know the mirror of the heart is infinite.
Either the understanding falls silent,
or it leads you astray, because the heart is *with* God,
or indeed the heart *is* He.

—Mathnawi I 3488-91

Those with mirror-like hearts
do not depend on fragrance and color:
they behold Beauty in the moment.
They've cracked open the shell of knowledge
and raised the banner
of the eye of certainty.
Thought is gone in a flash of light.

—Mathnawi I 3492-94

Just as your two eyes are under the control of the heart
and subject to the spirit's command,
all five senses move as the heart directs.
Hand and foot also move
like the staff in the hand of Moses.
If the heart wills, at once the foot begins to dance,
from neediness towards abundance.

—*Mathnawi* I 3562, 3566-69

Why Are You Milking Another?

Strip the raiment of pride from your body:
in learning, put on the garment of humility.
Soul receives from soul the knowledge of humility,
not from books or speech.
Though mysteries of spiritual poverty
are within the seeker's heart,
she doesn't yet possess knowledge of those mysteries.
Let her wait until her heart expands and fills with Light:
God said, *"Did We not expand your breast. ..?* [Quran 94:1].
For We have put illumination there,
We have put the expansion into your heart."
When you are a source of milk, why are you milking another?
An endless fountain of milk is within you:
why are you seeking milk with a pail?
You are a lake with a channel to the Sea:
be ashamed to seek water from a pool;
for *did We not expand your chest. ..?*
Again, don't you possess the expansion?
Why are you going about like a beggar?
Contemplate the expansion of the heart within you,
that you may not be reproached with, *Do you not see?* [51:21]

—*Mathnawi* V 1061, 1064-72

The Kernel and the Shell

When the kernel swells the walnut shell,
or the pistachio, or the almond, the husk diminishes.
As the kernel of knowledge grows,
the husk thins and disappears,
because the lover is consumed by the Beloved.
Since the quality of being sought is the opposite of seeking,
revelation and divine lightning
consume the prophet with fire.
When the attributes of the Eternal shine forth,
the garment of time is burned away.

—*Mathnawi* III 1388-91

A Word to the Heart

That which God said to the rose,
and caused it to laugh in full-blown beauty,
he said to my heart,
and made it a hundred times more beautiful.

—*Mathnawi* III 4129

From *The Rumi Collection: An Anthology of Mevlana Jalaluddin Rumi*, selected and edited by Kabir Helminski (Boston: Shambhala, 1999), pp. 78, 79, 80, 82, 84.

•

CHAPTER SIX

THE PATH TO GOD

One night a man cried, "Allah, Allah!"
until his lips became sweet with the sound.
The Evil One approached him as he stood chanting,
and asked "How now, chatterbox?
Where is the answer to your insistence?
Who replies to you 'Here am I?'
No answer comes from the Throne:
how long then will you mindlessly go on crying 'Allah?'"

Broken-hearted, the man ceased his chant and lay down to sleep.
In that sleep he dreamed a dream, and in that dream the
holy mystic Khazir appeared before him in a green garden. The saint spoke:
"Why have you desisted from the mention of God?
How is it that you now despair of calling on Him?"

The dreamer replied,
"I ceased because no 'Here am I' was coming to me.
I fear therefore that I may be turned from His door."

Khazir answered, "God says: 'Your cry of "Allah" is itself My "Here am I,"
just as your pleading and agony and fervor are My messenger.
All your twistings and turnings to come to Me were
My drawing you that set you free.
Your fear and love are the snares to catch My grace.
Under each "Allah" of yours whispers many a "Here am I.""" [13.2] [1]

—Rumi

I was the Sin that from Myself rebell'd:
I the remorse that tow'rd Myself compell'd. ...
Pilgrim, Pilgrimage and Road
Was but Myself toward Myself: and Your
Arrival but Myself at my own door.[2]

—Fariduddin Attar

Relationship persists so long as subsidiary cause persists,
and subsidiary cause persists so long as quest persists,
and quest persists so long as thou persistest,
and thou persistest so long as thou seest Me not;
but when thou seest Me, thou art no more,
and when thou art no more,
quest is no more, and when quest is no more,
subsidiary cause is no more, and when subsidiary cause is no more,
relationship is no more, and when relationship is no more,
limit is no more, and when limit is no more, veils are no more.[3]

—Niffari

Parabola
Volume: 11.1
The Witness

SHAHADAH

Victor Danner

Like other spiritual ways, Sufism speaks of an interior, conscious reality that is the ultimate and unique Witness (*shahid*) of all things within and outside man. It is identified with the Divinity, or *Allah*; but here, in this aspect of things, God is seen as being immanent, that is to say, within the universe and therefore within man, in contrast to the complementary view of the transcendence of God, which pictures Him as beyond the universe and man.

In both cases, we are in the presence of a spatial symbolism: To speak of God as being within or beyond the universe is but a figure of speech, although based on the intrinsic symbolism of things. The two aspects are indeed complementary, but Muslim theologians stress transcendence in order to avoid the danger of pantheism, or the identification of God with the world.

The Sufis, for their part, stress the immanence of God within man and the universe, but without this implying any material identification at all. Transformations and changes in the world do not affect God, even if He dwells within man in his innermost heart as the Spirit, the ultimate Witness of all things. Because this can easily give rise to misconceptions among those who do not have a contemplative bent of mind, many Sufi expressions, such as the famous *Ana'l-Haqq* ("I am God," or "I am the Truth") of al-Hallaj, will seem blasphemous in the light of exoteric Islamic law and theological dogma. But from an esoteric perspective the same expressions will be understood as the formulations of the inner Spirit speaking through saintly persons.

From the above, we can discern that Islam has two levels of comprehension, the exoteric and esoteric—the Law and the Path—that do not see the Quran and the Prophet in the same way. Even the fundamental sacred formula of Islam, "There is no divinity other than God," which is called the *Shahadah* ("Testimony," or "Witnessing"), can be interpreted in a purely external and literal sense to mean simply that there is only one God; or it can be given metaphysical and spiritual interpretations that go all the way to the negation of one's ego and the affirmation of the Divine Ego.

Needless to say, the exoteric interpretation lacks the depth and wisdom of the esoteric Sufi viewpoint. Thus, since the term Shahadah also means "Witnessing," one can be a witness, in a purely verbal sense, to the Oneness of God, rejecting all polytheistic attempts to ascribe divinity to other beings and things, and this is what characterizes Islamic exoterism. Or one can carry one's witnessing much further: For the Sufis, the Ninety-Nine "Most-Beautiful Names" of God in the Quran can be interpreted as paraphrases of the Shahadah. We then have: "There is no guide other than the Guide"; "There is no light other than the Light"; "There is no creator other than the Creator," and so on. Among those Divine Names is "the Witness" (*ash-Shahid*): from the Sufi metaphysical viewpoint, the phrase "There is no witness other than the Witness" means either that all empirical witnesses in the universe are reducible to the one Divine Witness or else that He alone is the real Witness in the particular consciousness of each being, whether that being is aware of this or not.

The Quran says of *Allah*: "Thou art a Witness to all things" (5:117). We are reminded here of the silent Witness (*saksin*) of the Hindu Vedanta; and hence it is not surprising that the Sufis should have developed interpretations for such verses that are reminiscent of Hindu and other Eastern mystical positions. Just as Hinduism teaches that the Intellect (*buddhi*) in man discerns the movements of his mind, but is above them, unruffled in its calmness, so likewise Sufism says that the Intellect (*aql*) in man is the faculty that witnesses all things in his soul. Hinduism makes a distinction between the individual buddhi that connects man with the *mahat-buddhi* ("Universal Intellect"); and Sufism says, in a similar fashion, that the individual Intellect in man issues from the Universal Intellect (*aql kulli*).

According to a statement of the Prophet Muhammad, "The first thing created by God was the Intellect" (or "the Spirit," in a variant version, for Spirit and Intellect are synonymous). The Spirit is both uncreated in its essence and created at one and the same time. In the Prophet's sentence, the created Universal Spirit is the luminous center of the entire creation, which then issues from its central point like rays of light moving in different directions. One of those rays of light intersects with the plane of man's soul, in the innermost heart. Because man's Spirit can return to its universal source—as if it were a ray of sunlight reabsorbed back into the sun—we speak of "spiritual realization," namely, the awareness that we are united with God through the Spirit.

But the quest does not stop with reabsorption into the Universal Intellect (or Spirit). It goes back all the way to the uncreated Divine Intellect that is both the origin and the end of the Path. That is no doubt the significance of yet another statement made by the Prophet, but this time it is *Allah* speaking through him: "The heavens and earth contain Me not, but the heart of My believing servant does contain Me." By "heart" we must understand Intellect or Spirit, which plunges into the depths of the Divine Essence. "Intellect," affirms Meister Eckhart, in a corroborative remark, "is the temple of God and nowhere does He shine more holy than there." This is the Intellect in the heart, it is not reasoning in the brain; the first is unitive and intuitive, the second is separative and dualistic. It is the Intellect alone that reaches God, not reasoning, for the latter can never transcend its limitations, especially the subject-object duality.

We can therefore appreciate that there are degrees to the question of Witnessing, depending upon what faculty we use. If we witness orally that God is One, that is purely verbal; if we witness with reasoning that God is One, that is rational discourse based on a mixture of faith and reason; but if we transcend these limitations and witness through the illuminative knowledge of the Spirit, then our witnessing is no longer an individualistic perception. Instead, it is an intellectual intuition that unites the subject-knower with the object-known in a single flash of certitude that admits of no doubt or hesitation and that engenders a luminous peace in the soul.

In a sense, the whole point of the Sufi Path is to reach that interior Witness through experiential knowledge of the Real, or through what is called gnosis. The Sufis are unanimous in saying that this knowledge cannot be reached through merely rational discourse proceeding from reasoning. This type of mental activity is indirect and reflective; but it does have a function, like man's other powers, in preparing the way for the purification of the Intellect, which lies buried in the layers of illusion and forgetfulness that cloud its solar radiance, preventing it from shining forth in man's soul. Let the dark clouds that hide the intellective Witness be purified from the soul and it will radiate within man as the sun does when the clouds hiding it on a gloomy day are banished.

Ibn Ata'illah, the Egyptian Sufi, poses this question to the beginner anxious to attempt the spiritual ascension all the way back to the One: "How can the heart be illumined while the forms of creatures are reflected in its mirror?" What this means is that the heart is really a mirror-like substance, luminous by nature, that needs to be purified of the multiplicity of forms reflected on its surface by the forms coming from the world within the mind. A mirror that reflected no creatures would be an undifferentiated light, like the Divine Essence itself, which is said to be the very ground of the Intellect.

In another aphorism, Ibn Ata'illah provides the clue to understanding the origins of multiplicity when he says, "That which shows you the existence of His Omnipotence is that He veiled you from Himself by what has no existence alongside of Him." This important maxim tells us a number of things. First, the world has an illusory aspect to it which arises from the actual creative Omnipotence of God; it is not, therefore, an accidental feature of the creation that we witness with our everyday minds the multiplicity and other-than-Godness of all beings and things, for all of this has its origins in the Divine Art of the Creator. Second, that illusory side to things does not mean that they have no real existence, as if they were mere nothings; on the contrary, they have been given existence and are real at their appropriate level. And third, while they are real, they are immediately reduced to nothingness alongside of the Divine Reality, for there can be no reality competing with the One, otherwise there would be two or more ultimate realities, two or more eternals, and so on, which would destroy the metaphysical uniqueness of the One, *Allah*.

Speaking of God, the Quran says, "Vision grasps Him not, but He grasps vision" (6:103). The vision in question is of course spiritual; the verse is stating an axiom in all Sufism: One cannot grasp the Divine Witness for the simple reason that it is He who "grasps" all things. Nevertheless, the actual process of witnessing does necessarily start out with an empirical, individualistic awareness that is separated from its Object, which is God. The infinitude of the Object rules out the possibility of a limited, finite mind grasping the Infinite; but the reverse is not to be ruled out, according to the Quranic verse. How to understand this in a way that does not harshly confront the Infinite with the finite, but that allows for an intermediate stage between the two that gives to the finite the possibility of an expansion into a semi-infinite reality, and to the Infinite a contraction into a more limited state? Previously, we had spoken of the human Intellect as being an individuated ray of Light coming from the Universal Intellect, that spiritual Sun at the center of the created universe. Beyond that Intellect is the uncreated Divine Intellect of God, which has none of the limitations of the other two. As the divine consciousness moves down the ontological plane towards man, it contracts first into the Universal Intellect, and then afterwards into the particular Intellect of man, which transcends him and all his powers of the soul. Somewhere between the divine plane, on the one hand, and the human plane, on the other, there is that intermediate spiritual world of the Universal Intellect where the divine breaks through into the human and the human into the divine in a mysterious fashion defying all comprehension or articulated analysis.

As a result, the mirror in the heart can be taken on all three planes simultaneously or otherwise, according to case. When Ibn al-Arabi suggests to us that "when looking at yourself in the mirror, try to see the mirror itself, and you will find that you cannot do so," he means the Intellect by the physical mirror. So long as the empirical self, which is a form, is present to your view, you cannot see the mirror. In the inner life of the Spirit, we cannot reach its mirror so long as creatures are reflected on it, as previously noted. But in the sage, the Intellect acts as a mirror on all three planes, which is evidently what Ibn al-Arabi had in view when he says elsewhere, "In seeing your true self, He is your mirror, and you are His mirror in which He sees His Names; now His Names are not other than Himself."

The Intellect, in other words, is the "eye of the heart" that permits the sage to see himself in God and God to see Himself in man. Purification in the Sufi Path is often referred to as the "polishing of the mirror" in the heart, so that the eye of the heart can see spiritual realities previously veiled from it by the imperfections and multiple veils in the soul. That polishing is accomplished by meditational exercises and the well-known Sufi practice of remembering the One through the invocation (*dhikr*) of one of the Ninety-Nine Names of God, such as *Allah*. With time, the veils are gradually gotten rid of, allowing the mirror of the inner heart—the interior Witness—to shine without obstacles. It is this which leads to the realization of the supreme identity between God and man, an awareness of which must obviously be present even in the first steps of the Path, an awareness that becomes increasingly concrete in the later stages.

In a famous statement wherein the Divinity speaks through the mouth of the Prophet, the supreme Identity is described in the following terms: "My servant draws nigh unto Me, and I love him; and when I love him, I am his ear, so that he hears by Me, and his eye, so that he sees by Me, and his tongue, so that he speaks by Me, and his hand, so that he takes by Me." Strictly speaking, without the presence of the Spirit in man's innermost being, he could not function at all, for he would have no life nor consciousness nor even individual existence, since all of those traits come to him from the Spirit, death being the departure of the Spirit from man's body, taking the soul with it for judgment. That is what Rumi is saying in the following remark, when he talks about the Mind (or the Spirit): "Were not the shadow of the Mind over man, all his members would become atrophied; the hand would not grasp in due manner, the foot would not go straight upon the road, the eye would not see anything, whatever the ear heard it would hear awry." In short, all of the powers of our soul are ontologically dependent on the transcendent Mind. But this is evidently not the same thing as the Prophet's statement: therein the realized sage is described, for he knows that it is indeed the Spirit that operates through the powers of his soul and body, something that he had not concretely known before beginning to tread the Path. That treading is referred to in the beginning of the statement with the words, "My servant draws nigh unto Me, and I love him." The effort to draw closer to the inner Witness yields interior graces that in turn attract the soul even more.

At what point in the Path the Spirit takes over the powers of the individual is another question. The inner Witness is present at the first steps, as was said; at the end, we are aware that it has always been there and has never been absent. That awareness of the unique Reality leads to what the school of Ibn al-Arabi calls "the Oneness of Being" (*wahdat al-wujud*), or the realization that all being or existence stems from the one absolute Being of *Allah*. While we are cognizant, in this world of multiplicity, of myriads of beings, this is an illusion, for all being is One, even though it might be refracted by the surfaces of the different levels of reality. The sun's rays are multiple and are reflected off the waves of a lake, giving the impression of an endless series of suns; but in reality there is only one sun that is at the origin of the countless rays of light that strike the constantly shifting waves on the lake's surface. We see the multiplicity of suns, but the doctrine of the Oneness of Being insists that there is but one sun reflected everywhere.

Instead of the Oneness of Being, we could have spoken of "the Oneness of Witnessing" (*wahdat ash-shuhud)*, or of "the Oneness of Consciousness," which is the other great school of Sufi metaphysical thinking that stresses, not the Object of knowledge, but the Subject. There is the witness, the object witnessed, and the act of witnessing—a familiar trio of terms, as is the lover, the beloved, and love, or the knower, the known, and knowledge. The point is that the real Witness in everyone who witnesses is God; the real Object witnessed in everything is God; and the real Witnessing in all individual acts of witnessing is God. It is *Allah* who is the real Lover, Knower, and the like; it is He who is the real Beloved and the Known; and He is the ultimate Love and Knowledge. The Subject is its own Object. Unlike the school of the Oneness of Being, which stresses the objectively Real, this school accentuates subjective knowledge, or consciousness, that has its ontological roots in the absolute Witness, the ultimate Subject, who is God. The multiplicity of witnesses, due to the innumerable mirrors reflecting the one solar Witness, give us the same image as above, but seen this time as multiple subjectivities that reflect the one unique Subject. The two perspectives are complementary: everything depends on whether one wants to emphasize the divine Object as the unique Reality or the divine Subject as the unique Knower or Witness.

The Quran, in one of the verses often quoted by the Sufis, says, "Wheresoever ye turn, there is the Face of God" (2:115). This can be understood from the vantage point either of the Oneness of Being or of the Oneness of Witnessing. If the former, then all beings are reflections of God's Being, His "Face," as the text says; if the latter, then we witness, through the connection of our intellectual faculty with that of God's, that all forms in this world come from the "ideas" in the Divine Intellect, the Mind that is in all things, the unique Subject.

In this connection, the Prophet's remark, "Whosoever knows himself knows his Lord," is also bound up with the two schools just mentioned. It is sometimes interpreted in the sense that, once aware of the limitations of our individual selves, we know that our Lord's Self is unlimited. But seen in the light of the Oneness of Being, the remark means that he who knows the being of his soul knows that it comes from the pure Being of his Lord; or, in the perspective of the Oneness of Witnessing, it means that the consciousness of the soul can come only from the Consciousness of the Lord.

To arrive at the awareness of the Oneness of Being or of Witnessing, Sufism proposes to the beginner that he tread the Path under the guidance of a teacher, the Sufi Shaykh or Pir. It is the Shaykh who furnishes his disciples with the teachings and practices of the Path, the weapons he will use to combat and vanquish his ego, the dragon within. But it is the Witness within us who, like the full moon at night, lights our way from the beginning to the end: "*Allah* is the Light of the heavens and the earth," the Quran tells us. "Light upon Light! God doth guide whom He will to His Light" (24:35).

Parabola
Volume: 10.1
Wholeness

THE LONG JOURNEY

Interview with Seyyed Hossein Nasr

Today newspapers, magazines, and bulletin boards bristle with advertisements for spiritual guidance, and it sometimes seems as though anyone who knows how to sit in the lotus position feels qualified to hang out a shingle as a teacher of wisdom. It is a relief, then, to hear in the midst of this babel the clear and reasoned voice of Dr. Seyyed Hossein Nasr, for twenty-one years a professor of Islamic philosophy and the history of science at Tehran University, and founder and first president of the Iranian Academy of Philosophy.

Dr. Nasr met with me in his book-lined office in the Gelman Library at The George Washington University in Washington D.C., where he is University Professor of Islamic Studies. As he spoke with quiet authority of the Islamic approach to wholeness, and of his firm belief in the necessity of rooting spiritual search in one of the great religious traditions, it became clear that Dr. Nasr brought to our discussion not only the erudition evinced in his many books—the most recent of which (as of 1985) are The Writings of Frithjof Schuon: a Basic Reader *(Amity House, 1985) and* Islamic Art and Spirituality

•

(Golgonooza Press, 1985)—but something more: a firsthand experience of the struggle towards wholeness.

Jeff Zaleski: *In your essay "Sufism and the Integration of Man," which appears in your book* Sufi Essays, *you write that "Islam is the religion of unity ..." and that "... the whole programme of Sufism ... is to free man from the prison of multiplicity, to cure him from hypocrisy and to make him whole, for it is only in being whole that man can become holy." How would you define the whole man? What are his attributes?*

Seyyed Hossein Nasr: The whole man is a person who realizes fully what it means to be man. That is, he has, or she has—and throughout this essay when I say "man" I mean both sexes—within himself realized all the possibilities of existence, the perfection of all the qualities with which God—ultimate Reality—has embellished human nature, but which is not fully manifested in all members of the human race. This idea goes back, of course, to the central Sufi doctrine of the Perfect Man or the Universal Man, *al-Insan al-kamil,* according to which every creature reflects in its own way some aspect, or quality, of the Divine Nature, some Divine Name or Divine Quality in its specific Islamic reference (*al-Asma wa's-Sifat*). Only man is the mirror of all the Divine Names and Qualities. Therefore, to say "Man" is to say "totality" and "wholeness"; that is, all aspects of the Supreme Divinity which have manifested themselves in the cosmos, all that which is not within the Divine Nature in its metacosmic reality, all that radiates from the Face which God has turned towards the created order, all that is already contained in a reflected fashion in what is implied by being man, by being *insan*. Now, to be whole is to realize this fullness of our own nature. The Sufi answer to your question would be very simple: in order for a man to be whole, all he or she has to do is to be himself or herself; that is, to realize what we really are in our ultimate reality, which is to be the total reflection, total image, total theophany of God's Names and Qualities.

JZ: *How do we realize what we really are? I may have an idea about wholeness, about the perfect man, but I see myself fragmented. How does one become whole?*

SHN: This is a very interesting question from the point of view of the everyday consciousness of human beings. The very fact that we pose such a question means that there exists within our mind and soul an echo, no matter how faint, and a light, no matter how dim, of that wholeness. Why is it that we who are fragmented even talk about wholeness? It means we have a reminiscence in our being of being whole. Now here lies in fact the key to your question: namely, wholeness brings with it a certitude of its own reality, precisely because the human being is composed of multiple levels of existence, of different powers—physical, mental, psychological, spiritual; and this is very important, not to mistake the spiritual for the psychological, or the mental for the intellectual, which is the other aspect of the spiritual. Because man possesses all of these faculties inwardly, unless he gains access to them there is always a sense of loss.

It's as if you asked me the question, "How do I know when water quenches my thirst?" If you get hold of real water and have real thirst, the very drinking of the water will quench your thirst, and nothing else. There is within the nature of man a quest for wholeness, which is itself a great miracle because we are not whole. Where do we get this urge? Where did we find the origin of the idea of wholeness? Deep down within ourselves, that wholeness from which we have become separated by our externalized existence beckons us. It calls upon us. And the call continues until we hearken to its voice and are able to live in such a way as to fulfill the innate need for wholeness; and questions as to how we reach it are really theoretical. The thirst we have to externalize ourselves—the need for satisfaction through an action which is external to ourselves and therefore which is against what wholeness really implies—continues in us. We all have it; it is the root of all our miseries. But it is never fulfilled unless it turns upon itself, moves in an inward direction—rather than outward—and reaches wholeness. Therefore, the very ceasing of this craving for externalization is proof that we have reached wholeness. Unless a person reaches wholeness, that craving never ceases. Its goal may change, but the fire is never extinguished except through the proximity of the Sacred which wholeness implies.

JZ: Is it possible for an ordinary person leading an ordinary life in an honorable and just way to achieve wholeness, or is special guidance necessary? Is a teacher necessary?

SHN: If we could only break the ice which separates our everyday awareness of ourselves from the spring of eternal life which resides at our heart, in the center of our being, we would neither need a teacher nor a revelation. But man, that is, man in the present cycle of humanity—at the time of Adam all men were prophets—man in this day and age cannot break that ice without the help of God—without the help of the ultimate source of our own being—and without the help of a teacher. Wholeness on the highest level belongs only to a great saint in the sense that everything that a person does always comes from a single center; and that is why only a saint is beyond hypocrisy. But that highest level of wholeness is not achievable for everyone. There are lower levels, however; there's a kind of hierarchy of wholeness. On a more restricted level there are the teachings of religion, which are meant for everyone; for example, the Divine Law in Islam, the *Shari'ah*, if practiced faithfully, produces a degree of wholeness and of integration in life which is sufficient for a man to live happily and to die in felicity, but not sufficient to realize wholeness on the highest level, which is union with the Divine and all that implies: the integration of all aspects of our being and the awareness of the One at the highest level. For that stage to be attained there's always need of a teacher, and if there are exceptions, it is only to prove the rule.

I always come back to the beautiful saying of the Gospels, when Christ mentions, "The wind bloweth where it listeth." I learned the significance of this many, many years ago, from a writing of Frithjof Schuon, where he spoke about the possibility of the Spirit manifesting itself where God wills, outside the ways in which we would expect. And this saying has many applications, one of which is the answer to your question: that it is possible for certain exceptional individuals to be pulled by the attraction of Heaven without a human teacher. But that possibility, although it might be realized in certain cases, is not an excuse for not having a spiritual teacher, nor does it manifest itself very often. So one comes back to the famous saying of Bayazid, the great Sufi of Khorasan, of the ninth Christian century, who in talking about people who seek this ultimate wholeness said that the spiritual master of those who have no spiritual master is the Devil. This integration of the higher faculties of the soul, which surely belong to God, is impossible without the help of a person who has already undergone the process of this integration, because one otherwise deals with very powerful and dangerous forces which often, under the guise of integration, lead to disintegration and permanent damage to an aspect of the soul which really only God and the Sacred can mold and remold.

JZ: *Is it possible for those who are not following a particular religious path to achieve any degree of wholeness?*

SHN: If I can emphasize "any degree," then yes. There are people, especially in this day and age in which many, because of the loss of the more metaphysical dimensions of the Western religions, have fallen out of their traditions and are looking for something, who may live close to nature and its beauties; and having a kind of simple soul which is satisfied with the grace emanating from the natural environment, they may attain through that a certain degree of wholeness. But man is not just a "natural" being in that sense. Such people carry within themselves, of course, those deeper layers of the soul, and the problem of not having integrated those elements into the conscious aspect of their being manifests itself sooner or later. To integrate those elements requires a mandate from Heaven; that is, one has to live according to one of the traditions, one of the religions which God has revealed. I do not believe that wholeness, in the higher levels of the meaning of this word, and as it gradually becomes synonymous with holiness, is possible without the door having opened from the heavenly side towards humanity. Man cannot force this door open by himself, and the door always opens from the divine side. You might say it is the Logos that descends—that Avatar that descends from heaven—who then opens up the path which we then follow from this side.

JZ: *What are the chief obstacles that a man will face on the path towards wholeness? What is it in ourselves that keeps us from wholeness?*

SHN: This is of course a very profound theological question which can be answered in many different ways. Christianity would say that it is original sin; Islam does not believe in original sin, but believes that the chief impediment is forgetfulness. But I want to answer this in a kind of present-day, "existential" manner, as it concerns the predicament of modern man. If you'd asked this question of me a hundred years ago, when my ancestors lived in Kashan—if God had willed that I'd be teaching there then, rather than a hundred years later, here in Washington—I would have answered that the chief impediment, of course, is this veil of forgetfulness which covers our inner nature. This veil has to do with our passions, with what the Quran calls *al-nafs al-ammara*; that is, the part of our soul which commands us to do evil—the passionate, externalizing, dissipating aspect of our soul. That would be the major obstacle, and always there would be a kind of contention between it and the Will of God, which one must follow.

Today, however, there's another very major obstacle which the men of old did not face. Then, human beings—in normal situations, at least— knew that there was such a thing as wholeness. Today men face first of all the obstacle of not even being clear as to the existence of wholeness, to say nothing of its attainment. If you were a Muslim, or a Christian, or a Hindu, living traditionally, you would not ask yourself the question, "Is there such a thing as wholeness, and is there a path towards it?" You would ask yourself the question, "Do I want to follow this path or not?" You knew that a path was there; for instance, if you were in the Islamic world, you knew that the khanaqah or zawiya, the Sufi center, was there, that there were people who followed the path of wholeness. Today the first obstacle is that many human beings are forced to ask, for the first time in the history of the world as we know it, "What is the meaning of life, anyway?"; that is, having to discover the questions of certitude and doubt, of truth and falsehood, by themselves. And therefore the first obstacle is precisely to remove our ignorance of the nature of Reality, if I can express it in an intellectual language; or, in a religious manner, to discover the goal of life: that it is in fact possible to be whole, and therefore it is a desirable goal. And once decided which goal to follow, whom should I choose as master? Now there is a more universal choice which did not even present itself to any humanity before us, and that is the possibility of even choosing one's religion. Except in rare situations, such as Kashmir in the thirteenth century, this was never a choice to be made by human beings.

There is of course also a great compensation in all of this, in that since this first obstacle presents an exceptional challenge, once it's overcome God makes the second obstacle much more easy to surmount. A traditional Muslim, Hindu, Jew, or Buddhist accepted with certitude the truth of their religion. In the traditional situation the skeptic was not the one who doubted God or his tradition, but who within that world of certitude might be skeptical about certain schools, certain trends of thought. And therefore to follow the spiritual path, to be placed under the direct beam of the Divine Grace which shines upon us, was a much more difficult feat to achieve. Today attraction of Divine Grace is made easier by the very difficulty of our predicament, the difficulty of the human situation. And for that reason, although the obstacles have changed, perhaps because of God's justice, the attainment is not that much more difficult. It's just the type of difficulty which is altered with present-day humanity.

JZ: The first obstacle you speak of, the difficulty of people today to begin focusing on their internal situation, is a serious one. There are fewer and fewer nations where true spiritual teaching is available. Why is this? Is this a consequence of an internal flaw in religions themselves, that people are less and less interested in their teachings?

SHN: This is again a question which can be answered in two different ways. From one point of view one could say that the inner meaning of religions becomes less and less accessible, to the extent that human beings become less qualified to understand that inner meaning. Secondly, in fact present-day humanity doesn't deserve anything more than it is able to attain. That is, it is the externalization of man today which makes the inward less accessible. But having said that, I want to add that in fact the inner dimension is not completely inaccessible. There is again a kind of divine compensation, putting aside all the pseudo-teachers and pseudo-gurus who provide a kind of spiritual guidance in reverse, from below rather than from above, and whose teachings correspond in effect to the subversion of so much of what remains of religion in the modern world. Putting that phenomenon aside, I would say that, first of all, authentic spiritual instruction can never cease completely without the world collapsing. There's a saying in Arabic according to which the earth shall never become empty of the person who's witness to God, who is a true spiritual teacher. That cannot happen; that's not metaphysically possible.

And at a more external level, precisely because you have this eclipse of the normal methods of attaining spiritual instruction, there is a kind of casting of the inward outward by the authorities of tradition, in the highest sense of the word: an externalization which has never been available before. Before this day and age you never had a humanity which could read the greatest pearls of wisdom of all the religions just by going into any bookstore, like the Yes! bookshop three blocks from here, and being able to read Lao-Tse and the Upanishads and Sufi masterpieces and Meister Eckhart and Hasidic writings and the Kabbala and God knows what. What does this phenomenon mean? Why is it that the most gifted spiritual person in even a country like India, or Persia, which have been great centers of mysticism in days gone by, did not have such a possibility? It means that you have again, because of this compensation which exists in the Divine and the human order, a kind of availability of things which in themselves were difficult to access before. Look at Judaism: if you were living in Spain in the fourteenth and fifteenth centuries, you would have belonged to a Jewish community which represented one of the peaks of Jewish culture. And at that time there were masters of Lurian Kabbala. What would you have had to do in order to be able to read some of these texts? After perhaps twenty years of studying Hebrew with this teacher and that teacher, finally you might be taught Lurian Kabbala. And now any kid as a college freshman can go and pick up the Zohar or the books of Lurian Kabbala in a bookstore.

This is not equal to instruction, of course, but even the theoretical exposition of that type of doctrine in the modern world has something to do with the question you posed, and this instruction has not become completely unavailable. To the extent that humanity falls spiritually and becomes more and more externalized, less and less interested in the inner dimensions of religion, these dimensions recede, without dying out completely. Those inner dimensions have receded most for that humanity which has externalized itself most: Europe and Western civilization. And to the extent that Islam, Hinduism, Buddhism, or Oriental Judaism undergo the same process, the inner dimension of the religion becomes less and less accessible. But by means of the compensation of which I've spoken, the door always remains open; and that is because ultimately we are responsible before God, and God is just. From the spiritual point of view you cannot stand on the Day of Judgment before the Lord and say, "O Lord, because I could not find Meister Eckhart in New York I stopped believing in you." For the person who seeks, the saying of Christ, "Seek and ye shall find," will hold true until He returns. That was not a temporal statement. But where you have to knock, and where you will find, may be different from days gone by.

JZ: *Assuming one begins to walk towards the open door of which you speak, one examines oneself and sees one's fragmentary nature. You spoke earlier about the passions. What is a useful attitude towards our fragmented nature, towards our passions? How should we eradicate them, or use them? How does remembrance, of which you also spoke, enter in here?*

SHN: I'm always very careful when questions like this are asked of me. It is necessary to mention a point which is absolutely crucial: spiritual instruction is not meant for general public consumption. Religions, in their exoteric form and with their general instructions, are. Commandments such as: you should be good, you should not lie, you should be humble, and the Ten Commandments: these are for all men. But how to control the passions? What to do with them? The alchemy of the transformation of human passions is not exactly the same for all human beings. Traditional science of the soul was like traditional medicine: it did not give the same prescription to every patient. But today many people who try to play the role of pseudo-guru commit the mistake of modern medicine, of giving an aspirin to whoever has a headache. The patient is considered to be an "it," as if this were a science of physics, where calcium has a specific weight whether it is in Washington or Kansas City or San Francisco. So I am opposed to giving a generalized answer to these questions, except as it concerns general principles. The case of each aspirant is different.

But in a general sense, there is a stage in the spiritual life when one has to slay the dragon. At some point St. George or St. Michael have to come along to slay the dragon in our soul—not the Chinese dragon, which in Chinese alchemy means the power of the soul as it grows wings and flies, but dragon in the sense of a sort of fiendish demonic force which prevents the hero from reaching the treasure, as in our children's stories in Western Europe and Asia as well as in America. This dragon has to be slain by the spiritual power which St. George or St. Michael represent; and their lance represents a direct Divine Presence without which it is not possible to slay this dragon. The dragon is *much* more powerful than we are. We are swallowed up very easily. That's why we can read a book about all these things and feel we have mastered the subject; we may be very disciplined for fifteen or twenty minutes or even longer, but then the first wind that blows topples us over, because we have not as yet slain the dragon. It is therefore necessary that, at the beginning of the path, you be able to slay the dragon, to subdue this passion. The Sufis refer to this principle by saying that we have to make the devil in us Muslim; that is, make that rebellious nature in us surrender itself to God.

Now, this process implies a kind of death. When we say "life," what do we mean by it? We mean this everyday consciousness, which is really the forgetfulness of God. We remember our everyday ambitions—to eat, to enjoy ourselves in the evening, to get up in the morning; we remember everything except the one thing that Christ said you should remember, the one thing necessary. And therefore to kill this consciousness is really "to die." So the first stage is a death, a purgation. That is universal in all spiritual paths. But that death does not kill our immortal soul; it leads to its coming to life. So the next stage is the stage of expansion, of the coming to life of the inner aspects which had been hidden by the force of this dragon which was suffocating them. And that in turn leads to union, to the fruit of the path, which is knowledge of God and love of God. So I would say that the three universal stages of contraction, expansion, and union, as Evelyn Underhill, the famous classical writer of the Western mystical tradition, mentions, pertain in one way or another to all spiritual paths.

But how in each individual case the passions are transmuted, what passion it is that a particular individual must try to work against, for that there is no general formula. Certain human beings have a false pride, and this pride itself hides itself in the form of a false humility. There are other human beings in whom this is not the sin; the sin is, let's say, that of carnal passions. Their case is very, very different and it is totally wrong and in fact very dangerous to try to give a general formula for the instructions needed as far as the spiritual path is concerned.

JZ: *In "Sufism and the Integration of Man" you mention Rumi writing that the adept in the spiritual retreat must invoke the Holy Name until his toes begin to say "Allah." What is the role of the body in the search for wholeness?*

SHN: I shall speak here from the point of view of the Islamic metaphysical tradition, but what I have to say can also be found, *mutatis mutandis*, in the spiritual teachings of Christianity, where the dichotomy between body and soul is emphasized much more, especially in the mainstream of Augustinian theology. In Islam, as in the other two monotheistic religions, wholeness includes the body. Why is it that all three religions believe in the resurrection of the body on the Day of Judgment? When we stand before God, in that final moment of encounter which determines the whole destiny of human beings—all of this life is a journey towards that one moment of encounter with God—our body, according to those theologies, is present along with our soul. Take the Christian case: Christ ascended to heaven bodily. The Catholics believe that the Virgin Mary also ascended to heaven corporeally. Judaism has the chariot of Elias. Islam has the ascension of the Prophet, *al-mi'raj*, which was a corporeal ascent, not just a spiritual one, the latter being open to everyone—*al-mi'raj ar-ruhani*. So the body is somehow part of that whole of which we are speaking.

Sufism emphasizes this a great deal. Rather than basing itself on a dichotomy between body and soul, it might begin at a particular stage, especially in ascetic Sufism, with a negation of the body. As I have said, somewhere along the way you have to die. One has to avoid, let us say, this or that passion, but always realizing that it is not the body that is the culprit. It is the concupiscent soul as it's attached to the body. It is not our hand or our mouth that commits an illicit act from a religious point of view; it is the intention behind it, within our soul, that does so. And what Sufism tries to do is to disassociate the soul from excessive attention to the bodily passions, while the body remains, in a sense, neutral. The body is in fact from another point of view very positive, because it is created by God and doesn't have the independence which our soul has to rebel against God. Say you have an atheist who says, "I don't believe in God." His pulse continues to beat, however, and his liver continues to function. And that organic functioning is seen from the Islamic point of view as meaning that these organs are following God's command, irrespective of the conscious mind which might deny God or His Will. That's why on the Day of Judgment each part of our body will bear testimony against us, independent of ourselves, according to famous eschatological descriptions that we have in the sacred scripture.

Now, in the second, later stage of the path, as the soul becomes purified it does not leave the body—the body is still there, we're still alive—and it realizes the significance of the body as God's creation and as a temple of the spirit. The idea of the body as a temple is very, very important, for it is related to the great influence and effect that a transmuted sensuality, which is also spiritual, has upon the spiritual life. Man is the bridge between heaven and earth. On the one hand, he is to leave earth for heaven; on the other, he is to bring back heaven on earth. He is to serve as a conduit, a channel, for Divine Grace, *baraka*. And this sensualized spirituality—which is so important in Sufism and which often is manifested in the forms of eroticism, and the love for perfume, for beauty, especially for female beauty, and all that which is mentioned in Sufi poetry—has to do with the positive function that the body then plays in this very important duty of the spiritualized man to transmit the Divine Presence to the world about him, including the world of nature.

At the same time, the body represents the outer limits of our individuality, and therefore when it participates in the divine rites we are sure that we are participating wholly in them. That is why Rumi says that you should sit down and invoke the name of God until your toes say "Allah, Allah"; this incredible poem in the *Mathnawi* refers to the very esoteric and of course never publicly divulged practices according to which, finally, the body participates in the prayer of the heart, and man realizes the function of the body as an extension of the heart, of our inner center, and therefore an *extremely* important container of what we call the soul. I'll give you an example. All of us are aware that we have a body, of course, and from one point of view it's an impediment, if seen only as passion and veil. On the other hand, just imagine what kind of people we would be if we could always remain in our bodies. In the Hesychast tradition there's a saying, "Only the saints can remain in their bodies." If we were to remain only in our bodies we would become perfect masters of meditation; because the one thing in us which never stays put is our mind. That's one aspect of its wonder, but on the other hand, it's the unbridled mental passion which makes it impossible to concentrate, to submit oneself to God and to open up the heart as the seat of contemplative knowledge. And the body can play an important role in the actual process of bridling the mind. If we could only live our mental life within the body we would become masters of the contemplative path. All one has to do is place oneself in God's Name and place the Name in the heart. But how hard it is to achieve this apparently simple action.

JZ: *It has been said, "Be aware of every breath."*

SHN: Yes, that of course is an allusion to the spiritual technique of the invocation of the Name of God, which in fact has to do with the expansion of the breast, since the lungs exist within the breast, and each breath expands the lungs. Breathing is not only related to the fundamental pulse which enables human life to continue, it also is the rhythm which, in the Sufi who's aware of the presence of God, relates him to God. So every time you breathe and you don't remember God, in a sense you've failed to achieve wholeness, and have fallen below the perfection of wholeness.

JZ: *In the search for wholeness, do men and women have different paths to travel? Or is the path the same for both?*

SHN: First of all, the male and female natures are not accidental. The differences are not only biological, and not only psychological. The differences do not stop even on the spiritual level, but have their roots in the Divine Nature itself. The principles of male and female represent essentially a complementarity which goes back to God Himself. All this debate now about God as Himself or Herself is due to the forgetting of the metaphysical doctrine of the Divine Nature which always embraces both aspects or poles. God in His Essence—or Its Essence—is above all duality; at the same time, God's Infinitude is the principle of femininity *in divinis*, while God's Absoluteness is the principle or Divine Prototype of masculinity. At the root of what appears on the human plane as the male and female stands the Divine Nature, and there is nothing at all accidental about the male-female distinction. There is such a thing as female spirituality. There is such a thing as male spirituality. Of course, all human beings also contain both of these elements within themselves to some degree.

As far as the practices of Sufism are concerned, they are the same for men and women. Both are seen as immortal beings with the possibility of reaching the Divine. And that is because men and women complement each other and reflect their common androgynic origin. They're both whole and segmented. That is why the possibilities of both celibacy and of sexual union have spiritual significance: because both realities are present in human nature. A person who lives a celibate life wants to show that he or she is, in fact, an image of the whole without the need of the other sex; that is the basis of celibacy in Buddhism and Christianity. Whereas in the other philosophy, as it exists in Islam and Judaism and Hinduism, in which sexuality is positive and in which one encounters a powerful current of spiritualized sexuality, it is sexual union which symbolizes the complementarity of the male and female, and hence wholeness. So both of these possibilities are realizable and have to be contained in any spiritual path, such as Sufism; but by and large Sufism, as the esoteric dimension of Islam, a religion in which spiritualized sexuality is emphasized, leans upon the pole of the importance of the complementarity of the sexes. This does not mean that there are two different programs, one for men and one for women. In the same way that on the level of Divine Law all of the injunctions of the Shari'ah are the same for men and women, all the fasting, the daily prayers, the paying of alms, the going on pilgrimage, the responsibility for moral action, the question of the judgment of God—except during the menstrual period of a woman, when she does not perform her daily prayers and does not fast—the general instructions and practices are the same. But the nuances, the delicacies of what spiritual instruction is given to a particular individual, are not the same. They are not something to be promulgated in a general manner for everyone whether man or woman. It's like what I said before about the differences between individuals. Every serious Sufi master takes into consideration the differences between his or her male and female disciples as well as between members of each sex. It needs to be mentioned that there are also women spiritual masters in Sufism, not just disciples. Perhaps the number has been less but there have been some very great women spiritual masters and saints. So while there is no black and white difference of spiritual techniques for men and women in Sufism, at the same time male and female spirituality are recognized for what they are, and that in some way, in every human being who's of a spiritual nature, these elements are intertwined.

JZ: You speak of every human being who's of a spiritual nature. Why are some people called to seek a spiritual way, and others not?

SHN: The question you pose is a very important one. The non-monotheistic religions, especially those of India, give the answer of the chains of life and death, of birth and rebirth and where we are in that cycle. Islam, like Christianity and Judaism, does not accept that perspective, because these three religions emphasize the present state of the human being and the importance of being able to reach God from the present state. They do not therefore emphasize meditation upon how we have reached the present state. Nevertheless, there are many esoteric teachings, especially in Islam, which allude to the fact that we had some kind of reality before we were born into this world, and that we were born with a certain nature that defines us. The moment of history in which we entered the temporal cycle, where we were born, and with what powers and possibilities, are all related to the state that we had before we came into what we call the terrestrial life. It is very difficult—in fact, impossible from the point of human intelligence—to give the exact reasons why you were born in New York, I was born in Tehran, a third person in Belgium; why you and I were born in the twentieth century, someone else in the thirteenth century; why you may be a very good musician and I a very bad one; or, why a particular person has a deep love for God and some other person doesn't. It seems that the moment we enter into the terrestrial life, what we bring to this world already depends on who we are. Astrology tries to deal with this a bit, relating it to the progression of the stars. But it needs much more than astrological knowledge to be able to relate what one is and the situation of one's life. Of course, heredity has a lot to do with it. But the question remains, "Why is it that we are born of a particular father and mother?" These questions are not easy to answer in the context of our discussion because they need a great deal of metaphysical preparation. They are not impossible to understand, but they're difficult to explain without that preparation.

What I can say, however, is that not all human beings start from the same point either intellectually or spiritually. But because we are human, because we all have the imprint of the Divine upon our forehead, God's justice requires that we all have the same access to Him. And that is why religion in its general formulation never excludes any of its followers.

But the inner teachings of a religion have to be for those who are prepared to receive them. If all human beings had the same yearning or love for God, then the inner teachings would be for everyone; but that is not the case of human reality. And no religion can fail to cater to the needs of the few who seek God here and now, for such a failure would mean that religion destroying the equilibrium of the whole collectivity, exactly as it has happened to the Western world—because it always is those few who seek God who are like the salt of society. The religion which cannot cater to the needs of its potential saints and sages gradually ceases to have saints, and then fissures begin to appear in its walls, leading to its collapse. The exoteric body of the religion begins to decompose. Therefore the need for that inner teaching reserved for the few is present because of the different capabilities of human beings. It seems that human beings stand in different points on this long journey of man from God and to God. We are all equal in that we shall stand before Him on the Day of Judgment and will be judged accordingly—His laws are for all of us—but how close we are to Him now and what knowledge of Him we have now and our love for Him now—those are not equal.

JZ: *Does a person who's achieved wholeness, or a great degree of wholeness, have a particular role to play towards his or her fellow humanity?*

SHN: In all the debate which goes on in the modern world between those who would like to debunk the contemplative ideal and in a kind of Aurobindean manner to think that perfection consists in coming back into the world and remaking it, and those who uphold the traditional ideal, what is really forgotten is that it is the human being's vocation which determines what he should do—what the Buddhists would call his *dharma*. We must follow our own nature. There are those whom God has willed simply to be, which is a very, very important manner of serving mankind. Like the light above our heads: it doesn't *do* anything, but it illuminates this whole room. It is this function of wholeness which has been belittled in the modern world, to the great detriment of the modern world, with its over-emphasis on action. And there are other human beings whose vocation it is to *make*; that is, people who are artistic.

So I do not want to give a single answer. There are three different modes of reflecting wholeness. One is through service, charity on all levels; for example, Christian saints who created hospitals for the poor—and that must not be mixed up with the kind of atheistic charity in the modern world which wants to be good despite God. I'm speaking of traditionally religious charity and living a life of service, like the Karma Yoga of the Hindus. A person who is whole lives this life in a manner that is whole, and there's tremendous effect in the actions which such a person performs. That's something which many people forget: the quality of the action of a person who is whole differs from the quality of others' actions. What he says, the way he looks at people: the deep effect that is left is due to the fact that it comes from a different source of action, a different layer of inner being.

The second mode is the mode of making, the whole field of *ars*—not art in the modern sense, but the Latin *ars*. Such a person might be simply a gardener, or the holder of some small job; it doesn't need to be grandiose art in the modern Western sense. A person with wholeness would bring this quality to whatever he would make or do. All his activity would be "art." In traditional civilization, a gardener or a woodcutter could be a man who had a great deal of wholeness, and whatever he did would reflect this wholeness in a manner which benefited those around him.

And the third is what is called the mode of being, that of those whose whole function it is either to disseminate knowledge—whose act of charity it is to teach—or simply to be a presence, not "to do anything" but simply to be a sort of silent witness to God. They're like a window onto the world of light.

There is no rivalry between these various models, and it's a great tragedy that there has been polemical writing during the last century over this issue, with people attacking even the great medieval saints, because they did not cater to the needs of the poor. This modern aberration is due to a total misunderstanding of the nature of the world of man and of God. It has led to this terrible situation today when much of theology is destroyed in the name of human service, without human service in fact getting any better despite this sacrilegious sacrifice as a result of which the functions of theology have become nearly forgotten.

JZ: Do you have any practical advice for someone who's beginning to sense the need for more wholeness in his or her life?

SHN: The person who already feels a lack of wholeness has received a gift from heaven. We say in Sufism that the only person whose ignorance is incurable is a person who doesn't know he is ignorant. To know that one is ignorant is already the first stage of cure from ignorance. In the same way, to realize that one is lacking in wholeness is already a blessing from heaven, even if it comes from such a little thing as wanting to eat wholesome and natural food. Like everything else, this can become a fad; nevertheless, it is a positive sign. But the important thing is, to be true to one's self; never to relent in one's quest for wholeness. Never to be lazy until one really finds wholeness. The great danger is a kind of momentary and passing state which appears as equilibrium or a small degree of wholeness, and which leads to forgetting that this was just a step or a station house on the path, not the goal. The danger is to become consolidated and petrified in that station. It is said in Sufism that any person upon the spiritual path who pays attention to the extraordinary powers, or even the great visions, that he or she may receive, will be barred from the vision of God. You might even be able to walk on water, but that's not the purpose of following Sufism. We're not following Sufism to walk on water or to do other miracles, but to be able to reach God. In the same way, the quest for wholeness, which enters into the heart of a person—which is itself a blessing from Heaven—should never come to an end unless one really gains wholeness in its ultimate sense. One must examine oneself, be always true to oneself, be honest with oneself; until, of course, one finds the path. One must find the way which suits one's nature and for which one is made. Once this occurs, it is the path which will decide for us. But of course from an inner point of view it's always the path that chooses the man, and not the man who chooses the path.

Parabola
Volume: 7.2
Dreams and Seeing

THE NIGHT JOURNEY

Abu Yazid al-Bistami

I dreamed that I ascended to the Heavens in quest of God, seeking to be united with God, who is glorious and exalted, on the terms that I should abide with Him unto everlasting; and I was put to a trial which the heavens and the earth and they that inhabit them would not withstand, forasmuch as He spread before me the carpet of His gifts, one kind after another, and offered to me the kingdom of each Heaven; and meanwhile I was closing mine eyes to them, because I knew that He was testing me therewith, and in reverence for the holiness of my Lord I paid no heed to them, saying all the while, "O my Beloved, what I desire is other than what Thou offerest me."

I dreamed that I ascended to the Heavens; and when I came to the Nearest Heaven, lo, I saw a green bird; and it unfolded one of its wings and mounted me thereon and flew with me till at last it reached the ranks of the angels who stand with burning feet on the stars, glorifying God at morn and eve. I saluted them and they returned my salutation; then the bird set me down amongst them and departed. I continued to glorify God amongst them and praise Him in their language, whilst they were saying, "This is a son of Adam, not a creature of light, since he hath taken refuge with us and talked with us." And I was inspired with certain words and said, "In the name of God, who is able to relieve me from want of you." Then

He kept offering me such a kingdom as no tongue can describe, but I knew that He was testing me therewith, and all the while I was saying, "What I desire is other than what Thou offerest me," and in reverence for His holiness I paid no heed to it.

Then I dreamed that I ascended to the Second Heaven; and lo, there came to me troops and troops of angels, regarding me as the people of a city regard a prince who entereth it. Then came unto us the Chief of the angels, whose name is Lawidh, and said, "O Abu Yazid, thy Lord greeteth thee and saith, I have loved thee and thou hast loved Me." And he brought me into a green meadow, where was a flowing river, and around it flying angels who fly to the earth every day a hundred thousand times to look upon the friends of God. Their faces were like sunbeams. They had known me according to the knowledge of the earth, that is, on the earth; and they came to me and greeted me and led me down to the bank of that river; and lo, on either side of it were trees of light with many boughs drooping in the air, and on every bough thereof the nest of a bird, that is, one of the angels; and in every nest was an angel bending low in worship. And all the while I was saying, "O my Beloved, my desire is other than what Thou offerest me. Be Thou to me, O Beloved, a protector instead of all them that grant protection and a companion instead of all them that accompany!" Then from my inmost heart was kindled a fiery thirst of longing, so that the angels and these trees withal became as a single gnat in comparison with my aspiration; and they were all gazing on me, astounded and amazed by the greatness of that which they saw in me. Then He continued to offer me a kingdom such as no tongue can describe, but all the while I knew that He was testing me therewith, and in reverence for the holiness of my Lord I paid no heed to it, saying "O my Beloved, my desire is other than what Thou offerest me."

And when God knew my true will to seek Him and my detachment from other than Him, lo, I saw an angel who stretched forth his hand and drew me. Then I dreamed that I ascended to the Third Heaven; and there were all God's angels, according to their several descriptions, who had come to me and were saluting me. Amongst them was an Angel with four faces. He said, "Dost thou wish to look on the wonders of God?" I said, "Yea." Then he unfolded one of his wings, and lo, upon every single feather was a lamp by whose light the radiance of the sun was darkened.

Then he said, "Come, O Abu Yazid, and take shelter in the shade of my wing, that thou mayst glorify and magnify God until death." But I said to him, "God is able to relieve me from the want of thee." Then from my inmost heart was kindled the light of my knowledge, by the radiance whereof their splendor, that is, the splendor of the lamps, was darkened; and the Angel became as a gnat in comparison with my perfection. Then He continued to offer me a kingdom such as no tongue can describe, but all the while I knew that He was testing me therewith, and in reverence for His holiness I paid no heed to it, saying all the while, "O my Beloved, my desire is other than what Thou offerest me."

And when God knew my true will to seek Him, lo, I saw an angel who stretched forth his hand and lifted me up. Then I dreamed that I ascended to the Fourth Heaven; and there were all the angels, according to their several attributes and guises and descriptions, who came to me and greeted me and looked at me as the people of a city look at one of their princes when he entereth it, raising their voices in glorification and praise of God because of my great devotion to Him and the small heed that I paid to them. Then He continued to offer me a kingdom such as no tongue can describe, but all the while I knew that He was testing me therewith, and in reverence for His holiness I paid no heed to it, saying, "O my Beloved, my desire is other than what Thou offerest me."

And when God knew my true and single devotion to Him in the search after Him, lo, I saw an angel who stretched forth his hand and lifted me towards him. Then I dreamed that I ascended to the Fifth Heaven; and there I saw angels standing in the sky, with their heads in front of the Sixth Heaven, from whom fell drops of light that made the heavens to shine. They all saluted me in diverse languages, and I returned their salutation in every language with which they addressed me; whereat they marveled. Then they said, "Come, O Abu Yazid, that thou mayst glorify and magnify God, and that we may help thee to win thy desire"; but from reverence for my Lord I paid no heed to them. And thereupon springs of longing rose from my inmost heart, and in comparison with that which flashed from me the light of the angels became as a lamp placed in the sun. Then He continued to offer me a kindgom such as no tongue can describe, but all the while I knew that He was testing me therewith, and I said always, "O my Beloved, my desire is other than what Thou offerest me."

And when God knew my true will to seek him, lo, I saw an angel who stretched forth his hand and lifted me towards him. Then I dreamed that I ascended to the Sixth Heaven; and there I saw the longing angels, who came to me and greeted me and boasted to me of their longing; and I boasted to them of some of the flutterings of my inmost heart. Then He continued to offer me a kingdom such as no tongue can describe, but all the while I knew He was testing me therewith, and paid no heed to it, saying, "O my Beloved, my desire is other than what Thou offerest me."

And when God knew my true will to seek him, lo, I saw an angel who stretched forth his hand and lifted me. Then I dreamed that I ascended to the Seventh Heaven; and there were a hundred thousand rows of angels, each row coming to meet me in numbers like unto the worlds of men and spirits multiplied a thousand thousand-fold. With each angel was a banner of light, and beneath each banner a thousand thousand angels, the tallness of every angel being the distance of a journey of five hundred years; and at their head was an Angel named Barya'il. They saluted me in their tongue and speech, and I returned their salutation in their own tongue whereat they marveled. And lo, a crier who cried, "Stop, stop, O Abu Yazid, for thou hast attained unto the goal," but I paid no heed to his words. Then He continued to offer me a kingdom such as no tongue can describe, and all the while I knew that He was testing me therewith, and I kept saying, "O my Beloved, my desire is other than what Thou offerest me."

And when God knew my true will to seek Him, He changed me into a bird, and every feather of my wings was farther than from the East to the West a thousand thousand times. And I ceased not from flying in the worlds of Malakut and Jabarut and traversing realm after realm and veils after veils and field after field and seas after seas and curtains after curtains until I was met by the Angel of the Footstool (*Kursi*), who had with him a pillar of light. He saluted me; then he said, "Take the pillar." So I took it, and lo, the Heavens with all therein sought shelter in the shadow of my knowledge and sought light by the light of my longing, and all the angels became as a gnat beside the perfection of my aspiration in the search after Him. And all the while I knew that He was testing me therewith and I paid no heed to it in reverence for the holiness of my Lord the most high God.

Then I ceased not from flying and soaring through realm after realm and veils after veils and field after field and seas after seas and curtains after curtains until I reached the Footstool. And lo, I was met by angels whose eyes were in number as the stars of heaven. From every eye shone a gleaming light, and those lights became lamps, and from the interior of every lamp I heard "Glory unto God" and "There is no god but God." Then I ceased not from flying on that wise until I arrived at a sea of light, its waves dashing against one another; and in comparison with it the radiance of the sun would be dark. And lo, on the seas were ships of light: beside their light the splendor of those seas was darkened. I went on, crossing seas after seas, until I reached the Greatest Sea, upon which is the Throne of the Merciful (*Arsh ar-Rahman*); and I ceased not from swimming therein until all between the empyrean and the lowest depth—the Cherubim and the Bearers of the Throne and all others whom God hath created in heaven and earth—seemed less than a mustard-seed betwixt heaven and earth to the flight of my inmost heart in its quest of Him. Then He continued to offer me of the graces of His loving kindness and the perfection of His power and the grandeur of His kingdom such gifts as no tongue can describe; but all the while I was saying, "O my Beloved, my desire is other than what Thou offerest me," and in reverence for His holiness I paid no heed to them.

And when God knew my true will to seek Him, He called unto me and said, "O chosen one, approach Me and look upon the belvederes of My Glory and the spacious fields of My Splendor, and sit on the carpet of My Sanctity, that thou mayst behold the subtleties of My Doing in My (appointed) Times. Thou art My chosen and My beloved and My elect from amongst My creatures." And thereat I was melting as lead melts. Then He gave me a draught from the fountain of grace in the cup of friendship; then He changed me to a state which I have no power to describe; then He brought me nigh unto Him and brought me so nigh that I become nigher to Him than the spirit to the body. Then I was met by the Spirits of all the Prophets, and they saluted me and magnified my case and spoke with me and I spoke with them. Then the Spirit of Mohammed—God bless and save him!—came to meet me and said, "O Abu Yazid, welcome! Be glad and rejoice! Great is the preferment that God hath bestowed on thee above a multitude of His creatures."[1]

Note:

1   "An Early Arabic Version of the Mi'raj of Abu Yazid al-Bistami," translated by Reynold A. Nicholson, *Islamica* 2 (1926).

Parabola
Volume: 23.3
Fear

THE BLESSED STATE

Gray Henry

There is only one Real Fear—that we do not fully avail ourselves of the opportunity afforded by the human state—that at the moment of death we are not content with the state or the degree of spiritual integrity we have realized. Once we are separated from our bodies, our vehicles of "doing" and change, we are left with who we *are*. Even knowing this we go along abusing the human state.

In the various spiritual traditions, fear and its related attitudes of contrition and repentance can be seen as the blessed impetus and key for the commencement of the spiritual life as fear incites the soul to move forward. In Islamic mysticism the movement of the soul towards it true nature is described in three stages: the first is called *makhafa* or Fear of God, the second is called *mahabba* which refers to the Love of God, and the last stage is the *ma'rifa* which means gnosis or Knowledge of God. According to Martin Lings, each of these stages has two aspects: "The domain of fear-action is that of 'must not' and 'must'; love has likewise, in addition to its dynamic intensity, the static aspect of contemplative bliss; and spiritual knowledge is both objective and subjective being ultimately concerned with the Absolute as Transcendent Truth and Immanent Selfhood. ... Fear of the Lord is the beginning of wisdom, and it is to fear that the first two stations are related. They are thus concerned with danger, and they are two because danger confronts man with two possibilities, flight or attack," that is, abstention and accomplishment. The aforementioned stations of wisdom "might be called dimensions of holiness."[1]

Also according to Lings, these same three principles of fear, love, and knowledge are apparent in Islamic art and Quranic illumination. The majority of calligraphers were Sufis who had a great fear of intruding on the perfection of the Holy Book with their art. In Islamic art, the geometric aspect corresponds with the principle of rigor and fear. The arabesque, or endlessly entwining plant tendrils represent love. Finally the calligraphy of the Revealed Word corresponds to the domain of knowledge.

Frithjof Schuon explains that "Every spiritual path must start with a 'conversion,' an apparently negative turning round of the will, an indirect movement towards God in the form of an inner separation from the false plenitude of the world. This withdrawal corresponds to the station of renunciation or detachment, of sobriety, of fear of God: what has to be overcome is desire, passional attachment, and idolatry of ephemeral things."[2]

The Sufi use of the rosary can in one sense be compared to the Christian rite of Holy Communion. Both begin with an attitude of fear and repentance—an emptying of one's Self of oneself. In the first stage of the rosary a Muslim repeats ninety-nine times "May God forgive me"; this is said with the intention of *tawba* or turning—that is, of sincerely desiring to change. The Christian, before approaching the altar to receive the sacrament, prays "Lord have mercy upon me, Christ have mercy upon me."[3] Both Muslim and Christian participate in an emptying—in a death of all that is unholy or low in themselves. This is the stage which might be referred to as the death St. John of the Cross describes: "Die before you die." But after death comes resurrection and in the third stage eternal life. After emptying comes re-formation, and according to Meister Eckhart, this leads ultimately to Union with the Godhead:

> *When I preach, I usually speak of disinterest and say that a man should be empty of self and all things; and secondly, that he should be reconstructed in the simple Good that God is; and thirdly, that he should consider the great aristocracy which God has set up in the soul,*

such that by means of it man may wonderfully attain to God; *and fourthly, of* the purity of the divine nature.

In the second stage of the rosary the Muslim asks God's blessings and praises upon the Prophet Muhammad with the idea that he himself may return to his own pure and primordial nature, the *fitra* or condition of True Man. The Christian, as he kneels now empty, waits to receive the bread and wine, whether understood symbolically or literally to be the presence of the Word of God. When the Logos is taken within his own emptiness he thereby regains his Christ-like nature. He has been *re*-formed for that moment on the Self which he hopes he will have realized for the time of his own resurrection.

Now the third stage of spiritual movement initiated by fear is that of the union or return to the Divine Source of all Being—the froth subsiding into the sea from which it has been manifested. One hopes that if purity of soul has not been realized—if one has not awoken to one's true state of being—God will bestow His Grace and His Mercy for the intention of sincere effort in His direction.

The Muslim in the final stage of the rosary repeats ninety-nine times, "There is no divinity save The Divinity," thereby attesting to the absence of anything but God. Neither the vessel full of itself nor the empty vessel filled with True Man survives; both have returned to the One. A painting by Raphael to be found at the Vatican provides an image for the Christian. In this painting we are before an altar upon which stands a chalice, and above this appears the dove of the Holy Spirit. At the top of the painting is a depiction of God in the company of heavenly personages including Mary, Jesus, John the Baptist, the Apostles, and angels. What we may understand from this is that after the worshipper has received the sacrament and kneels purified before the altar, his soul rises up through the medium of the Holy Spirit and back to God. This is a very powerful rite to experience and also reminds the believer on a weekly or more frequent basis of the very method and outcome he wishes for his human life. He practices death, resurrection, and eternal life, hoping that during his human state he purifies his being and in the end returns directly to his Maker.

So just as we see how fear is the blessed beginning, we must never forget its positive nature. Spiritual attainment has frequently been described in the terminology of the alchemical tradition whereby man's leaden, dull nature is returned to its golden original state. When any substance or entity (or even a relationship) undergoes dissolution, it must eventually be re-crystallized in a new form. In other words, the new entity has the possibility of being reconstituted in a higher and nobler state. What this means for any of us is that when we experience fear, when things seem to be coming apart, we should instead be joyful and grateful for the possibility of moving upward from our present plateau where we perhaps are too comfortably established.

"Lead represents the chaotic, 'heavy' and sick condition of metal or of the inward man," Titus Burckhardt explains, "while gold—'congealed light' and 'earthly sun'—expresses the perfection of both metallic and human existence." He goes on to say that the *re*-forming of the soul cannot take place until it is

> *freed from all the rigidities and inner contradictions [so that it may]
> become that plastic substance on which the Spirit or Intellect, coming
> from on high, can imprint a new 'form'—a form which does not limit
> or bind, but on the contrary delivers, because it comes from the Divine
> Essence. ... The soul cannot be transmuted without the co-operation
> of the Spirit, and the Spirit illumines the soul only to the extent of its
> passive preparedness and in accordance with its manners.*[4]

And so as the purpose of the human state of being is the sanctification of one's soul, and as one would desire to achieve this before death, I would like to conclude with an extraordinary description of the Saint who no longer *fears*—although this was the blessed state by which his spiritual life commenced.

> *The Saint hath no fear, because fear is the expectation of either
> some future calamity or of the eventual loss of some object of desire;
> whereas the Saint is the "son of his time" [resides in the Eternal Present/Presence]; he has no future from which he should fear anything
> and, as he hath no fear so he hath no hope since hope is the expectation
> either of gaining an object of desire or of being relieved from a mis-*

fortune, and this belongs to the future; nor does he grieve because grief arises from the rigor of time, and how should he feel grief who dwells in the Radiance of Satisfaction and the Garden of Concord?[5]

Notes:

1   Martin Lings, *Symbol & Archetype: A Study of the Meaning of Existence* (Cambridge, England: Quinta Essentia, 1991), pp. 114-115.

2   Frithjof Schuon, *Stations of Wisdom* (Bloomington, IN: Perennial Books, 1980), p. 148.

3   "Where reverence is, there too is fear." Plato, *Euthypho*, 12b.

4   Titus Burckhardt, *Alchemy—Science of the Cosmos, Science of the Soul* (Louisville, KY: Fons Vitae, 1997) pp. 24, 97, 111.

5   Al-Junayd, ninth century CE.

Parabola
Volume: 22.3
Conscience and
Consciousness

THE SAINT WITH SEVEN TOMBS

Tim Winter

"We were born to be the companions of the angels.
Let us go there again, friend, for that is our country."

—*Rumi*

The Sufi shrine which nestles near the Bosnian village
of Blagaj is well-guarded both by nature and by sacred,
enigmatic metaphors. The visitor follows the Buna River
upstream through a gorge shaded by willow and oak,
until, without warning, the river's source is attained. A
white cliff hundreds of feet high towers over the small
cave from whose living limestone rock the green waters
gush. Cantilevered over this cave is a whitewashed Sufi
tekke, or meeting house, built centuries ago by dervish
initiates of the secretive Bektashi order. From its windows one gains a heart-ravishing view of this mysterious
scene: the river that flows from nowhere.

During my visit in 1994 the madness of war was less
than a mile distant; yet within this blessed sanctuary
peace was everywhere. Great eagles circled above; the
occasional fish broke the surface of the river. Within the
tekke, a choir of four teenage girls was slowly exploring
the modulated, minor keys of Bosnian sacred music.

Why did fifteenth-century dervishes choose this place
to establish their shrine? Gazing from the window, I tried

to see it through their long-dead eyes. The girls, as though reading my thoughts, sang the old poem of Yunus Emre:

Those rivers of Paradise,
They flow, repeating the Name of God.

An image of celestial Eden? It was, I felt sure, nothing so hackneyed and conventional. The symbol must be something more devastating. Soon the girls, eyes distant as their souls resonated to the ancient words, changed keys and launched into the great hymn of Bayram Veli:

What ails this soul of mine?
Why overflows it with such pain?
My soul it burns, burns,
and in that very burning finds its balm.

A flash of intuition, and the answer came to me. The unknown dervishes had used the river which came from nowhere as a symbol of the miracle of existence. Their Bektashi brotherhood, like Neoplatonist philosophy, held that creation is continually renewed in every instant. The mystic wayfarer, the *yolcu*, voyages upstream until he reaches the point of the "Most Holy Effusion" (*fayd-i aqdas*), where the world and human spirits emanate from the Divine. As ensouled participants swimming in this great river, we dimly intuit that the river has a source. Consciousness of self remains an existential burning, a homesickness, until realization is attained: The human heart enshrines a spark whose light is from the divine Source. As ensouled creatures, we may swim upstream, against the flow; or we may allow ourselves to be carried along with the dead flotsam, until, at last, we become indistinguishable from it.

The tekke on the river Buna is built around one of the tombs of the dervish saint Sari Saltuk. I say "one of the tombs" because, like many saints, he was too important to have only one grave. Before he died, he ordered his disciples to construct seven tombs for his mortal frame, "so that ignorance of where my body lies will produce everywhere a pilgrimage that will uplift the souls." Hence tombs of Sari Saltuk are pointed out today not only in Bosnia, but in Romania and Turkey. Ottoman sources even insist that he has a tomb in Gdansk on the Baltic. The medieval Moroccan traveler Ibn Battuta found a sanctuary dedicated to him in the Ukraine. The total number is debated by scholars, and will probably remain "known only unto God."

Sari Saltuk exists mainly in legend. Folk tradition is not even sure he was a Muslim. Bosnian stories regard him as a dragon-slayer, and hence assimilate him to St. George. One Turkish historian identifies him with St. Nicholas; others conflate him with Elias. Peasant stories in Corfu associate him with St. Spyridon. Albanians, who visit his sanctuary in Kruje, once adopted him as the (Muslim) patron saint of the brewer's guild. A lover of the Quran, his sweet recital of the Gospels in the great church of Constantinople reduced the monks to tears. Perhaps these ambivalent memories would have pleased Saltuk himself, a wandering miracle-worker who, like all those brought close to God, had shed the coarser garments of his human identity.

As the saint had foretold, the tomb at the Buna sanctuary became a magnet for pilgrims. In the 1980s, the annual celebration of the Prophet Muhammad's birthday (*mevlud*) at the shrine drew many thousands.[1] The courtyard and riverbanks filled with families straining to hear the great *Nativity-Song*, written by Safvet-beg Basagic (d. 1934) and performed by one of Bosnia's great vocalists. The various Sufi orders were present, and held their ceremonies after the night prayers, illuminated by the full moon which symbolizes the light which the transfigured heart of the Prophet reflects from the divine Sun.

At other times, the tekke is peaceful, playing host to humbler local folkways. Village women come to light candles and then collect the wax, which they use as a healing ointment. A jug known as a *bardak* is filled with water and left near the tomb overnight, after which the water is used to cure various ailments. The custodian writes *zapis*, amulets to hang around the necks of babies, to ward off envious magic and the evil eye. Pilgrims stand by the cloth-covered sarcophagus of the saint who may or may not be there, and commune with his immortal spirit.

Set into the wall of the tekke is Sari Saltuk's famous wooden sword, given to him by Khizr, the "Green Man" who in the Quran appears as the mystical teacher who warns Moses about the limitations of a purely exoteric religion. In Balkan Sufism, weapons have a rich spiritual meaning. Two axes crossed symbolize the union of the two struggles: against injustice in the world, and against the egotistic passions of the lower self. A sword with two blades is known as Zulfikar, after the sword wielded by the Prophet's son-in-law Ali, who exemplified the virtue of *futuvvet*, spiritual chivalry. Just as the warrior for his nation abides by a complex Samurai-like code of honor, so too the inner warrior is a knight of faith, who progresses on the road to God by maintaining a scrupulous and dignified generosity with God's creatures.

Sufism differs from the great monastic traditions of Christendom in that it sees the world as a barrier to be traversed, not circumvented. The Sufi does not withdraw from the world outwardly, but is detached from it inwardly. Rumi speaks of *khalwat dar anjuman*, isolation in the midst of company, because the woman or man who quests for the Source of existence is in a state of *ghurba*, or exile. Following the Quran, the Sufis hold that the world is a manifestation of God's Names, but it is still not God. So Yunus Emre can sing:

> *Let us away, to look upon the Beautiful,*
> *The radiance of Whose face can famished thousands fill.*[2]

Sari Sultak possessed a further, more enigmatic weapon in his arsenal. *The Book of Saltuk*, penned by the sage Ebulhayr for the Ottoman prince Jem in the 1480s,[3] tells us that the dragon slayer traveled with a bow and seven arrows. The number seven resonates with many metaphors in Sufism. One thinks immediately of the Prophet's Ascension (*mi'raj*) through the seven heavens into the ineffable divine Presence, an experience of progressively transformed consciousness which is the archetype of all Sufi wayfaring.

The number seven also invokes the first chapter of the Quran, which contains this number of verses and is said mystically to encompass the remainder of the Book. And in Sari Sultak's Bektashi teaching, the shapes of the human face correspond to the letters of the Arabic alphabet. Hence the poet Balim Sultan could exclaim: "My face is the Seven Oft-repeated Verses."[4] The illumination of human consciousness "straightens" the features twisted by worldly ignorance, until the Quran's entire text can be read in the face of the perfect saint. At this exalted degree, the saint's identity has melted away into the Divine Word.

In Bektashi Sufism, seven is also the "number of generation." A whole genre of poems formerly sung at the Buna tekke, known as the Cycle Poems (*devrije*), develops the idea that every existent thing has four "mothers," which are the four elements of Earth, Air, Fire, and Water, through whose mingling are generated the "Three Children"—animal, vegetable and mineral things. The total is seven, and the human creature is the summit and purpose of this process of creation, for while other beings manifest some of the Divine Names, the human being manifests them all. Through the transformation of consciousness, the descendant of Adam and Eve turns away from the multiple phenomena of existence and faces the solitary Divine, hence becoming God's true deputy (*khalifa*) in the cosmos. Only humanity has the ability to do this; since only the human mind may achieve perfect consciousness.

It is true that animals also share in a kind of self-awareness. The Quran inquires of us: "Have you not seen that all that is in the heavens and the earth glorifies God? The birds as they spread their wings? Every creature knows its form of prayer and its praise; and God is All-Aware of what they do" (18:41). Hence the need to respect non-human lives: the Prophet taught, "You shall be rewarded for kindnesses done to any living thing," and he spoke of a harlot whose sins were forgiven when God saw her filling her shoe with water from a well, to quench the thirst of a dog.

And yet human consciousness is above that of animals, because it is gifted with choice, between good or evil, Reality or illusion, the Center or the endless periphery. The Prophet explained that human creatures enshrine more than an animal soul: "Each one of you has his creation gathered in his mother's womb for forty days. Then he becomes a clot for a like period. Then he becomes a piece of flesh. Then God sends the angel, which breathes in the Spirit." [5]

What is unique about human consciousness, in Muslim teaching, is not the mind but the Spirit (*ruh*). The Quran tells us how before God created the world, all spirits were summoned to appear before the Divine presence, and were asked: "Am I not your Lord?" "Yes, we testify!" they cried. And the Quran explains: "That was lest you should claim at the Resurrection, 'We were unaware of all this'" (7:172).

In this Quranic vision, then, our consciousness existed before we were born, and was only "breathed" into our mothers during pregnancy. Before then, in that pre-existent arena which the Prophet described as the World of Spirits (*alam al-arwah*), our consciousness was of a pure, quintessential nature, and our individual selfhood, which is the result of accumulated experiences and education, was only latent. Our full humanity, then, and our capacity to turn towards or away from the Real, can only come about when the Real plunges us into the world, or, as the builders of the Buna sanctuary might have put it, when we become fish in the river. The task and function of human consciousness, then, is to remember the Source. Ultimately, it has no other purpose.

The ascent from lower to higher states of consciousness is the process which the Sufis term Wayfaring (*suluk*); and it is here, surely, that we can best find the meaning of Sari Saltuk's seven arrows, and also of his seven tombs. The Prophet passed through seven heavens during his Ascension to God, and then affirmed that "prayer is the believer's Ascension." And the wayfarers, as they follow in his footsteps, and sit with eyes half-closed on their prayer-carpets in the Buna sanctuary, know that they too must fight seven battles and experience seven "deaths." The soul must perish seven times before it rises into the divine Presence from which it came.

Hence the Sufis often describe the Soul (*nafs*) as passing through seven "degrees" (*maratib*).[6] The lowest is the Inciting Soul (*an-nafs al-ammara*), which is the human consciousness helpless before the demands of the lower possibilities of our condition. This "bestial" soul is prey to arrogance, greed, bad character, gluttony, and the other familiar vices which the Prophet condemned. The cure is to compel oneself to recite certain Quranic litanies prescribed by a spiritual director.

Once overcome, the Inciting Soul is replaced by the Reproachful Soul (*an-nafs al-lawwama*). The soul in this condition is still vulnerable to the subtler vices, such as self-satisfaction and a yearning to be admired, but it recognizes these traits and does battle with them. At this level, the conscience becomes the chief weapon against flaws in the consciousness. The preferred litany at this stage is, in many Sufi Orders, said to be the simple repetition of the Divine Name, Allah: the keenest arrow in Sari Saltuk's quiver.

The third degree is the Inspired Soul (*an-nafs al-mulhama*). Here the beginner's vices have been scoured from the heart, and the divine Light begins to gleam. One sage remarks of this degree: "Its attributes are liberality, resignation, knowledge, forgiving people, inviting them to rectitude, accepting their excuses, and seeing that the Exalted God holds all things by their forelocks."[7] At this stage the heart, seat of the spirit, is, as the Prophet said, "like a feather blown about by the wind."[8]

The end of this station is the first Annihilation (*fana*), where the individual consciousness of the wayfarer is "noughted" by the Divine Presence. At the middle of the Path, this experience is fleeting, and it is followed by a return (*ruju*) to human consciousness. This is defined as the fourth degree: the Serene Soul (*an-nafs al-mutma'inna*). As the Real's trusted deputy, the possessor of such a soul can work wonders, breaking the laws of existence with God's leave. Sari Saltuk himself worked countless miracles: when the Mongols threatened Turkey, he flew to the Romanian coast on his prayer rug, followed by twelve thousand disciples. Merely hearing his voice could convert thousands of heathens to Islam; the sight of him would turn magicians into stone.

The final three stages are veiled in mystery, as the Sufi writers hold that language cracks and grows treacherous under the weight of such sublime realities. They are known technically as the Contented Soul, the Soul Found Pleasing, and the Perfect Soul. As the condition of Annihilation becomes more permanent, the saint increasingly exists only in a physical sense. This is what a Bosnian Sufi meant when he once shared with me this traditional paradox: "Know that although true saints do not exist, God has created many of them."

Seven degrees; hence seven deaths, and seven rebirths in God. "People are asleep," the Prophet said, "and when they die, they awake." But he also commanded: "Die before you die!" The journey is arduous, as Yunus Emre sings:

> *Long is the Road, and many the stages to be reached:*
> *No easy defiles, deep the torrents to be crossed.*[9]

And yet as this poet, so popular even today in Bosnia, reminds us, there are rewards incalculable:

> *My life together with the Friend is like the sun in swirling cloud.*
> *Moments there are his Face is veiled—then see, His beauty is revealed!*[10]

In a place such as the Buna tekke, the beauty of nature is invoked as a summons to introspection. It triggers a self-awareness in the hope that we will recall our glorious origins in the divine Fountainhead. The tekke, no doubt through the unseen intercession of Sari Saltuk himself, has survived the chaos of war, and once again hosts pilgrims who wish to travel against the stream, in the hope that they too shall confront the ultimate miracle and mystery of existence. May that journey be shortened, as the Sufis say, and may it continue forever.

Notes:

1   Tone Bringa, *Being Muslim the Bosnian Way* (Princeton: Princeton University Press, 1995), pp. 221-2.

2   *The City of the Heart*, translated by Süha Faiz (Shaftesbury, England: Element, 1992), p. 17.

3   *Saltukname*, edited by S. Akalin (Ankara and Istanbul, 1988-90).

4   A. Gölpinarli, *Alevi-Bektasi nefesleri* (Istanbul: Remzi Kitabevi, 1963), p. 24.

5   Muslim, Qadr, no. 1.

6   The clearest exposition is in A. al-Shabrawi, *The Degrees of the Soul* (London: Quilliam Press, 1997).

7   *Ibid.*, p. 36.

8   Ibn Maja, Muqaddima, no. 10.

9   Faiz, p. 18.

10 *Ibid.*, p. 14.

Parabola
Volume: 25.3
The Teacher

THE SPIRITUAL GUIDE

Rumi

The Prophet said to Ali: "O Ali, thou art the Lion of God,
    thou art a valiant knight,
But do not rely upon thy courage: come into the shadow
    of the Palm-tree of hope.
Come into the shadow (protection) of the Sage whom
    none can waylay.
His shadow on the earth is like Mt. Qaf, his spirit is like
    the Simurgh that soars aloft.
Though I should sing his praises until the Resurrection,
    do not look for any end to them.
The Divine Sun has veiled Himself in Man:
    apprehend this mystery, and God knows best
    what is the truth.
O Ali, above all works of devotion in the Way is the
    shadow of God's Servant.
When others seek to save themselves by religious works,
Go thou, take refuge in the shadow of the Sage
    against the enemy within thee."
Having been accepted by the Pir, give thyself up to him:
    submit, like Moses, to the Authority of Khizr.
Whatever thy Khizr may do, bear it patiently, lest he say,
    "Begone, *here we part*" [Quran 18:78].
Though he scuttle the boat, be dumb! Though he kill a
    child, do not tear thy hair!
God hath described his hand as His own, for He saith,

"*The Hand of God is over their hands*" [48:10].
This "Hand of God" slays his disciple, then brings him to life everlasting.

Mathnawi II 2959ff. From *Rumi: Poet and Mystic*, trans. Reynold A. Nicholson (London: George Allen and Unwin Ltd., 1950).

Parabola
Volume: 25.3
The Teacher

SHAMS AL-URAFA

Translated by Seyyed Hossein Nasr

The role of the Sufi master, to whom one must make perfect surrender, and his significance in delivering the disciple from bewilderment in the world of multiplicity to contemplation in the world of Unity are well exemplified in the spiritual testament of Shams al-Urafa ("the sun of the gnostics"), one of the leading Sufi masters of Persia. Shams al-Urafa describes his meeting with his master and subsequent transformations that overcame him.

This humble *faqir*, Sayyid Husayn ibn al-Rida al-Husayni al-Tihrani al-Ni'matullahi, was blessed with the divine favor in the year 1303 [1886] when I met his gracious Highness, the model of gnostics and the pole of orientation of the travelers upon the Path, the honorable direction of prayers Shaykh Abd al-Quddus Kirmanshahi. At this time all my attention was directed to the study of formal [traditional] sciences and I possessed some knowledge of medicine, philosophy, mathematics, geometry, astronomy and astrology, jurisprudence and its principles, grammar, geography and prosody and was occupied with studying and teaching. But I had no knowledge of the problems of Sufism and the laws of spiritual poverty and gnosis and was unaware of the science of the truth and the intricacies of Divine knowledge. My attention was turned only to the problems of the formal sciences and the debates and discussions of text-books but not to inner purification, embellishment, and contemplation. I had made no endeavor on the path of purifying the soul and cleansing the inner being, thinking that the way to know the truth is none other than pursuing the formal sciences.

Thanks to Divine Grace and the aid of the Pure Imams—upon whom be peace—I met that great man on the above-mentioned date near Imam-Zada Zayd. He did with me what he did. Again within the distance of a week I was blessed with his presence near Imam-Zada Zayd.

After some conversation I expressed the wish to become initiated. On Thursday night I went to the bath at his side and received the ritual ablutions that he had ordered. After the bath he took my hand in the customary fashion and after performing the formula of repentance he instructed and initiated me to the invocation (*dhikr*) of the heart with the litanies (*awrad*), the particular initiating acts and invocations. I obeyed. After fifteen nights [the minor retreat (*khalwat-i saghir*)] near the hour of dawn, while in contemplation, I saw all the doors and walls of the dark room in which I was placed participating in the invocation with me.

I fainted and fell. After sunrise my corporeal father, because of the great love he had for me, did not stop at any measure in bringing a physician and calling those who attract the *jinn* [psychic forces] or write prayers to cure illness. My corporeal mother also did all possible in the way of administering different medicines, fumigations, and nourishments.

For twenty days I was in such a condition. I could not perform the duties laid down by the *Shari'ah*, nor was I aware of formal customs. I spoke to no one concerning this matter. After this period my condition returned somewhat to normal and I became free from the state of "attraction" (*jadhba*). I went to the bath and purified myself. I felt the desire to meet that great master and for a few days I wandered as a mad man in the streets and bazaars seeking him. Finally I succeeded in meeting him. I kissed his hand and he expressed his benevolence towards me.

To summarize: for two years I traveled upon the spiritual Path under his care and following his instructions. I turned away completely from the formal sciences and endeavored to understand questions of gnosis and march upon the Path of certainty. Whatever he ordered I obeyed without saying yes or no. If some of the things I heard or saw appeared on the surface to be opposed to the Shari'ah, I considered it a defect of my own ears and eyes and did not fail in any way to serve and obey him. In service, conversation, solitude, and retreat I obeyed as completely as I could. I also obeyed all that he had ordered as necessary in the six kinds of invocation: the manifested (*jali*), the hidden (*khafi*), the informal (*hama'ili*), the obscure (*khumuli*), that connected with the circle (*halqa*) and with the gathering (*ijtima*). I was also made to realize the four houses of death. ...

Thanks be to God, through his spiritual will and the assistance of the saints I realized all the seven states of the heart and fulfilled in the way of actions and litanies whatever was required for each station. I performed the minor, middle, and major "forty days" (*arba'inat*) [of spiritual retreat]. In the year 1309 [1892] I accompanied him to the city of faith, Qum, and there performed two consecutive major "forty days." His Highness joined the Divine Mercy [died] there and I became very ill without my intimate friend and comforter. I passed days and nights in hardship at the corner of the mosque of Imam Hasan until my poor mother discovered my condition and sent someone to Qum who for a while treated me.

After some improvement I returned to Tehran with that friend. Thank God through the spiritual will of that great gnostic I came to know of the details of spiritual poverty, gnosis, the subtleties of realized knowledge and certainty, and reached the station of annihilation in God (*fana*) and subsistence in Him (*baqa*). I traveled the seven stations of the heart each with its special characteristics. With his esoteric aid and assistance from the intermediate world (*barzakh*), whatever order I received of commands or prohibitions, cleanliness, worship, asceticism, spiritual retreat, or self-purification I performed fully and did not fall short of serving God's creatures as far as I could.

From Seyyed Hossein Nasr, *Sufi Essays* (Chicago: ABC International Group, 1991).

The Tale of the Fish

Shah Da'i Shirazi

Now once upon a time a school of fish
had met in council to discuss the tale
(familiar to all) that fish had life
and breathed and took existence from one source:
The Water. Furthermore, that *all* which lives
from Water gains its living, finds its life
in Water. Water's fame fills all the world,
and Water fills the oyster's ear with pearl,
the eyes of heavy clouds with mercy, mouth
of dust with flowing bounty. All the earth
has pledged its soul as mortgage to this source,
this element which with one drop renews
the world—which with such light abounds, it seems
that Heaven's very eye is fixed upon it.
Man (so says the tale) appeared from but
a single drop of it, and from it sprang
the vasty ocean of all heart and soul.

The school of fish were puzzled by all this,
and thus began to argue what it meant:
one of them said, "Beware! What right have we
to sully with our words the bright-faced one,
His Majesty the Water?" Then a fish
(more optimistic) spoke and said, "But wait!
Such disappointment must be a mistake,

for what if the whole tale were true, what then?"
"There must be proof!" a third demanded, "for
without some hard facts, who knows what is true?"
A fourth burst out: "Ah! Now I see it all!
All is unveiled through intuition, for
on such a Path, mere thought has far less chance!"
"That would be fine, my friend," the fifth
fish said, "if everyone possessed, like you,
the eye of intuition; but in truth,
they simply don't—and there's an end to that."
"The Inner State! That's the real thing, not words,"
another shouted. "Only Water pure
will satisfy the thirsty ones."
"No, wait."
then spoke another delegate. "I think
that only Love can guide us now, and if
you do not have His Love, give up and call
the conference off." Thus spoke the fish, and thus
they wrangled, flinging forth opinions till
the sea grew warm with all their hot debate,
when from the circle of contention, one
of the companions stepped, and cleared his throat.
"I am the humblest and most ignorant
of fish, yet hear me, and if what I say
meets with approval, then abide by it
and put an end to strife"; thus was his speech.
"I know that in a distant quarter of
our sea, there lives an ancient fish, who more
than any here possesses wisdom. Truth,
sagacity. On all horizons of
our sea, in science there is none like him,
but listen: all his knowledge and degree
of wisdom does not spring from written page
or dusty book, for in his school (they say)
such seas of ink are but a vagrant stream,
and knowledge such as he possesses, from
the inmost level of the heart springs forth.

In deepest trenches of our unplumbed sea
he roams, and shuns the shallows and the shores.
Come, let us to him with our questions swim,
let all the drops return unto their source.
Perhaps our puzzle will be solved by him
and thereby all our hearts gain rest at last."
This sound advice at once infused the fish
with new enthusiasm, and as one
they clamored their acclaim and new-found hope
that promised a solution to their quest.
So, one by one they swam, set out towards him;
anxiety suffused their ears with blood,
their eyes with tears, their journey with dispatch.
Boundless hardship plagued their path—success
came only after infinite distress.
But finally they found the ancient one
who of all fish in that age was the Pole,
and to his august presence bowed themselves
in deep humility and courtesy
as well they might. Their spokesman rose and said,
"O Shaikh, O thou who sought and found
the secrets of the universe, now peer
into our hearts, for God's sake, hear our plea.
We have been told that Water is the source
and origin of all, the ferment of
all union and all separation; but
how strange this seems to us, how hard to grasp,
since we have never seen this Water, not
a one of us, not once in all our lives!
Towards thee we have been swimming day and night
yet from this ocean of perplexity
have found no exit. Not a trace of Him,
this fabled Water, not a single drop
before our eyes has fallen—and obsessed
by questing, tossed in raging floods of doubt
and torrents of dismay, we come to thee
as our last hope. Now could it be that thou,

for love of God and in thy grace, might feel
some pity for our plight, illuminate
the darkened minds of fish and demonstrate
this Water to us like a noble sun
in such a way that clouds might never veil
its face nor hide its brilliance from our sight."

The ancient fish was silent. On his breast
he sank the chin of meditation, till
at last from his communion with the world
of the Unseen, he raised his countenance
and spoke. "Ah, fish! If you could bring to me
from all existence one thing, and one thing
alone that is *not* Water, then I might
reveal to you the Essence which you seek.
But mark this well, that there is naught but He!
This endless ocean which surrounds us, that
is He, and so are we. We each came forth
from Water, and unto the Water shall
return." Upon the fishes' minds these words
worked miracles. Their hearts and eyes became
a veritable sea of lights. They cried
"So He it is who all this while hath sought
Himself: and He and I and we and thou
are but a pretext, subterfuge and trick!
Our doubts and questions rose from this one fact,
that Water's veil is Water—nothing more.
Thank God our troubling doubts are put to flight,
imagination and warped fantasies
dispelled at last and laid to rest. Now we
have learned that all our voyaging is but
an inward voyage, and in all our sea
none swim beside us. All, all, all is He!"

MORAL
The less, the more—the good, the bad—the sweet
and bitter: If we wish to pry within

the secrets of a thing, we must perforce
have recourse to its opposite, its twin.
But know that our Creation's eyes are blind
because HE has no opposite, no like,
comparison nor similitude; and in
His Essence, all such opposites are one.
How faint, how small our knowledge of this truth,
for knowledge is distinction, nor can we
distinguish aught except between two things.
The portals of Distinction have been closed
by Unity, and if you should attain
to gnosis in the One, then recognize
that though He be possessed of attributes,
His Essence is but one—"Say: He is One!"

Translated by Nasrollah Pourjavady and Peter Lamborn Wilson, *Studies in Comparative Religion*, Volume 10 (1976), pp. 102-05.

Parabola
Volume: 30.1
Awakening

SLUMBER SEIZES HIM NOT

William C. Chittick

A self-evident truth, a meditative technique, and a spiritual practice are at once embodied in a statement upon which the Islamic perspective is founded. This statement is the first of the two Shahadahs or testimonies of faith, the words "No god but God." The Quran tells us that it is the message of all the prophets, who are traditionally said to number 124,000, from Adam himself down to Muhammad.

To say that the first Shahadah is a self-evident truth may sound odd to those outside the tradition. As soon as we translate it into non-theistic language, however, it turns out to be something of a truism. It simply means that there is no reality but that which is truly real. Or, there is nothing real but the real. To understand how this apparently bland statement animates a major tradition, we need to consider its implications.

The first Shahadah is called *kalimat at-tawhid*, that is, "the sentence that asserts (God's) unity." This "assertion of unity" is typically taken as the first principle of Islamic faith, the second and third being "prophecy" and "the return to God" (or "eschatology"). In contrast to the second and third principles, unity stands outside history. It was not established by the Islamic revelation, nor does it depend in any way on the human situation.

It simply expresses the way things are, irrespective of human observers—or so it has always appeared within the tradition.

The Quran considers unity a universal truth, voiced in every prophetic message: "We never sent a messenger before thee except that We revealed to him, 'There is no god but I.'" The verse goes on to state the implication of unity, also voiced in every prophetic message: "So serve Me" (21:25). In other words, the awakening granted to prophets and sages conveys to them the certainty that the Supreme Selfhood is one and that all reality is subservient to it. The conclusion to be drawn is that people should acknowledge their subservience by acting appropriately, that is, by "service" (or "worship," *ibada*). Each messenger, however, establishes a distinct viewpoint and a unique form of service: "To each of you [messengers], We have given a law and a way" (5:48).

The first Shahadah provides Muslims with their primary technique of meditation. Islamic theology in all its varieties—including the Sufi and philosophical versions—describes reality in terms of the divine names. The Quran tells us that God possesses "the most beautiful names," and it cites as examples a great variety of ordinary words, such as alive, knowing, desiring, powerful, merciful, just, and forgiving. Traditionally these are said to number ninety-nine, though the actual lists established by theologians often mention fewer or more.

As a meditative technique, the Shahadah allows people to unpack the meaning of that most elusive of words, "God" (Allah). It asserts the unity of God by illustrating that all divine names and attributes, all real qualities on any level of reality, find their full and true meaning only in the One. To say that God is "knowing" means that there is none knowing but God. True knowledge belongs to God alone, not to anything in the created realm. So also with other divine attributes: There is none alive but God, none desiring but God, none powerful but God, none merciful but God. All attributes designated by the divine names belong to God in truth and are ascribed to created things in a conventional, not a true, sense.

If meditation on the first Shahadah were to stop here, we would be left with a transcendent, inaccessible God and a cosmos bereft of reality. But the Quran and the tradition also affirm the complementary perspective, that of God's immanence and omnipresence. The creatures manifest God's *ayat* or "signs"—a constant Quranic theme. These appear in four basic domains: the natural world, the human self, the activities of the prophets (e.g., their "miracles"), and scripture (ayat is precisely the word used for the "verses" of the Quran). The Book makes no distinction between natural and supernatural signs.

Whatever appears in creation signifies the divine Reality that gave it existence. Life, power, desire, and all other positive qualities lead back to their source in God. It is precisely through the qualities, attributes, and characteristics of created things that God discloses the reality of his infinite and absolute Self. "Wherever you turn, there is the face of God" (2:115). "Everything has its treasuries only with Us, and We send it down only in a known measure" (15:21).

Among the many Quranic names of God, one became current in Islamic languages as a virtual synonym for Allah itself, and that is *al-haqq*. Translators usually render this name as "the Truth," but it also means real, right, appropriate, just, and worthy (along with the corresponding nouns). It signifies, in other words, that there is nothing true, real, right, just, and worthy but God. The more we stress this point, the more we assert God's transcendence.

The Quran uses the word *haqq* about 250 times, but only a few of these instances designate God per se. It also uses the word to describe the appearance of the signs in various domains. Thus it makes haqq an attribute of the Quran and other scriptures. It says that God creates everything in the heavens and the earth "only with the haqq." In other words, all revelation and all things and acts in the universe accord with truth, reality, rightness, justice, and appropriateness. Everything is serving the purposes of God. As the Quran puts it, "There is nothing in the heavens and the earth that does not come to the All-Merciful as a servant" (19:93).

Human beings, however, prove to be a partial exception to the rule of universal servanthood. If not, there would be no need for the command-ment "serve God" in the prophetic messages. Humans (along with the *jinn*, who include Satan) have the option of rebelling against the Real, the Right, the True, and the Appropriate (even if, from another standpoint, this rebellion is itself a worthy sign of the Real's love for his creatures).

Human exceptionalism is observed plainly in the signs: "Have you not seen how to God prostrate themselves all who are in the heavens and all who are in the earth—the sun and the moon, the stars and the mountains, the trees and the beasts, and many of the people?" (22:18). "Many of the people," in other words, acknowledge the Right, the True, and the Worthy and act appropriately, but many do not.

In this way of looking at things, "submission" (*islam*) is a fact of existence. All things are "Muslims"—submitted to the Real—because "There is no god but God," no other means through which to partake of reality. "To Him is submitted whosoever is in the heavens and the earth, willingly or unwillingly" (3:83). The prophets and their followers acknowledge this universal submission and then add to it a particular submission. Knowing that they are submitted like plants and animals, sun and moon, they also freely choose to conform themselves to the Real. They do so by following specific sorts of service designated by revelation. The role of the prophets in human affairs is thus to lead the way to the Real, the Right, and the True.

If the word haqq means "right" in the sense of proper and correct, it also means it in the sense of what is rightfully due to someone or something, and hence it is employed in modern-day discussions of human rights. Muhammad had this meaning of the word in view when he said, "Your soul has a right against you, your Lord has a right against you, your guest has a right against you, and your spouse has a right against you, so give to each that has a right its right." But to say that someone has a "right against you" means that you have a responsibility toward that someone. In the pre-modern context of Islamic languages, it was impossible to disengage rights from responsibilities.

In short, the Quran and the tradition employ the word haqq in a variety of ways illustrating both the transcendence and the immanence of the Real. Meditating upon haqq in the context of tawhid allows people to understand that God alone truly possesses reality and rightness, that he parcels it out to creation, and that human beings have been given the freedom to accept it or reject it.

Human exceptialism has everything to do with the fact that Adam was created in the image of the Real and taught "all the names" (2:31). That he understood what he was taught and lived up to his responsibilities as "vicegerent" of God (2:30) is indicated by his being appointed prophet. His children, however, typically live in forgetfulness and heedlessness. Islam has no concept of original sin, but the Quran does say that Adam "forgot" (20:115), though he then repented and was forgiven. Even so, "Human beings were created weak" (4:28), and the frailty of forgetfulness appears in them as a matter of course. Surrendering to it is sufficient cause for downfall. "Those who stay heedless of Our signs—their refuge is hell" (10:7).

The remedy for forgetfulness is *dhikr*, a word that means to remember, mention, and remind. The Quran employs it as a designation for itself and other prophetic messages, all of which mention the Real and remind people of God's rights and their own responsibilities. On the human side, remembrance of God and mention of his names are the proper response to the signs: "He clarifies the signs for the people—perhaps they will remember" (2:221).

Scholars of Sufism often translate the word dhikr as "invocation." Invoking God—that is, remembering him and mentioning his name—is in fact the main duty that Sufism adds to the responsibilities explicitly set down by the revealed law. The act of remembrance transforms the Shahadah from a meditation into a spiritual practice. Any perusal of the Sufi manuals will show that the first Shahadah has been the most common invocation prescribed for disciples. The only rival is the name Allah itself, whose meaning the Shahadah explains.

In remembering God, the goal is to recognize the Real in both his transcendence and immanence and to be constantly mindful of the rights and responsibilities placed upon Adam's children by the manifestation of signs in the universe, society, and the soul. Worthy remembrance demands living in the world rightly and appropriately. In other words, the goal is to wake up fully to the way things are and to live in a constant state of wakefulness and mindfulness.

Given the meditative significance of the Shahadah, all those who strive for wakefulness know from the outset that "There is none awake but God." The Quran does not include "awake" among the divine names, but it does express the idea without ambiguity. The famous "Throne Verse," which is inscribed in the domes of myriad mosques, begins with the words, "God, there is no god but He, the Alive, the Ever-standing. Slumber seizes Him not, nor sleep …" (2:255).

Slumber and sleep are attributes of those who were created weak. Creatures who live and stand up also lie down, sleep, and die. God, in contrast, is "the Alive who does not die" (25:58), the Ever-standing who does not sit, and the Awake who never sleeps.

On the human side, waking up, like every other ascent in the direction of the Real, amounts to "assuming the character traits of God." This phrase, much discussed by theologians like *Al-Ghazali*, designates the process of actualizing the divine image latent in the human substance. In the same sort of context, Muslim philosophers often prefer the word "deiformity" (*ta'alluh*, derived from the same root as Allah). In both cases, the goal of human existence is understood to be conformity with the Real, for the Real alone is good, the Real alone is wise, and the Real alone is awake.

What then is awakening? It is to become aware of the Real, the True, the Right, and the Worthy. It is to act appropriately and worthily by giving all that have rights their right and by accepting one's responsibilities before God and creation. It is to affirm the unity of the Real with such incessant meditation and invocation that the Real totally dominates awareness. It is to see the face of the Real wherever we turn. It is to recognize in every fiber of our being that we are always and forever servants of the Real.

Everyone familiar with the teachings of Sufism knows that love frequently plays a central role in the process of bringing about conformity with the Real. The goal of lovers is to embrace their beloved. The more lovers grow in love for God, the more they embrace him by assuming his attributes and character traits, and the more difficult they find it to disentangle themselves from him.

The Sufi knows that he loves no one but God, even when he loves others, because there is no beloved but God. The Real alone is the source of beauty, good, and everything lovable. Whatsoever we love can be nothing but his sign, his face, his self-disclosure. Worthy love involves recognizing that we love only the Real.

The Prophet said, "God is beautiful, and He loves beauty." To say that God is beautiful means that no one is truly beautiful but God, and to say that God loves beauty means that no one truly loves beauty but God. If it is true that we love only the Real, it is even more true that the Real alone does the loving. As the Sufis put it, "None loves God but God."

The Real alone is true beloved and true lover, and all love is nothing but his love. Human uniqueness comes down to being able to make this discernment and to live one's life appropriately. The possibility of waking up to love explains why humans alone are true lovers of God and true objects of his love. As the Quran implies, however, his love precedes their love. "He loves them and they love Him" (3:119).

Rumi constantly sings of love's power to erase the distinction between lover and beloved. He points out that love is simply another name for the energizing force expressed by the first Shahadah:

> Love is that flame which, when it
>   blazes up,
> burns away everything except the
>   Everlasting Beloved.
> It strikes home the sword of "no god"
>   and slays everything other than
>   the Real.
> Look sharp—after "no god," what
>   remains?
> There remains "but God," all the rest
>   has gone.
> Bravo, O great, idol-burning Love!
> —Mathnawi 5: 588–90

One of the more important scriptural sources for the Sufi under-standing of love is the famous "hadith of voluntary works," an authentic saying of the Prophet that puts the following words into the mouth of God: "My servant never ceases approaching Me through voluntary works until I love him. Then, when I love him, I am the hearing through which he hears, the eyesight through which he sees, the hand through which he grasps, and the feet through which he walks." The more the servant assumes the character traits of God, the more beautiful and God-like he becomes, and the more the distinction between lover and beloved fades away.

Ibn Arabi, the greatest master of Sufism's theoretical teachings, cites the hadith of voluntary works more often than any other saying of the Prophet. On occasion he stresses the fact that the verb "I am" (*kuntu*) in the saying means literally "I was." In other words, God was the hearing and sight of the lovers before they ever came to know it. He also points out that this "was" has nothing to do with time, for temporality does not touch the Eternal. The Real is always and forever the lovers' hearing and sight, their hands and feet and, says Ibn Arabi, "Everyone in existence is a lover." It is we who need to wake up to the fact of love, not God.

The Real is the Awake who never sleeps, the Living who never dies. We are asleep, and we wake up by dying to forgetfulness and heedlessness. This is one of the meanings of Ali's famous maxim (often attributed to the Prophet), "People are asleep, and when they die, they wake up."

But to say that we wake up is not quite accurate. Rather, through the mystery of love, we somehow become aware that even now we sleep. Even now, the Real's wakefulness is all that there is. There is no lover but the Real, there is no beloved but the Real, and there is nothing real but the Real. No one hears but the Real, no one sees but the Real, and no one is awake but the Real.

CHAPTER SEVEN

•

THE WINE OF LOVE

I peered
    into the mirror
        of my beloved
gave witness as myself
    about the self
        to my self.
I looked closer:
    was there someone
        reflected
in my eye?
    I was alone.
        I saw myself in me.[1]

—Awhaduddin Kirmani

O lovers, O lovers, it is time to abandon the world;
The drum of departure reaches my spiritual ear from heaven.
Behold, the driver has risen and made ready the file of camels,
    And begged us to acquit him of blame:
why, O travelers, are you asleep? These sounds before and
behind are the din of departure and of the camel-bells;
With each moment a soul and a spirit is setting off into the Void. From these
    stars like inverted candles,
    from these blue awnings of the sky
There has come forth a wondrous people,
    that the mysteries may be revealed.
A heavy slumber fell upon thee from the circling spheres:
Alas for this life so light, beware of this slumber so heavy!
O soul, seek the Beloved, O friend, seek the Friend,

O watchman, be wakeful: it behoves not a watchman to sleep.
On every side is clamor and tumult, in every street are torches and candles,
For tonight the teeming world gives birth to the world everlasting.
Thou wert dust and art a spirit,
thou wert ignorant and art wise.[2]

—Rumi

Parabola
Volume: 3.2
Sacrifice and
Transformation

DIE AND BECOME

Sacrifice in the Poems of Rumi

Annemarie Schimmel

In East and West, Rumi has been acknowledged as the most influential figure in the development of Islamic thought and expression. His didactic poem, the *Mathnawi*, with its approximately 26,000 verses, was declared by his admirers as "the Quran in the Persian tongue," and is a storehouse of mystical ideas as they had developed up to the mid-thirteenth century. But even more fascinating for the modern reader are the more than 36,000 verses of lyrical poetry which were born out of his meeting with Shams-i Tabrizi, a wandering dervish of great spiritual power who kindled in him the fire of Divine Love.

Rumi is the poet whose vocabulary is more varied than any other writer in the Persian language. He used the language of the common people with as much skill as that of the mystics and theologians. The rich imagery of his verse reveals new meanings every time we return to it—what first seem to be very down-to-earth descriptions of daily life may suddenly change into touching love lyrics; rather crude remarks may lead to enraptured mystical sighs.

The diversity of Rumi's imagery and the vast range of his poetical work seems strangely diffuse to a Western reader and makes it difficult to give a full account of his main ideas. His own compatriots and later mystics in

Turkey, Iran, and the Indo-Pakistani subcontinent attempted to interpret his thought in the categories of *wahdat al-wujud*, "Oneness of Being," as developed by Rumi's contemporary, the Spanish-born Ibn Arabi. Dwelling upon the infrequent theoretical remarks found in the *Mathnawi*, they neglected the free flight of love in the earlier lyrics, which, after all, defies systemization. But Rumi was anything but a philosopher; in fact, his words about the "shabby little philosopher" do not lack spice. Yet one of his passages in the *Mathnawi* that has attracted the interest of Oriental and Western scholars alike is the famous sequence:

I died as mineral and I became a plant ...

in which Rumi describes the upward movement of everything created. Parallel verses in the third and fourth book of the *Mathnawi* seem to point to a more or less "automatic" upward movement that permeates creation. However, it seems to me that in the context of Rumi's work these passages can be interpreted differently, even if we take for granted that he, like his predecessors Sana'i and Attar, in fact believed in this steady upward movement and saw in it a hint of God's miraculous powers. After creating everything out of nothing, He can bring those who are like animals from an ordinary stable into His private pen and then give them higher and higher rank, as He promised in the Quran.

One of the passages which is often quoted to support the notion that Rumi's world view is mechanistic is the story of the chickpeas, which, put in a kettle of boiling water, complain of their sad fate. But the housewife tells them that they should behave like Isaac, who was ready to be sacrificed by his father; for only by sacrifice would they acquire a higher status. And he introduces into the rather amusing story a verse from the Divan of Hallaj, the "martyr of love" in Islamic mysticism:

Kill me, O my trustworthy friends, for in my being killed there is my life. ...

This line shows the context in which the chickpea story should be read, as well as related passages concerning growing and rising.

Rumi loved imagery from the kitchen, and it is small wonder that concepts like "raw" and "cooked" abound in his descriptions of life (Levi-

Strauss would be delighted!). Being a faithful follower of earlier ascetic ideas, Rumi knew of the necessity of breaking for the sake of rebuilding. Did not the Prophet say, according to mystical tradition, "Die before ye die"? The first step on the Path and the foundation of spiritual life in general is to break the *nafs*, the lower soul, or the base instincts, which are often compared to a restive horse, a donkey, or a disobedient wife—once they are broken they can be transformed into a useful instrument. As the Prophet said, "My *shaytan* (my lower self) has become a Muslim."

Likewise the hard shell of the walnut has to be broken in order to free the sweet kernel which, in turn, must be crushed to release the fragrant oil which is the innermost heart of the nut. Only when man has died to his lower qualities will he be able to develop higher and nobler ones; only when the tree sheds its leaves in the fall and suffers patiently the hardships of winter will God grant him paradisiacal green garments in the spring.

Rumi sees that everything follows the rule that sacrifice is necessary to reach a higher goal: the field has to be ploughed, be torn mercilessly so that it can receive the seed; the seed grows and is harvested and the grains are crushed under the millstone; the flour, then, has to endure the process of baking in order to become bread, which will be crushed again by man's teeth. But by this constant succession of sacrifices the grain will finally become part and parcel of human nature and will thus participate to a certain extent in the human soul and spirit. Thus it can eventually reach the angelic state or even complete "annihilation" in God. Or, to take another favorite image of Rumi: the house has to be destroyed so that man can find the treasure which, according to oriental folklore, is always buried under ruins. This comparison is all the more fitting as according to an extra-Quranic revelation God said: "I was a hidden treasure and wanted to be known; therefore I created the world." The whole world was created in order to worship God and to pay homage to His glory; but it can never encompass Him. There is only one place where He can be found, according to another extra-Quranic word: "I am with the hearts of My servants which are broken for My sake." The house of the heart, crushed and broken under the constant strokes of affliction, becomes finally the place under which the treasure "God" can be found; and would not such a treasure be a hundred times more valuable than all the houses in the world?

The prerequisite of this wonderful discovery is that the heart should accept the blows of suffering gladly and with gratitude. For it is not asceticism in itself or suffering for suffering's sake that leads man to the finding of the "hidden treasure" in himself; it is love that makes him capable of bearing afflictions gratefully:

> *Love makes dead bread into soul,*
> *Love makes the mortal soul immortal.*

Since love requires sacrifice and rewards man only later, it is often depicted by Rumi as cruel: for instance, as a ragman who carries away everything that is old in order to clean up the place; or as a judge who claims the payment of heavy taxes; as a dragon who wants to eat man; as a crocodile or as a black lion. Man is called to make himself a sweet morsel before this wild beast; he has to be well cooked and sweet so that the animal Love can devour him, while it will refuse to eat the raw. That is why the dragon Love particularly relishes the saints who have become soft and sweet under the blows of affliction. As for the lover, his only goal is indeed to become one with the object of his love; he wants to give up his self, his soul, everything. Who does not know Rumi's story of the lover who knocked at the beloved's door and was sent away, because he said, "I am here"? It was only on his return, after maturing for a year in the flames of separation, when he answered the question "Who is it?" by saying "It is you, beloved!" that he was then admitted. He had sacrificed his "I" in order that the beloved might be all. For who else but the Divine Beloved has the right to say "I"? Indeed, it is easily possible to see every act in life as a sacrifice. Rumi often uses the imagery of the Feast of Sacrifice during the pilgrimage to Mecca, and offers himself to the beloved as a fat and handsome sacrificial lamb; and though he has not used a pun which is found in an eighteenth-century Sindhi mystical poem, he would have liked it: there, the heroine wants to become a *qurban*, "sacrifice" in order to be *qaribani*, "near." That is exactly what Rumi felt. He expresses it in a symbol that was widely used by the mystics of Islam: the first word of the profession of faith, *la* (*ilah*), "There is no deity," lends itself in its calligraphic form to interpretation as a two-edged sword. The mystics would require that man should take this "sword of la" and slay with it everything that is not his divine beloved. Then, by adding the "letter of

Divinity," *alif*, to the la, they would reach the second, positive half of the profession of faith, *illa Allah*, "except God": By slaying everything that is not Him they would attain to the true existential experience of the Divine Unity, their own selves having been sacrificed on the journey to God. In the same way Rumi interprets also the ritual prayer. He tells a wonderful story of the mystic Daquqi who went out to lead the congregational prayer; when he spoke the introductory formula, *Allahu akbar*, "God is greater (than everything)," it was as if everyone fell as a sacrifice before God, because this formula is also used at the ritual slaughtering of an animal. And is not prayer an act in which man conforms to the Divine Will and gives up his own?

Persian poetry abounds in images and symbols for the necessity of sacrificing everything on the way toward the beloved, and has never ceased stressing the importance of suffering on the path that leads toward perfection. The classical symbol of this view is that of the moth and the candle, which was used for the first time in its mystical connotation in a work by Hallaj, the *Kitab at-tawasin*. He describes the moth's circling around the candle, its drawing near and its ecstatic death in the flame, which means its union with the Reality of Realities whence no one returns to give news about his journey. The moth and candle symbolism became most popular among the Persian, Turkish, and Indo-Muslim mystics, and reached Europe in the late eighteenth century to form, in Goethe's *West-Oestlicher Divan*, the foundation of his poem *Selige Sehnsucht* that speaks of the *Stirb und Werde*, "die and become." Here we are again close to Rumi's view which he expressed in his lines about the constant upward movement of everything created. What he intends is not a soulless development; rather, he believes that the power which makes itself felt in this movement is God's love.

It was once more Hallaj who formulated for the first time the meaning of *ishq*, "dynamic love," as the innermost essence of God, of that God who was a hidden treasure and wanted to be known. It is this dynamic love that uplifts everything to higher stages, provided that the object obeys the law of love, which means to be ready to die at the word of the beloved, to "die before dying," and to be revived, then, on a higher level. Did not God reveal to someone who asked Him about Hallaj's fate: "I am the blood money for those whom My beauty has killed"? The greater the sacrifice, the higher the reward—and death as a martyr of love entails the highest possible reward, that of the blessed vision of God. On the lower levels of existence this sacrifice may still be unknown and unfelt, but it operates nevertheless—whether by the melting of snow under the warm rays of the sun to become water and nourish the earth, or whether by the hard rock's crumbling to become soft dust so that flowers can grow out of it; whether plants are eaten by animals, or animals by man. Nothing returns to its former state:

No mirror becomes iron again, no ripe grape becomes sour again …

The changes may be hidden, yet they take place and justify the movement of the world. But it is only man, endowed with the gift of free will and able to recognize and respond to the dynamic Divine love, who is able to rejoice in tribulation and to sacrifice everything gladly, even his life, for the sake of the Divine Beloved—by whichever name this Beloved may have been called in the course of human history.

Parabola
Volume: 23.2
Ecstacy

"I Will Make Myself Mad"

Kabir Helminski

I have tried caution and forethought;
from now on I will make myself mad.
　　　　　　—Rumi

What is the place of ecstasy in a mature spirituality? Are there different states to be discerned beyond that over-arching label? Can it be reconciled with sobriety? Should ecstasy be pursued?

The poetry of Rumi and other Sufis often exudes a fragrance of ecstasy that has attracted generations of seekers. While this fragrance has spread far beyond the boundaries of its original homelands, its source is not merely cultural, historical, or geographic. The source of this ecstatic state is experiential, spiritual, ontological. The fragrance of ecstasy reminds some people of *home*. In the words of Rumi, one of the greatest saints and mystical poets of all time:

The Drunkards and the Tavern

> *I'm drunk and you're insane.*
> *Who's going to lead us home?*
> *How many times did they say,*
> *"Drink just a little, only two or three at most?"*

In this city no one I see is conscious;
one is worse off than the next, frenzied and insane.

Dear one, come to the Tavern of Ruin
and experience the pleasures of the soul.
What happiness can there be apart

from this intimate conversation
with the Beloved, the Soul of souls?

In every corner there are drunkards, arm in arm,
while the Server pours the wine
from a royal decanter to every particle of being.

You belong to the tavern: your income is wine,
and wine is all you ever buy.
Don't give even a second away
to the concerns of the merely sober.

Have I lived among the lame for so long
that I've begun to limp myself?

What is this drunkenness? What kind of sainthood is this? What is the role of ecstasy in Sufi spirituality, and what could these words mean in our own contemporary culture?

Rumi's time was no less complex than our own. In his world there was neither peace, nor security, nor a monolithic belief system. Within the Islamic society of his time, diverse ways of seeing the world naturally flourished. Conventional religious piety, legalistic rigidity, cultic heterodoxy, philosophical cynicism, and what I will call orthodox Sufi mysticism breathed the same air.

Before our own cultural assumptions project Rumi as a spiritual renegade who stood outside all beliefs, it is worth noting that Sufis like Rumi never relinquished their claim to represent the heart and soul of Islam. Both Rumi and his teacher, Shams-i Tabrizi, walked in the footsteps of Muhammad, and said so clearly. When they were irreverent, it was against rigidity and hypocrisy. Yet within the essential boundaries of Divine Law, they found an approach to Truth by the ecstasy of Love.

We live in a time of practically institutionalized nonconformity, an unprecedented era of personal freedom and unrepression. We live in a time when ecstatic experience is compulsively sought. Ecstasy suggests being outside of one's ordinary state, overcome with rapture. Today the flight from self-existence, from the burden of egoistic preoccupations, strategies, and ambitions is accomplished through sensuality, intoxication, and mass entertainment.

Rumi's call to drunkenness should not be confused with these dissolute or superficial intoxications. Ecstasy, like any precious commodity, will have its imitations and counterfeits. The authentic ecstasy of the Sufi is not based in emotionalism. Ecstasy is not a feeling to be pursued; rather, it is the freedom from all self-seeking pursuits. It is madness in the sense that it opposes one's apparent self-interest. The *nafs*, the ego-self, is viewed as something to be opposed rather than accommodated.

> *The nafs is a sea of calm deception until it roars.*
> *The nafs is a Hell that radiates little heat.*
> *The nafs is an ankle-deep river you drown in.*
> *Better to be ignorant of worldly concerns,*
> *better to be mad and to flee from self-interest,*
> *better to drink poison and spill the water of life,*
> *better to revile those who praise you*
> *and lend both the capital and the interest to the poor,*
> *forgo safety and make a home in danger.*
> *Sacrifice your reputation and become notorious.*
> *I have tried caution and forethought;*
> *from now on I will make myself mad.*
> —*Rumi,* Mathnawi *II 2290-91, 2305, 2328-32*

The key to the drunkenness advocated by Rumi and other Sufis lies in understanding the educational and transformational process of Sufism. "The Tavern of Ruin" is the Sufi *dergah* in which this education is carried out. In the ideal of the dergah, seekers came to lose the passions of the self and to experience the ecstasy of selflessness. This education was in every respect a dismantling of the false self.

I am not aware of any book, or even chapter, in all of classical Sufi literature that specifically addresses the subject of ecstasy, although there are many terms in the Sufi "glossary" that relate to the subject of extraordinary spiritual experience. The Sufi technical term closest to ecstasy, *wajd*, is derived from a root meaning "to find." The great formulator of Sufism, Ibn Arabi, defined it as "a state formerly hidden from the heart that now confronts its perception."[1] The experience of ecstasy is the discovery (wajd) of true being (*wujud*). In this discovery the seeker is lifted to a transpersonal state of consciousness in which individual existence is seen for what it is: a provisional being, an existence dependent upon another order of Reality.

> *O you whose selflessness and intoxication are Our Self.*
> *O you whose existence derives constantly from Ours.*
> *Now I will tell you without speech and with constant renewal*
> *The ancient mysteries: Listen!*
> —Mathnawi III 4682-84

It is also worth mentioning that there is a term, *tawajud*, which signifies pretending ecstasy, or attempting to summon ecstasy without ecstasy itself.

The everyday training of the Sufi was framed by the boundaries of Divine Law and the model of Muhammad's behavior (*sunna*): ritual prayer, fasting, remembrance, the development of virtues (*akhlaq*). Within the Mevlevi tradition, community service, the study of sacred literature, and the cultivation of the arts (calligraphy, design, music, poetry, Quranic recitation) completed the curriculum. The culmination of all these practices might be the *sama*, a weekly event in which chanting, sacred music, mystical poetry, and various movements might lift the heart to a true spiritual ecstasy.

Within the later Sufi tradition, sama was routinely forbidden to those who were dominated by their worldly selves, because the music and movements were likely to magnify whatever qualities predominated in the soul. On the other hand, Rumi and his companions would sometimes spontaneously engage in samas lasting for days.

Such activities were radical behavior in the context of the religious orthodoxy, in which the mixing of music and spirituality was suspect.

Because the original impulse and inspiration of Islam was meant to offer human beings a purified spirituality, it is understandable that there would be some resistance to the employment of secondary means of achieving interiority. This had the advantage of fostering a religious culture relatively free of poor taste, mawkish art, and spiritual materialism. Within the sacred context, visual art became abstract design, and musical expression was channeled into Quranic recitation. Music and representational art were generally discouraged as a *means* to spiritual experience.

Nevertheless, among the mystics, the positive effects of Sama and ecstatic experience were recognized.

> *The effects of Sama can be very different, depending on one's degree of spiritual realization. For the penitent, Sama brings remorse. For those longing for God, it increases their yearning. For the believers, it strengthens their certainty. For the disciple, it verifies what has been taught. For the lover, it helps to cut off attachments. And for the selfless Sufi, it is the basis of his loss of faith and trust in the world, enabling him to give up everything including himself.[2]*

Music, whirling, chanting, and spontaneous poetry were the expression of the state of spiritual love in those early days, but gradually these practices were formalized and ritualized, becoming a means toward the state of spiritual love, rather than the spontaneous expression of it.

Because many human beings could not grasp the mysteries and pleasures of selfless ecstatic experience, the work of mystics and ecstatics was often guarded and protected from the intrusion and meddling of those whom the Sufis call "raw."

> *Listen to the words of Sana'i from behind the veil:*
> *"Rest your head where you have drunk the wine!"*
> *Any drunk who strays from the tavern*
> *becomes the fool and the laughingstock of children.*
> *He stumbles in the mud at the sides of the road*
> *and every fool laughs at him.*
> *He continues on his way, the children following behind,*
> *ignorant of his drunkenness and the taste of wine.*
> *All of mankind are children,*

except for those who are drunk with God.
No one is mature who is not free of self-will.
—Mathnawi *I 4326-30*

To misunderstand or exaggerate the place of ecstasy in Sufism is to diminish and distort the wholeness and balance that characterizes the Path. I once heard Sufism defined by an outsider as "a body of techniques for producing ecstasy," but ecstasy is not the goal, even if it sometimes is a byproduct.

There is a creative tension in Sufism between enlightenment and maturity. By enlightenment we mean those higher states of consciousness that bring light and life into the soul. By maturity we mean that overall development of character and virtue, including the ability to express oneself and participate effectively in the life around us. The ultimate expression of maturity is "servanthood," not in the menial sense but in the way of dauntless friendship and generosity. And yet the servant assumes a kind of "ordinariness," an invisibility within society.

In the whirling ritual of the Mevlevi, or "whirling dervishes," there are symbolic actions which suggest a balance of ecstasy and the containment of ecstasy. The ceremony is punctuated by "stops," in which the participants come to stillness, hands upon their shoulders, forming the letter *alif*, the number one. Instead of pursuing ecstasy, they are called back from the brink of ecstasy to testify to the oneness of God. The dervish recalls his or her "nonexistence." God is everything; the ultimate state for the human being is conscious servanthood, which continually recalls the Being of God as the Source of everything. It is utter humility and abandonment of self. Near the end of the ceremony the *shaikh* turns slowly and majestically in the center of the floor, his right hand holding open his robes just slightly. This gesture is a reminder of the early days when people uncontrollably tore their robes in a state of abandonment.

While it is true that many who are attracted to the path of Sufism are ecstatics by nature, just as many are sober and practical. Rumi's teacher, Shams-i Tabrizi, said of his own teacher, Shaikh Salabaf, that he attained intoxication but never reached sobriety! Within the tradition it is no secret that spiritual maturity is a state of sobriety that encompasses intoxication.

There have always been and will always be a percentage of the mystically inclined who may be somewhat dissolute. Faced with the hypocrisies of conventional social life and the traumas of periodically arising social disruption and mass insanity, it isn't surprising that more sensitive souls would turn to transcendence in whatever form might be available. It is no less true today. And yet the widespread misinformation, especially in contemporary Islamic societies, that Sufis are irresponsible, indulgent, or dissolute belies the facts: In the history of Islamic cultures, a majority of the most creative and accomplished minds and the most sanctified souls have been affiliated with Sufi orders, and founders of them.

In the higher forms of Sufism there is a fastidious purification of experience from all subjective, personal concerns. Shams of Tabriz commented regarding those who might be inclined to pursue their spirituality in conjunction with the use of cannabis: "We do not accept the fantasies of the angels. How much less have we to do with the fantasies of the devils."[3]

The ecstasy that is sought for the purposes of escaping the burden of egoism cannot emancipate us from that egoism because the one is a direct expression of the other. Real spiritual ecstasy may occasionally come to those who have learned the lessons and art of sacrifice.

Ecstasy (wajd) is strangely associated with agony. To the outside observer the signs of ecstatic transport may even look like torment. To the extent that any self-awareness remains, to the extent that there is an experiencer of the experience, there is the possibility of bewilderment, unfulfilled longing, and even awesome dread.

The original and pure Islam called the average human being toward the depths of mystical experience by inviting him to contemplative prayer five times a day. The ritual was meant to awaken a state of presence. Muhammad said, "One moment of conscious reflection [tafakkur] is more valuable than seventy years of [unmindful] ritual prayer." But Islam also calls the mystic to rejoin the human community by melting in the bioenergetic ritual of surrender, by being grounded in the ranks of congregational prayer, by participating in the equalizing spirit of collective worship.

Sufism, as with any complete spirituality, is the integration or synthesis of the mystical and the prophetic consciousness, of ecstasy and practicality, of enlightenment and maturity. The mystic is inclined to explore states of consciousness, the prophet to bring earthly life more into harmony with higher states of consciousness. What we mean by a Sufi is one who has attained something that could be called "functional nonexistence," a grounded selflessness, a practical enlightenment.

> *God! God! Don't expect the qualities of wine*
> *From the self-existent.*
> *Behold its all-encompassing Gentleness*
> *in the eyes of the drunk!*
> —*Rumi,* Diwan *23311*

Notes:

1 From *al-Istilahat al-Sufiyyah* by Ibn Arabi, in *What the Seeker Needs* (Putney, VT: Threshold Books, 1992).

2 Hujwiri, *Kashf al-Mahjub* (London: E. J. W. Gibb Memorial Trust, 1959).

3 Shams-i Tabrizi, *Maqalat*, unpublished translation by Kabir Helminski and Refik Algan.

Parabola
Volume: 4.2
Sacred Dance

The Ritual of Rebirth

Annemarie Schimmel

Sama *(mystical dance) is the food of the soul!*
Thus sing the Mevlevi dervishes at the end of their whirling dance, taking up an old Arabic saying and repeating
it in Turkish, as generations of Sufis in the Muslim world
had poetically paraphrased it in Persian. And it is told
that a Sufi in Sind, the Lower Indus Valley, once asked
an orthodox theologian whether there would be dance
in Paradise, and upon the theologian's negative reply he
sighed: "Then, what have we to do with Paradise?"

The lover who enters the mystical dance is higher
than heaven, loftier than the spheres, for while the call
to sama comes from heaven, the dancer reaches a place
that is even beyond the Divine Throne. Wherever God
manifests Himself, the cosmic dance will begin. Mount
Sinai, split asunder under the impact of overwhelming
revelations, means for Rumi that it performed a dance of
ecstasy during which the mountain unriveted itself and
attained annihilation and was scattered piecemeal in the
Divine Presence, just as man is annihilated in God as a
result of his dance. Once the spirit is freed from the fet-
ters of worldly density and has attained a life in union
with the spiritual center, he sees that every tree, every
plant in the garden of this world, is dancing, touched by
the spring breeze of love.

•

For as dance is connected with perfect annihilation in God it is also connected with creation. One of Rumi's most powerful poems describes how he turned his ear towards the unseen to listen to the Divine address "Am I not your Lord?", understood by the Sufis as the first Song that set the not-yet-created souls in motion. And as the human souls answered this Divine call by responding "Yes, we witness it," everything else that was to be created responded in its own way and began to dance joyfully out of non-existence to adorn the world with tulips, willows, and sweet basil. When the soul of music is heard, or the spring breeze touches the gardens and fields, they are reminded of God's primordial address and again participate in the cosmic dance:

> *The twigs start dancing like novices,*
> *the leaves clap their hands like minstrels ...*

It goes without saying that the imagery of dance is most outspoken in Rumi's work. Cast into deepest spiritual crisis after his mystical beloved Shams-i Tabrizi had disappeared from Konya for the first time, Rumi gave himself to music and dance, and tradition tells how throughout his later life he would fall into an ecstatic state whenever he heard some lovely sound, whether the melodious hammering of the goldsmiths in the bazaar of Konya, or the voice of the watermill on the hillslope of Meram; then he would begin the spinning movement and recite poetry full of love and longing. At other times his friends would arrange musical parties for him during which he whirled around, the ladies throwing roses over him. The funeral of his friend Salahuddin the goldsmith was celebrated with a wonderful sama, as was the birth of his youngest son or the wedding of family members. All this, of course, deeply shocked the orthodox inhabitants of Konya; but so great was the fire of his love that even they had to accept the great theologian's strange ways. Rumi's poetry is a result of the whirling dance, and a careful analysis of his lyrics reveals that many of them were born in the throes of rhythmical movement.

Rumi knew that the "water of life" will gush forth from the soil which the lover touches with dancing feet, as he also saw in sama the ladder that leads to heaven, to the roof where the beloved shows his radiant face. Therefore he can compare the sama also to a window that opens toward the heavens. Rumi compares the spinning of the lover around the Beloved to the movement of the spheres around the moon or the sun; the fact that the highest mystical guide is called *qutb*, "pole" or "axis," fits very well into this symbolism. Therefore the interpretation of the Mevlevi ritual as a cosmic dance is found quite frequently in later treatises dealing with the deeper meaning of the ritual. The *Sphärenreigen*, the round-dance of the spheres, is a beautiful ancient symbol of the harmony that governs the created world, in which Rumi firmly believed. Part of this harmony is the dance of the dust particles, *dharra*, or, as we may translate it into a modern concept, the atoms, which are attracted by the sun and dance around it: Only the attraction by the sun gives them a common direction, orders their lives, and transforms them into a well-organized community that participates in the eternal dance and thus becomes united in a certain sense with the center, the sun which is the cause of their dance.

Dancing means both annihilation and resurrection, being born and dying. The dialectical movement of *fana*, annihilation in God, and *baqa*, duration in the Divine Presence, is symbolized in the dancing movement which takes man out of himself, makes him die to his lower attributes, and grants him life in a higher sphere. The garments of the Mevlevis point to this truth. The dance begins in long black coats which represent the dark earthly existence; but once the music becomes faster and the threefold greeting ceremony is over, the coats are thrown aside and the dervishes start whirling in white robes, comparable to big white moths whirling around the central candle; they are now clad in the "dress of resurrection," the spiritual body. It is no accident that the greatest Muslim mystic, Husayn ibn Mansur al-Hallaj, danced in his chains when he was led to the place of execution—he was aware of the truth that death in love means union with the beloved. And it was he who invented the allegory of Moth and Candle.

The moth that turns around the flame; Majnun who dances in the desert in search of his beloved Layla; the pilgrim who circumambulates the Ka'bah in deep devotion, clad in the shroud-like *ihram*; the young pigeons that flutter around the balcony of the beloved, or the nightingale which with a thousand beautiful songs surrounds the rose, symbol of the face of the Beloved—all of them participate in the mystical dance, like the atoms that spin around their nuclei, or the stars that form wonderful patterns in the heavenly sphere; or man himself, yielding to the attraction of a center outside himself, namely, eternal Love—an experience that means death and resurrection in one. As Rumi says in one of his poems:

> *Who knows Love's mazy circling, ever lives in God,*
> *For Death, he knows, is Love abounding:* Allah Hu.

Parabola
Volume: 12.2
Addiction

Intoxication and Sobriety in Sufism

Victor Danner

Over the course of time, the Sufis have developed a rich technical vocabulary to express their gnostic doctrines on the nature of the Real and the method of spiritually realizing it. Very often we find pairs of contrasting terms, such as expansion and contraction, presence and absence, and union and separation, that might at first sight lead us to think that one of the terms is positive and the other negative in all situations and at all times. Then we learn from the various contexts of certain Sufi works that this is simply not so at all. On the contrary, shifts of perspective can make the positive term negative, the negative positive.

That is precisely the case for the famous pair of contrasting terms, intoxication (*sukr*) and sobriety (*sahw*), which the Sufis have used to denote various states in their spiritual psychotherapy. The baneful results of intoxication from wine-bibbing are such that we naturally assume that in the mystical life intoxication, however defined, is hardly an ideal, and that sobriety must necessarily take precedence over it. Yet, that is not what we find with certain Sufis, who prefer intoxication with the fiery wine of gnosis over the rather frigid, greyish world of reasoning, with its puritanical sobriety. Other Sufis see things in a completely different light: Serene, luminous sobriety must prevail over the demential states resulting from

•

uncontrolled intoxication, which wipes out our discernment and self-control, leaving us like drunks reeling from tavern to tavern.

In one of his works, Omar Khayyam, the great Persian Sufi poet of medieval Islam, alludes to a period in mankind's distant past when wine-drinking was a sacred act. As in the case with carnal love, it still had a symbolic element in it that precipitated in the mind of the drinker a concrete intuition of the Divine Reality. Then, with the passage of time, and the embroilment of man in the passions of the flesh that obscured the inner light of the Spirit, the symbolic content of wine gradually disappeared. The vine became a noxious plant; the tavern, a raucous assembler of seedy topers; and the drunk, the embodiment of the man addicted to the attractive lure of the world in all its pure magnetism. No doubt, the bacchanalia of Antiquity had been in more primordial days a mystical cult of Bacchus that went awry through the injection of passionate elements that wiped out the original signification and turned a noble, sacred deed into an ignominious vice. Perhaps that is what Omar Khayyam meant.

The notion of addiction in itself is not unilaterally negative. In the past, one could still be addicted to a noble cause, even to God, because the verb conveyed the ideas of being devoted to someone or something, or of being delivered to someone under a court decree, or of applying oneself habitually to someone or something. Addiction came to mean an indulged practice, and thus habituation: "His addiction was to courses vain," as Shakespeare wrote. In our day, we no longer close our letters with "Yours most addicted," nor can we say, as did an old English author, that "we sincerely addict ourselves to Almighty God." In the more archaic sense of addiction, there is the notion of adjudgment or devotion, which reappears in the modern meaning of habituation; the addict is adjudged by the authority of habit to be under the sway of his addiction; he is devoted to it. So we say, "So-and-so is addicted to drugs," and in this case addiction has a nasty connotation, whereas in the past we could also have said, "So-and-so is addicted to God," because in both instances someone is handed over to a stronger power; he is adjudged to fall under its sway; he becomes devoted to it.

"Wine, women, and song," these were the primary addictions of the Arabs on the eve of the Quranic revelation heralding the coming of Islam. The sacred Law of Islam abolished wine-drinking altogether, perhaps because the addictive nature of the vine had plunged the Arabs into utterly crass forms of immorality; but the same Law was much more lenient in formulating the relations between man and woman, and wound up sacralizing conjugal love, thus restoring to sexual love its Edenic symbolism; and as for "song," which was the Arab cult of poetry, the Law was much more muted and tolerant, for the Arab soul was of old addicted to the word, which in the Quran became the Word of God. Thus, of the trio, "wine, women, and song," only wine was abolished from the sacred precincts of the Islamic community and relegated to the category of prohibited actions.

But it was not altogether abolished from the consciousness of the believer; for, if he could not drink wine in this world, he could look forward to drinking it in the Hereafter. The blissful, in Paradise, have radiant faces, and, according to the Quran. "They are given to drink of a pure wine, sealed, whose seal is musk. For this let all those strive who strive for bliss!" (83:22-26). This wine is the mystical wine of Omar Khayyam and of the Sufis, "delicious to the drinkers, wherein there is no headache nor are they made mad thereby" (37:42-47). We know what this wine is: It is a powerful, living spiritual reality. "If they watered the earth of a tomb with such a Wine, the dead would recover his soul and his body revive," says the thirteenth-century Egyptian Sufi Ibn al-Farid. It is to this celestial wine that Omar Khayyam refers in one of his quatrains:

> *You know, my Friends, with what a brave Carouse*
> *I made a second marriage in my house;*
> *Divorced old barren Reason from my Bed,*
> *And took the Daughter of the Vine to spouse.*

The gnostic symbolism of wine leads to the positive interpretation of intoxication, for the mystic's worldly addictions are now cut off; he is now addicted to God, who is the wine of pure Love. "Wine," says the Syrian mystic Nabulusi, of the eighteenth century, "signifies the drink of divine Love that results from contemplating the traces of His beautiful Names. For this love begets drunkenness and the complete forgetfulness of all that exists in the world." By the "traces of His beautiful Names," Nabulusi has in mind the manifestations of the Divine Beauty as opposed to the wrathful operations of the Divine Majesty. But note that the intoxication with God annihilates one's previous forgetfulness of Him. Formerly, one remembered the world and forgot its Creator; now, one remembers the Creator and forgets His creation—and not just the painful aspects of the creation; it is the entire creation that is forgotten in the intoxication with God.

In this respect, sobriety is a very unfortunate state of the soul; it characterizes the person who is uninterested in the heavenly cup of wine and who cares not to indulge his mystical bent, if he has one. "Joyless in this world is he that lives sober," notes Ibn al-Farid, "and he that dies not drunk will miss the path of wisdom." Dying drunk means either actually dying after following the lifelong discipline of the mystical path, culminating in the inebriated state of union, or else it means spiritual death through self-extinction (*fana*) which comes about through quaffing the cup of gnostic wine. It is this wine of pure Love that dissolves in its igneous reality all egocentric limitations, thus opening up the soul to the radiant effusions of the Spirit within the heart, and these in turn sanctify the soul and confer wisdom upon the seeker.

That wine is a metaphysical reality that is prototypal to the earthly vines we see around us. Here in this world, the cupbearer (*saqi*) is distinct from the wine he serves us, while in the Hereafter, says Rumi, "God is the Saki and the Wine." There is an uncreated wine that pre-existed the entire universe; as mystics, we can sip from its cup and get utterly drunk even before the appearance of the vine on the face of the earth. "In memory of the Beloved," chants Ibn al-Farid, "we quaffed a vintage that made us drunk before the creation of the vine." The Beloved in this verse is either God or the Prophet as Logos in the uncreated Divine Reality. What is evident in all this is that the metaphysical wine is a reality that escapes all the limitations of the cosmos. One sip of this wine of gnosis and the seeker is subjected to an "expansion" (*bast*) that breaks through all the previously limited "contraction" (*qabd*) of his egocentric self. It is the infinitizing expansion that engenders intoxication and madness in the adepts. In this sense, madness is a positive trait, for as the Persian Sufi Ansari put it:

> *Whom Thou intoxicatest with Thy love*
> *On him bestoweth Thou both the worlds.*
> *But Thy mad devotee,*
> *What use hath he for both the worlds?*

The madness that comes from this inebriation is not a mental disequilibrium calling for some kind of therapy; it is, rather, a state of mind that prefers God to the world and that restores the normal hierarchy of things broken by the Fall. In his *Phaedrus*, Plato notes that, "The madness that comes of God is superior to the sanity that is of human origin." That is so because *sanity* here (which is the same as *sobriety*) is simply a collective judgment of conduct based on criteria derived from an equally collective form of forgetfulness. The "original sin" in all of this is, of course, forgetfulness, which is fueled by the fallen state of soul common to all; and the end result is a kind of worldly wisdom, in the light of which the Sufi madness seems like sheer foolishness. But, as the Gospel would put it, "The wisdom of this world is foolishness with God."

For the mystical treader of the path, a veritable reversal of priorities, values, judgments, and convictions takes place. Within the categories of thought cultivated by the nonmystical mass of humanity, on the other hand, such a reversal cannot but appear to be a real disequilibrium, a mental fissure. Even the concept of mysticism in our days has taken on the ancillary notions of something irrational and obscure, at least in the West and wherever the West has gone in the East. But irrational and obscure in relation to what? Irrational and obscure in relation to the rationality and clarity of the average man, the man of the Fall. Al-Hujwiri, the Persian Sufi of medieval Islam, tells this story: "It is related that one day when Shibli came into the bazaar, the people said: 'This is a mad man.' He replied, 'You think I am mad, and I think you are sensible. May God increase my madness and your sense!'" In other words, the reversal of the poles of consciousness in Shibli had reached such a point that he knew instantaneously the sheer futility of attempting to clarify things to people at large. Instead, he took them at their word; if their behavior is what is called sensible, and his is madness, then let both camps increase in their respective states! Clearly, for Shibli, theirs was a condition of sober ignorance, devoid of the intoxicating delights of mystical perceptions; for them the world was opaque and even massively so; their minds, veiled by ignorance, could not discern the fiery essences that ignited all the earthly forms around them. Yes, they had a kind of wisdom, but it was a frigid, worldly wisdom that stopped at the surface of forms and could not penetrate to the universal realities alive in every existing thing. "It behooves us," warns Rumi, "to become ignorant of this worldly wisdom; rather must we clutch at madness." Madness results from the repentance, the change of mind, that the seeker experienced when, one fine day, he perceived the Beloved masked by the multiplicity of the world; he intuited Something behind the facade of forms. There was no turning back; for, as the Persian Sufi Shabistari says:

> From drinking one cup of the pure wine,
> From sweeping the dust of dung-hills from their souls,
> From grasping the skirts of drunkards,
> They have become Sufis.

The drunkards referred to in the poem are the Sufi shaikhs of the path, who are drunk with the wine of Love. Grasping the skirts of such drunkards means following the discipline of the path that they impose on their disciples, or else it means frequenting the God-lovers among the Sufis.

Enough has been said to show that intoxication seems to have a certain preeminence over sobriety, although that is not always the case. But when it is, then intoxication, the tavern keeper, the cup, the wine, the cupbearer, the dancing girl, and even the tavern as such, all become symbols of otherworldly realities or of spiritual things: Intoxication is ecstasy; the tavern keeper, the shaikh of the path; the cup, the soul; the wine, gnosis; the cupbearer, the Spirit; the dancing girl, God; and the tavern, the world. And all of these symbols can change into yet other significations, depending on context.

Sometimes the wine symbolism joins forces with another powerful theme, that of human love, and in this case the intoxicating fires of erotic love and wine-drinking are commingled in an imagery that the unwise can easily take as sheer libertinism. The Persian quatrains of Omar Khayyam deal with both themes with unparalleled beauty; but stripped of their Sufi content, they are reduced to a glorification of hedonistic existence. It is significant, in any case, that both themes result from an intrinsically ennobling element in wine and human love that allows of their being exalted to a higher plane of interpretation. A kind of madness stalks the lover and his beloved in ordinary life, and this is similar to the state of the soul that comes over the seeker of God; and the carnal union that love in this world inevitably provokes is an earthly reminder of mystical union in the spiritual world. Since this is so, we are tempted to conclude that things in this world impose upon us certain views about things in God's world, and His world then becomes the image of our world. But this is so only as a preliminary assumption and as seen from the outside, so to speak, and superficially, for it is not the view of the Sufi sages. In reality, the prototypes of all things in this world are contained in the Divine Intelligence from all eternity, as the Sufis would say: The embrace of one's beloved is but a reflection, in this world, of Divine Love; and indeed, taken to their ultimate roots in God, the lover, his beloved, and their love would not even exist if God were not the absolute Lover, Beloved, and Love.

Because of their use of erotic and wine symbolism, the Sufis have sometimes been taxed by the religious scholars with the charge of being unrestrained libertines who actually indulged their carnal pleasures and wine-drinking delights. This, of course, is not true at all. In the case of the great Ibn al-Arabi, whose *Tarjuman al-Ashwaq* ("The Interpreter of Desires") was a long ode cast in an erotic form that provoked the ire of religious scholars who found it to be scandalous, we are in the presence of a saintly sage whose reputation is faultless. Even so, events compelled him to write a commentary to his poem that showed its mystical and esoteric meanings, so much so that his foremost critic amongst the religious authorities who had criticized him became his disciple eventually.

Seen in the light of human experience, the Sufi use of wine and erotic symbolism to express spiritual realities is really a matter of pedagogical strategy. One could, of course, speak about these things in the abstract, somewhat like the philosophers when they hold forth on ontological questions; but the net results are not as convincing, because they are not drawn from the concrete data of human experience. The drunk emerging from a tavern is a common sight; the lovers who embrace are an everyday fact. While it is true that in medieval Islam one found a greater conformity to the prescriptions of religion, that civilization was not in the least puritanical; on the contrary, it was extremely tolerant, charitable, and self-confident. The drunkard strolling about with a goblet in hand was not necessarily a Christian image, otherwise Rumi would not have employed it when he said, "Come drunk and strolling, goblet in hand—let it not be lawful for Thee to be the Saki and us to be so sober!"

It is only in a puritanical age that the wine symbolism of Sufism falls to the wayside, rejected out of hand by sober-minded religious scholars whose impoverished minds cannot see God as the generous Saki. But there is also an element of scandal in the wine and erotic symbolism that serves to shock the dull mind into an awareness of spiritual dimensions not easily perceived otherwise. For the Saki is God; why am I then sober? "Since Thou art the Saki," says Rumi, "'unbelief' is to remain sober." The poetical imagery of wine, intoxication, the Saki, and the like, contrives to communicate an intuitive perception in the reader or listener that has something of that spiritual "wine" in it, and he becomes intoxicated in his own way. If he has understood the imagery, he becomes what he has understood, for we are what we know to be true. Thus, in the concrete image of wine, there are a thousand concepts unleashed in the mind, and these in turn force a thousand conclusions. The process of purification begins by merely hearing or reading the wine poem: We now know, in some mysterious way, what we must be. A degree of intoxication results from the "wine" conveyed by the poet.

The point just made is of great importance: There are degrees of intoxication, just as there are degrees of sobriety. We are not all equally matched in our inebriated states. Similarly, we are not all equally mad, given that there are shades of madness. When, consequently, does sobriety end and intoxication begin? That is a question that can be answered best by taking the case of the person who suddenly becomes aware of the mystical content of existence. Until then, he was quite sober, that is to say, he had not been even moderately fired up by the doctrinal wine of Sufism, for he had never been exposed to it. Then comes the exposure in the form of a poem, a treatise, a word from an adept, an intuition in the mind, and suddenly a degree of intoxication with the One sets in upon the soul; yet, for all that, the old sobriety is still there, but less intense, less characteristic of the man. The upshot of all this is that, if intoxication admits of degrees ranging from the finite to the infinite, then even the doctrinal comprehension of the path is already an intoxication that leads, or should lead, to a steady increase in the addiction to God; but this is the liberating addiction of the Spirit to its Divine Source, a liberating addiction because no longer enveloped by the constraints and limitations of the empirical self. Since the Object of the Spirit is God and cannot but be God, this implies that the Spirit is necessarily under the power, always and everywhere, of its Object: It is subject to God, devoted to Him, attached to Him through intrinsic habituation, which is the definition of addiction along spiritual lines in the old sense; the modern sense has retained only the fact of being subject to a drug, devoted to its usage, attached to it, and this out of habituation. The process of being addicted to the wine of Allah begins only when one perceives that it is absolutely different from worldly wine. As Rumi says, "How is this pure wine related to the wine of the grape? This is the Water of Life, that other, carrion." Sufi teachings embody the essence of life-giving, spiritual wine. To understand them in a correct way is to participate to a certain degree in the ultimate Reality to which they refer.

Addiction to the Divinity is not at all like addiction to things sensual or material in our world. The reason lies in this, that addiction of the usual worldly sort blots out man's discernment, which comes from his intellectual faculty: He can no longer discern the Real from the unreal. But it also blots out the celestial gropings of his will, which then becomes enmeshed in the trappings of this world. As Rumi would put things: "Know that every sensual desire is like wine and hashish—it veils the intelligence and stupefies rationality." In other words, addiction to worldly habits, such as wine and hashish, far from being positive in all aspects of their symbolism, are extremely negative precisely because they efface the unique function of man's intelligence, which is to discern the being of God in all things. The addiction itself, whether to wine, women, or song, to use the current expression, is a noble symbolism, for it represents the addictive tendency of the Spirit to its Divine Source; but the results of this-worldly addiction are diametrically opposed to other-worldly addiction. In the latter, the intelligence is rendered more luminous and diamondlike in its purity; the "eye of the heart" is more and more unveiled, and with this unveiling comes the liberating gnosis of the Infinite.

Addiction to "wine, women, and song," from another point of view, is but a specious way of transcending the self without really doing so. Everyone carries within himself the imperishable Spirit, the inner Observer of all that goes on in the mind and psyche of man and in the operations of his organs of sensation and action. Because of its presence within the innermost heart, and however veiled it might be through the effects of forgetfulness, it nevertheless still communicates to the soul a thirst for transcendence. In the ignorant, this thirst is manifested in deviated fashions, in ways that are merely counterfeits or parodies of the real transcendence that comes through the ascension of the Spirit back to its divine origin, which is what realization is all about. Addiction to "wine, women, and song" in a worldly sense comes about through a failure to see them as symbols of the Hereafter. Instead of their universal essences being intuited by the mind of man, he senses only their most external forms and uses these to escape from the drudgery of his own self, a false expansion, or a false intoxication, being substituted for the real thing. One might even say, in passing, that in our days trips to the moon or to outer space are substitutes for the inner voyage of the Spirit, which transcends the entire physical universe; but these physical voyages are proofs that the thirst for transcendence is imbedded in the very nature of man. Still, it is only in the inner flight of the Spirit, retracing its vertical path back to God, that man can truly transcend himself, all other forms of transcendence being pale reflections of this one. As Rumi says:

> *Men incur the reproach of wine and drugs*
> *That they may escape for a while from self-consciousness.*
> *Since all know this life to be a snare,*
> *Volitional memory and thought to be a hell.*

In some Sufi schools of thought, the intoxication of ecstasy is followed by a sobriety that constitutes a collapse into selfhood. Sobriety, in such a state, is normal consciousness, which veils the mystic from the vision of God seen in the ecstatic raptures of intoxication. There is a kind of contraction in sobriety that alternates with the expansion of intoxication. Or again: Intoxication has to do with union with God; sobriety is then separation from Him. Whereas there is self-effacement in intoxication, there is self-restoration in sobriety. In all of these states, there is a constant succession or alternation that ceases only with the cessation of one's selfhood, one's egocentric existence.

In other schools of Sufism, intoxication as a state of self-effacement, or extinction, is only the beginning of the spiritual life. In their view, the perfection of the spiritual life comes finally with "at-one-ment" with God, which is possible in sobriety alone. But in this manner of looking at things, sobriety is no longer the privation of intoxication, the autumn or winter of the soul as compared with its spring or summer. It is, instead, the state of lucid consciousness that faded away into absence. This, at any rate, is what the Sufi school of Ibn al-Farid maintains. In the following verses, Ibn al-Farid outlines this teaching; but we must bear in mind that the feminine pronouns refer to the Divine Essence:

> *And in the sobriety following my intoxication I retained the Object, which, during the effacement of my self-existence,*
> *I contemplated in Her by whom it was revealed.*
> *So that in the sobriety after self-effacement I was none other than She, and when She unveiled Herself my essence became endued with my Essence.*

Whereas intoxication is equated with self-extinction, or what the Sufis call *fana* (similar to the Buddhist *nirvana*), sobriety is equated with the enduring state of permanence (*baqa*) in God, an abiding awareness resulting from union with the One, which in the above imagery is represented by the unveiling of the feminine reality of the Essence, feminine because of its attractive and irresistible beauty, similar in this regard to feminine beauty in this world.

In still another type of spirituality, that of the Shadhili adepts, whose path was founded in the thirteenth century by the famous imam Abu'l-Hasan ash-Shadhili, we find a different viewpoint altogether. One of the Shadhili masters, Shaikh Ibn Ata'illah, speaking about the blessings of God, divides mankind into three groups. The first group is forgetful and sees God's blessings as coming from mankind and not from God. The second group is that of the travelers on the Path; and of any person belonging to this class, we can say that "His intoxication prevails over his sobriety, his union over his separation, his extinction over his permanence, and his absence over his presence." This, however, is not ultimate perfection, which is to be found in the third group, the adept of which is described in this fashion: "He drinks, and increases in sobriety; he is absent, and increases in presence; his union does not veil him from his separation, nor does his separation veil him from his union; his extinction does not divert him from his permanence, nor does his permanence divert him from his extinction." What has happened is that the strict dichotomy of the contrasting pairs, or the predominance of one state over another, and even the alternation of the two elements like the movements of a pendulum, all this has been transcended through the infusion of an intellective dimension of gnosis that effectively mixes the dosages of intoxication and sobriety, not to mention the other pairs, without doing violence to the serenity of the soul.

It could be argued that an intoxication that increases sobriety is no longer an intelligible concept, at least from a logical standpoint; but then, we could also take our point of departure in an intuitive perception of things that allows us to reconcile seemingly contradictory notions. Has not God been defined at times as "the union of opposites"? So, similarly, at some point, the distinction between intoxication and sobriety, which initially is almost absolute, becomes less so as we move back into their common origin in God, and there we can conceive of an intoxication that increases sobriety, and vice versa. But if we conceive this in the metaphysical order, we might also perceive it in this world, in sensorial phenomena: Was not the white man's intoxicating drink called "fire water" by the red man?

In the end, the mind of man seeks that blissful state wherein the dualities of the created world no longer have the power to alter the harmony of his inner Spirit. Religion provides an approximate equilibrium; but the mystical life in the great religions is what leads to the ultimate union that transcends all dualities. While the Sufi Path is indeed built on the sacred Law of Islam, without which it would stand suspended in a void, it is nevertheless true that the Path itself leads to a Reality that is beyond intoxication and sobriety, beyond this or that, even though we are forced, by the nature of things, to reach that Reality through a skillful blend of intoxication and sobriety, and to say of ultimate Reality, at least temporarily, that it is this or that.

GLOSSARY

Ahl-i Haqq (Ahl-i Ḥaqq) - a branch of Shi'ite Islam with strong esoteric leanings and centered in Kurdistan

Ahsa'i, Shaikh Ahmad (Aḥsā'ī, Shaykh Aḥmad, d. 1826) - an Iranian philosopher and spiritual teacher who founded the Shaykhi branch of Shi'ism

akhlaq (akhlāq) - character traits; virtues, praiseworthy moral and ethical qualities; the science of ethics

alam al-arwah ('ālam al-arwāḥ) - the world of the spirits, contrasted with the world of the bodies; often called *malakut* (q.v.)

Ali ('Alī) - the cousin and son-in-law of Muhammad, the fourth caliph, the first Shi'ite imam, and a pillar of Islamic spirituality

Allah (Allāh) - God; the supreme or all-comprehensive name, the referent of all the ninety-nine divine names

Ansari (Anṣārī, 'Abd Allāh, d. 1088) - influential author of Arabic and Persian works on Sufism, especially the stages of the path to God

aql ('aql) - intelligence, intellect, reason; macrocosmically, the first creation of God, and microcosmically the divine light of guidance innate in every soul

Arsh ('arsh) - the Throne of the Merciful, which encompasses the cosmos

asma wa'l-sifat (al-asmā' wa'l-ṣifāt) - the names and attributes of God, typically said to number ninety-nine; contrasted with the Essence (*dhāt*), which is God in himself, beyond name and designation

Attar, Fariduddin (Farīd al-Dīn 'Aṭṭār, d. 1221) - one of the greatest of the Persian Sufi poets, author of a divan and several long didactic poems, the most famous of which is the *Conference of the Birds*

Avicenna (Ibn Sīnā, d. 1037) - the foremost of the Muslim Aristotelians and a great physician, well-known to the medieval West

ayat (āyāt) - "signs" of God; a Quranic term that designates natural phenomena, prophetic miracles, and the Quran's own verses

baqa (baqā') - subsistence, permanence, remaining; contrasted with *fana*, annihilation, impermanence, disappearance (the two terms are taken from Quran 55:26); in Sufism, the replacement of human limitations by the divine attributes in the image of which man was created

baraka - divine grace, blessing; the presence of God that is sensed in holy people and places

barzakh - "isthmus"; the intermediate realm where people are "located" between death and resurrection; also, the World of Imagination, between the World of Spirits and the World of Bodies

bast (basṭ) - expansion; contrasted with *qabd*, contraction (both terms being derived from Quranic divine names); in Sufi psychology, a state of elation, joy, and melting, as opposed to sadness, darkness, and hardening

batin (bāṭin) - the Inward, a divine name that the Quran pairs with the Outward (*zahir*); the invisible, spiritual side of things, as opposed to the visible and corporeal sides; the esoteric as opposed to the exoteric

Bayram Vali (d. 1430) - Turkish saint and founder of the Bayramiye Sufi order

Bektashi - one of the Sufi orders, prominent in Turkish-speaking parts of the Islamic world

Bistami (Abū Yazīd al-Bisṭāmī, d. ca. 874) - one of the greatest of the early Sufi shaikhs, source of numerous pithy sayings

dar al-islam (dār al-islām) - the "house of Islam," that is, realms under Muslim rule

Dar as-Salam (dār al-salām) - the "house of peace," a Quranic epithet for Paradise; a place that participates in the peace of the Divine Presence

dergah (Persian dargāh) - originally, royal court, threshold; in Turkey, a Sufi center.

dervish (darwīsh) - a poor person, the Persian equivalent of *faqir* (q.v.).

dhikr - reminder, remembrance, mention; the message of the prophets, and the human response; methodical repetition of one of the names of God, similar to the Hindu mantra

divan (dīwān) - the collected short poems of a poet

fakir - see *faqir*

fana (fanā') - see *baqa*

faqir (faqīr) - a poor person; a practitioner of Sufism

Farabi, al- (al-Fārābī, d. 950) - one of the greatest of the early Muslim philosophers

fayd-i aqdas (fayḍ-i aqdas) - Most Holy Effusion; Ibn Arabi's term for God's awareness of himself and of all that will ever be

fikr - thought, reflection, meditation; in Sufism, the complement of *dhikr*

fitra (fiṭra) - human nature as originally created by God, rooted in *tawhid*

futuvvet (futuwwa) - spiritual chivalry, magnanimity; a general designation for good character

Ghazali (al-Ghazālī, Abū Ḥāmid, d. 1111) - famous theologian, jurist, and Sufi; author of numerous works

ghurba - exile; our situation in this world, distant from our true home with God

hadith (ḥadīth) - a saying of Muhammad; distinguished from the Quran, the revealed words of God

hadith qudsi (ḥadīth qudsī) - a saying of Muhammad in which extra-Quranic words of God are quoted

Hafiz (Ḥāfiẓ, d. 1389) - outstanding Persian lyric poet and master of Sufi lore

hajj (ḥajj) - the pilgrimage to Mecca that is one of the five pillars of Muslim practice

Hallaj, al- (al-Ḥallāj, Ḥusayn ibn Manṣūr, d. 922) - celebrated Sufi martyr, famous for his utterance, "I am the Real"

Halveti (Khalwatī) - a Sufi order, prominent in Turkey

Haqiqah (ḥaqīqa) - reality, truth; God as the Supreme Reality and the goal of the Tariqah

ḥaqq (ḥaqq) - real, reality, truth, right; a Quranic name of God

harem (Arabic ḥarīm, ḥaram) - sacred place, sanctuary, forbidden area; the private rooms of a house; the women's quarters

Hayy ibn Yaqzan (Ḥayy ibn Yaqẓān) - "Alive, son of the Awake," a character in a story by Avicenna and elsewhere representing the fully actualized intelligence of the sage

Hazrat (ḥaḍra) - "presence"; title given to respected persons

Hu (hū, huwa) - the Arabic pronoun "he," a divine name that refers to the unknown and unnamable Essence of God

hudur (ḥuḍūr) - presence of mind, collectedness, awareness of God's presence

Hujwiri, al- (al-Hujwīrī, d. ca. 1072) - author of *Kashf al-mahjub*, the earliest Sufi text in Persian, Trans. Nicholson

Hurqalya (Hūrqalyā) - the celestial earth, the place of true visions and the Resurrection, the World of Imagination

Husamuddin (Ḥusām al-Dīn, d. 1284) - a disciple of Rumi and the inspiration for his *Mathnawi*

husn (ḥusn) - beauty, goodness, virtue

ibada ('ibāda) - worship, service

Ibn (al-)Arabi (Ibn al-'Arabī, d. 1240) - the "Greatest Master" of Sufi teachings, famous among other things for elaborate discussions of the Oneness of Being and the Perfect Man

Ibn al-Farid (Ibn al-Fāriḍ, d. 1235) - the foremost Sufi poet of the Arabic language

Ibn Ata'illah (Ibn 'Aṭā'illāh, d. 1309) - an important Shadhili shaikh and author

Ibn Battuta (Ibn Baṭṭuṭa, d. 1377) - a North African scholar and geographer who journeyed throughout the Islamic countries as far as Beijing and recorded his observations in his *Travels*

Ibn Sina (Ibn Sīnā) - see *Avicenna*

ihram (iḥrām) - special clothing worn during the hajj

insan (insān) - "man" in the nongendered sense, human being

insan al-kamil, al- (al-insān al-kāmil) - "Perfect Man," the fully realized human being, exemplified by prophets and great saints

Inshallah (in shā' Allāh) - God willing, *Deo volente*

ishq ('ishq) - love, transformative love for God

Ishraq (ishrāq) - illumination, the school of philosophy established by Suhrawardi

Ishraqiyyun (ishrāqiyyūn) - followers of Ishraq

islam (islām) - submission, surrender (to God); the ontological situation of all creatures; the voluntary surrender to God of prophets and their followers; the religion that goes by the name

isra (isrā') - night journey; the *mi'raj*

Jabarut (jabarūt) - "mightiness," the intelligible, spiritual world; commonly contrasted with *malakut* ("the dominion," the intermediate realm of the soul) and *mulk* ("the kingdom," the bodily realm)

jadhba - "attraction," the divine power that draws people to God; contrasted with *suluk* (q.v.)

jan (jān) - Persian for soul, spirit, life

jihad (jihād) - struggle; striving on the path to God; warfare

jihad al-akbar (al-jihād al-akbar) - "the greater struggle," striving to overcome one's own self-centeredness and negativity

Ka'bah (ka 'ba) - the House of God in Mecca toward which all Muslims pray

kalimat at-tawhid (kalimat al-tawḥīd) - "the words declaring (God's) unity", that is, the first formula of the Shahadah

khalifa (khalīfa) - vicegerent, deputy, representative; the human function of representing God in His creation; the representative or deputy of a Sufi shaikh

khalwat - retreat, withdrawal from society to focus on spiritual exercises and inner purification

khalwat dar anjuman - "retreat within society," living in the presence of God while participating actively in the community

khanaqah (khānaqāh) - a Sufi center

khayal (khayāl) - imagination, image; the intermediate realm of the soul, between spirit and body

Khazir (Khaḍir) - see *Khizr*

Khizr (Khiḍr) - the teacher of Moses in Quran 18:65-82; a saint who drank the water of life and lives among us, appearing occasionally as a spiritual guide

khutba (khuṭba) - address, sermon

Kirmani, Muhammad Karim Khan (Muḥammad Karīm Khān Kirmānī, d. 1870) - the second successor of Shaikh Ahmad Ahsa'i as leader of the Shaikhi school

Kubra, Najmuddin (Najm al-Dīn Kubrā, d. 1220) - Sufi teacher, founder of the Kubrawi order

kufr - unbelief, ingratitude, impiety

Kursi (kursī) - the "Footstool" of God, mentioned in the Quran as embracing the heavens and the earth; located cosmologically right below the *arsh*, the Throne of the Merciful

La ilaha illa'Llah (lā ilāha illa'Llāh) - "(There is) no god but God," the formula of *tawhid* that is uttered in the Shahadah

madda (mādda) - matter (in the Aristotelian sense)

mahabba (maḥabba) - love, the sole divine attribute that the Quran ascribes equally to man and God: "He loves them, and they love Him" (5:54)

Mahdi (mahdī) - "the guided one," a descendent of Muhammad who will appear along with Jesus to bring about the end times

majlis - session, sitting place; a gathering of Sufis, or the room where they gather

makhafa (makhāfa) - fear, specifically of God

Malakut (malakūt) - the spiritual realm (when contrasted with *mulk*); the imaginal realm (see *Jabarut*)

ma'na (ma 'nā) - "meaning"; the spiritual, intelligible, invisible dimension of a thing; contrasted with *surat*

maratib (marātib) - degrees, levels, of spirit or being

ma'rifa (ma 'rifa) - recognition, knowledge, gnosis; direct, spiritual perception as opposed to indirect knowledge or book learning

Mevlevi (Mawlawī) - the spiritual lineage of "Mawlānā" (our master) Jalaluddin Rumi; the Sufi order that he founded

mevlud (Ar. mawlūd) - birthday; celebration of the birth of a saint

minbar - pulpit

mi'raj (mi 'rāj) - ascent, ladder; Muhammad's ascent through the seven spheres into the divine presence

mi'raj ar-ruhani (al-mi 'rāj al-rūḥānī) - the spiritual ascent to God available to the Prophet's followers

Muhasibi (Muḥāsibī, Ḥārith al-, d. 857) - important early Sufi author

mulk —kingdom; the universe; the corporeal world

Nabulusi (Nābulusī, 'Abd al-Ghanī, d. 1731) - Syrian author of Sufi works in the line of Ibn Arabi

Nafas ar-Rahman (nafas al-raḥmān) - the Breath of the Merciful, the cosmos as the infinite words of God articulated within His own breath

nafs - self, soul; used without qualification in Sufism, it means the ego, the negative tendencies that pull us away from God; typically understood as having several stages of growth leading to perfection

namaz (namāz) - the Persian word for *salat*, the daily ritual prayer

Niffari (Niffarī, d. ca 970) - great Sufi teacher and author of two books of conversations with God

Omar Khayyam ('Umar Khayyām, d. ca. 1130) - philosopher and mathematician, famous in the West for his Persian quatrains as Trans. Fitzgerald

Pir (pīr) - the Persian word for shaikh

qabd (qabḍ) - see *bast*

Qaf (Qāf) - a mythic mountain, said to surround the world

Quran (Qur'ān) - the Word of God revealed to Muhammad by means of the angel Gabriel

qutb (quṭb) - pole, axis; in Sufism, the greatest shaikh of the age; the living master around whom all spiritual teachers revolve

Rahma (raḥma) - mercy, compassion; the primary attribute of God and the source of the world

ruh (rūḥ) - spirit; the divine inblowing that animates the universe; the Breath of the Merciful

ruju (rujū') - return; coming back to normal consciousness

Rumi, Mevlana ("Our Master") Jalaluddin (Mawlānā Jalāl al-Dīn Rūmī, d. 1273) - outstanding poet and spiritual teacher; founder of the Mevlevi Sufi order; author of the *Mathnawi* and a divan

saki - see *saqi*

salam (salām) - peace, freedom from strife and defect

salat (ṣalāt) - ritual prayer, the daily performance of which is the second pillar of Islam

sama (samā') - "listening"; listening to the recitation of Quran or poetry; listening to music; music accompanied by ritual dancing

Sana'i (Sanā'ī, d. 1131) - the first of the great Persian Sufi poets

saqi (sāqī) - cupbearer; the one who pours the wine of love; an image derived from Quran 76:21, "Their Lord pours them pure wine [in paradise]"

sema - see *sama*

semahane (samā'-khāna) - "house of listening," where Sufis perform *sama*

Shabistari (Shabistarī, d. 1320) - Sufi teacher in the line of Ibn Arabi; author of the 1000-verse poem *Gulshan-i rāz*, "The Rosegarden of Mystery"

Shadhili, Abu'l-Hasan ash- (Abu'l-Ḥasan al-Shādhilī, d. 1258) - eponymous founder of a major Sufi order

shahadah (shahāda) - "bearing witness"; testifying that there is no god but God and that Muhammad is His messenger

shaikh (shaykh) - "elder," teacher, Sufi master

Shaikh al-Ishraq (Shaykh al-Ishrāq) - "the master of Illumination," title of Suhrawardi

Shari'ah (sharī'a) - "wide road"; the revealed law of Islam as codified by the jurists; contrasted with Tariqah

Shibli (Shiblī, d. 945) - one of the early Sufi masters

Shirazi, Shah Da'i (Shāh Dā'ī Shīrāzī, d.1465) - disciple of Shah Ni'matullah Wali (founder of the Ni'matullahi Sufi order) and author of a divan of Persian poetry and several prose works

Simnani (Simnānī, 'Alā' al-Dawla, d. 1336) - Sufi teacher and theoretician of the Kubrawi order

Simurgh (sīmurgh) - the griffen, the king of the birds; symbol for God as the goal of the spiritual path

Sufi (ṣūfī) - an advanced adept of the inner journey; loosely, an initiate into a Tariqah

Suhrawardi (Suhrawardī, d. 1191) - Shaikh al-Ishraq, founder of the Illuminationist school of philosophy and author of many books in Arabic and Persian

suluk (sulūk) - wayfaring, traveling on the path to God

sunna - "custom, wont"; the exemplary behavior of Muhammad

surat (ṣūrat) - form; the form in which God created Adam; the outward appearance of a thing; contrasted with *ma'na*

ta'alluh - deiformity, theomorphism; becoming qualified by the attributes of God

tafakkur - reflection, meditation; a Sufi practice

Tariqah (ṭarīqa) - (narrow) path; the road to God; contrasted with Shari'ah and Haq-iqah; a Sufi "order"

tawba - repentance; turning toward God as a result of His turning toward you

tawhid (tawḥīd) - declaring oneness, asserting the unity of God; the first principle of Islamic faith

tekke (from Arabic *takya*) - a Sufi center

Umar ('Umar, d. 644) - important Companion of the Prophet, Islam's second caliph

ummah, al- (al-umma) - community; the community of all Muslims

wahdat al-wujud (waḥdat al-wujūd) - "oneness of Being"; the assertion that there is only one true Being, that of God; a doctrine that is famously but misleadingly attributed to Ibn Arabi

wajd - ecstasy, finding the Being of God

wujud (wujūd) - being, existence; the Being of God, other than which there is no true being

Yunus Emre (Yūnus Emre, d. ca. 1321) - a great Turkish Sufi poet

zahir (ẓāhir) - outward, apparent; God as the Manifest; contrasted with *batin*

zakat (zakāt) - the alms tax, paying of which is one of Islam's five pillars

zawiya (zāwiya) - literally "corner"; a Sufi center

CONTRIBUTOR PROFILES

Iraj Anvar is a theatre director, actor, performer of Persian music, and translator who has been active in spreading Sufi teachings in New York for many years.

Coleman Barks is an emeritus professor of English at the University of Georgia and has published many successful translations of Rumi's poetry, such as *The Essential Rumi*.

Titus Burckhardt (1908-1984), a Swiss German, was initiated into the Darqawi order of Sufism in Morocco in 1934 and subsequently published numerous books on art and the principles of traditional thought, including *Alchemy*, *Moorish Culture in Spain*, and *Sacred Art in East and West*.

William C. Chittick, professor of Religious Studies at Stony Brook University, is author of twenty-some books on Islamic thought and Sufism, such as *The Self-Disclosure of God* and *The Heart of Islamic Philosophy*.

Emma Clark teaches in the Visual Islamic and Traditional Arts Department of the Prince of Wales Foundation in London. Among her books is *The Art of the Islamic Garden*.

Henry Corbin (1903-1978), French philosopher and professor at the Sorbonne, devoted his life to introducing the intellectual riches of Islamic philosophy and Sufism to the West; he is author of many ground-breaking books, including *Creative Imagination in the Sufism of Ibn Arabi* and *The Man of Light in Iranian Sufism*.

Victor Danner (1926-1990), a professor at the University of Indiana, Bloomington, is best known for his translation of Ibn Ata'illah's *Book of Wisdom*.

Gai Eaton is a prominent British convert to Islam, a former diplomat, and author of books such as *The King and the Castle, Islam and the Destiny of Man*, and *Remembering God*.

Shems Friedlander is a designer, artist, and poet who was active for many years in New York City and is now senior lecturer in The Adham Center for Television Journalism at the American University in Cairo. Among his books is *Rumi and the Whirling Dervishes.*

Camille Helminski is co-founder with her husband Kabir of the Threshold Society, a non-profit educational foundation. She has been affiliated with the Mevlevi Sufi order for many years and is the author of *Women of Sufism.*

Kabir Helminski is a shaikh in the Mevlevi tradition. He has published translations of Rumi and has authored several books on Sufism, such as *The Knowing Heart.*

Gray Henry is co-founder of the Islamic Texts Society and for many years has been the director of Fons Vitae, a publisher of books on spirituality and Sufism.

Sheikh Tosun Bayrak al Jerrahi has led the Jerrahi Order of the Americas since 1977 and has translated and interpreted several important Sufi texts.

Shaikh Ali Jum'a has been a professor at al-Azhar University and is now Grand Mufti of Egypt.

John Moyne, a scholar of Persian, is emeritus professor and former head of linguistics at the Graduate School of the City University of New York. He has collaborated with Coleman Barks on several books.

Seyyed Hossein Nasr, University Professor of Islamic Studies at George Washington University, is a former chancellor of Aryamehr University in Iran. He has published fifty books and hundreds of articles on Islamic topics, focusing on the metaphysical and cosmological dimensions of Islamic philosophy and Sufism. He has delivered the Gifford Lectures (Knowledge and the Sacred) and was honored with a volume in the Library of Living Philosophers.

Reynold A. Nicholson (1868-1945) was a professor of Persian at Cambridge University and is the man most responsible for bringing Rumi into the English language with his edition and translation of the *Mathnawi*.

Nasrollah Pourjavady is professor of philosophy at Tehran University and a foremost historian of Sufism; among his books in English are a translation of Ahmad Ghazali's classic work on love, *Sawanih: Inspirations from the World of Pure Spirits*, and, in collaboration with Peter Lamborn Wilson, *Kings Of Love: The History and Poetry of the Ni'matullahi Sufi Order of Iran*.

Carol Ring has a doctorate in Middle Eastern Studies from the University of Pennysylvania; she lives and works in the hills of Galilee.

Annemarie Schimmel (1922-2003) was a professor at Harvard and a prolific author of books in German and English on Islamic literature, Sufism, and especially Rumi. Among her outstanding books are *And Muhammad Is His Messenger* and *Deciphering the Signs of God*.

Jean Sulzberger, a senior editor of *Parabola*, has traveled extensively in the Middle East and Central Asia.

Peter Lamborn Wilson is an American poet, essayist, and philosopher and has collaborated in many translations of Persian poetry, such as *The Drunken Universe*.

Tim Winter, also known as Abdal-Hakim Murad, is the Sheikh Zayed Lecturer in Islamic Studies, and Fellow of Wolfson College, University of Cambridge. He is General Editor of the Islamic Texts Society's al-Ghazali series and has translated two of its volumes, including *On Disciplining the Soul*.

FOR FURTHER READING

Of the many translations of the Quran available in English, *The Koran* interpreted by A. J. Arberry (London: George Allen & Unwin, 1955) does the best job of preserving the literal meaning and simultaneously catching the poetic nature of the text. For Hadith, the best collection in English is *Mishkat al-Masabih* by James Robson (four volumes, Lahore: Ashraf, 1963-65).

General Accounts

Abou El-Fadl, Khaled. *The Search for Beauty in Islam: A Conference of the Books.* Lanham, MD: Rowman & Littlefield, 2006.

Armstrong, Karen. *Muhammad: A Prophet for Our Time.* New York: HarperCollins, 2006.

Danner, Victor. *The Islamic Tradition.* Ghent, NY: Sophia Perennis et Universalis, 2005.

Ernst, Carl W. *Following Muhammad: Rethinking Islam in the Contemporary World.* Chapel Hill: University of North Carolina Press, 2003.

Fitzgerald, Judith and Michael Oren. *The Universal Spirit of Islam.* Bloomington, IN: World Wisdom Books, 2006.

Lings, Martin. *Muhammad: His Life Based on the Earliest Sources.* London: Allen & Unwin, 1983.

_____. *Splendours of Qur'an: Calligraphy and Illumination.* Liechtenstein: Thesaurus Islamicus Foundation, 2006.

Murata, Sachiko and William C. Chittick. *The Vision of Islam.* St. Paul, MN: Paragon House, 1994.

Nasr, Seyyed Hossein. *The Heart of Islam: Enduring Values for Humanity.* San Francisco: Harper, 2002.

Renard, John. *Seven Doors to Islam: Spirituality and the Religious Life of Muslims.* Berkeley: University of California Press, 1996.

Schuon, Frithjof. *Understanding Islam.* Bloomington, IN: World Wisdom Books, 1998.

Sufism

Addas, Claude. *Quest for the Red Sulphur: The Life of Ibn `Arabi.* Cambridge, Eng.: The Islamic Texts Society, 1993.

Awn, Peter. *Satan's Tragedy and Redemption: Iblis in Sufi Psychology.* Leiden, Neth.: Brill, 1983.

Chittick, William C. *Sufism: A Short Introduction.* Oxford: Oneworld, 2001.

_____. *The Sufi Path of Knowledge: Ibn al-'Arabi's Metaphysics of Imagination.* Albany: State University of New York Press, 1989.

_____. *The Sufi Path of Love: The Spiritual Teachings of Rumi.* Albany: State University of New York Press, 1983.

Chodkiewicz, Michel. *An Ocean Without Shore: Ibn Arabi, the Book and the Law.* Albany: State University of New York Press, 1993.

Cutsinger, James S. *Paths to the Heart: Sufism and the Christian East*. Bloomington, IN: World Wisdom Books, 2002.

Ernst, Carl W. *The Shambhala Guide to Sufism*. Boston: Shambhala, 1997.

Izutsu, Toshihiko. *Sufism and Taoism*. Berkeley: University of California Press, 1984.

Lewis, Franklin. *Rumi: Past and Present, East and West*. Oxford: Oneworld, 2000.

Lings, Martin. *A Sufi Saint of the Twentieth Century*. Berkeley: University of California Press, 1971.

Morris, James Winston. *The Reflective Heart: Discovering Spiritual Intelligence in Ibn 'Arabi's Meccan Illuminations*. Louisville, KY: Fons Vitae, 2005.

Murata, Sachiko. *Chinese Gleams of Sufi Light*. Albany: State University of New York Press, 2000.

Nasr, Seyyed Hossein. *In the Garden of the Truth*. San Francisco: Harper, 2007.

Schimmel, Annemarie. *Mystical Dimensions of Islam*. Chapel Hill: University of North Carolina Press, 1975.

_____. *The Triumphal Sun: A Study of the Works of Jalaloddin Rumi*. London: East-West, 1978.

Siraj ad-Din, Abu Bakr. *The Book of Certainty: The Sufi Doctrine of Faith*. London: Tauris, 1995.

Translations

Abd al-Qadir al-Jaza'iri. *The Spiritual Writings of Amir Abd al-Kader*. Trans. Michel Chodkiewicz. Albany: State University of New York Press, 1995.

Abd al-Qadir al-Jilani. *The Sublime Revelation*. Trans. Muhtar Holland. Fort Lauderdale: Al-Baz, 1993.

Aflaki. *The Feats of the Knowers of God: Manaqeb al-Arefin*. Trans. John O'Kane. Leiden, Neth.: Brill, 2003.

Ali ibn al-Husayn. *The Psalms of Islam*. Trans. William C. Chittick. London: Muhammadi Trust, 1988.

Ansari, Abdallah. *Intimate Conversations*. Trans. Wheeler Thackston. New York: Paulist Press, 1978.

Attar, Fariduddin. *The Conference of the Birds*. Trans. Afkham Darbandi and Dick Davis. London: Penguin, 1984.

_____. *The Speech of the Birds*. Trans. Peter Avery. London: The Islamic Texts Society, 1998.

Darqawi, Shaykh al-Arabi ad-. *Letters of a Sufi Master*. Trans. Titus Burckhardt. Bedfont, Eng.: Perennial, 1961.

Ghazali, Abu Hamid al-. *Deliverance from Error*. Trans. Richard McCarthy. Louisville, KY: Fons Vitae, 2004.

_____. *The Niche of Lights*. Trans. David Buchman. Provo, UT: Brigham Young University Press, 1998.

_____. *The Remembrance of Death and the Afterlife*. Trans. T. J. Winter. Cambridge, Eng.: Islamic Texts Society, 1989.

Ibn Abbad ar-Rundi. *Letters on the Sufi Path*. Trans. John Renard. New York: Paulist, 1986.

Ibn Arabi. *The Ringstones of Wisdom*. Trans. Caner Dagli. Chicago: Kazi Publications, 2004.

_____. *Sufis of Andalusia*. Trans. R. W. J. Austin. London: George Allen & Unwin, 1971.

Ibn Ata'illah al-Iskandari. *The Subtle Blessings in the Saintly Lives of Abul-Abbas al-Mursi and His Master Abul-Hasan*. Trans. Nancy Roberts. Louisville, KY: Fons Vitae, 2005.

Iraqi, Fakhruddin. *Divine Flashes*. Trans. William C. Chittick and Peter Lamborn Wilson. New York: Paulist Press, 1982.

Maneri, Sharafuddin. *The Hundred Letters*. Trans. Paul Jackson. New York: Paulist Press, 1980.

Muhammad Ibn al-Munawwar. *Secrets of God's Mystical Oneness: Asrar al-Towhid*. Trans. John O'Kane. Costa Mesa, CA: Mazda, 1992.

Nizamuddin Awliya: Morals for the Heart. Trans. Bruce Lawrence. New York: Paulist Press, 1992.

Qushayri, al-. *Principles of Sufism*. Trans. Barbara von Schlegell. Berkeley: Mizan Press, 1992.

Razi, Najmuddin. *The Path of God's Bondsmen from Origin to Return*. Trans. Hamid Algar. Delmar, NY: Caravan, 1982.

Rumi, Jalaluddin. *Mystical Poems of Rumi*. Trans. A. J. Arberry. 2 vols. Chicago: Chicago University Press, 1968; Boulder, CO: Westview, 1979.

Sells, Michael. *Early Islamic Mysticism: Sufi, Qur'an, Mi'raj, Poetic and Theological Writings*. New York: Paulist Press, 1996.

Shams-i Tabrizi. *Me & Rumi: The Autobiography of Shams–i Tabrizi*. Trans. William C. Chittick. Louisville, KY: Fons Vitae, 2004.

Suhrawardi, Shihabuddin Yahya. *The Mystical & Visionary Treatises of Suhrawardi*. Trans. Wheeler Thackston. London: Octagon, 1982.

Sulami, as-. *The Subtleties of the Ascension*. Trans. Frederick S. Colby. Louisville, KY: Fons Vitae, 2006.

Chapter Citations

Call of the Tradition

1. *Ta'rikh al-Rusul wa'l-muluk* from *Sacred Texts of the World: A Universal Anthology,* Ninian Smart and Richard D. Hecht, eds. (New York: Crossroad, 1982), p. 131.
2. From Annemarie Schimmel, *Mystical Dimensions of Islam* (Chapel Hill: The University of North Carolina Press, 1975), p. 213.
3. A. J. Arberry, *The Koran Interpreted* (New York: Simon & Schuster, 1955).
4. Fariduddin Attar, *The Conference of the Birds,* Trans. Edward Fitzgerald (Boston: L. C. Page, 1899), pp. 172-74. Quoted in Whitall Perry, *A Treasury of Traditional Wisdom* (London: George Allen and Unwin, 1971), p. 375.
5. *Hadith qudsi,* from Muslim as quoted in *Mishkat al-masabih.* Cited in *Islamic Spirituality: Foundations,* edited by Seyyed Hossein Nasr (New York: Crossroad, 1987), p. 201.

Chapter 1

1. Al-Ghazali, *The Alchemy of Happiness* (New York: Orientalia, 1964).

Chapter 2

1. From R. A. Nicholson, *Studies in Islamic Mysticism* (London: Cambridge University Press, 1921), p. 55.
2. R. A. Nicholoson, *The Kashf al-Mahjub: The Oldest Persian Treastise on Sufiism* (London: Luzac, 1911), p. 39.

Chapter 3

1. *The Mystical Poems of Rumi,* trans. A. J. Arberry (Chicago: The University of Chicago Press, 1968), p. 70.

Chapter 4

1. From Stephen Mitchell, *The Enlightened Heart: An Anthology of Sacred Poetry* (New York: Harper & Row, 1989), p. 58. Trans. Robert Bly.

2. Seyyed Hossein Nasr, *An Introduction to Islamic Cosmological Doctrines* (Boulder: Shambala Publications Inc., 1978).

Chapter 5

1. From Nicholson, *Kashf al-Mahjub,* p. 368.
2. A. J. Arberry, trans., *Discourses of Rumi* (York Beach, ME: Samuel Weiser, Inc., 1972), p. 33.

Chapter 6

1. Adapted from A. J. Arberry, *Tales from the Masnavi* (London: George Allen & Unwin, 1963).
2. *The Conference of the Birds,* in Ananda Coomaraswamy, *Coomaraswamy: Collected Papers, Metaphysics,* ed. Roger Lipsey (Princeton: Princeton U. Press, Bollingen Series LXXXIX, 1977).
3. A. J. Arberry, *The Mawaqif and Mukhatabat of Muhammad ibn Abdi'l-Jabbar al-Niffari* (Cambridge: Cambridge University Press, 1935), pp. 73-74.

Chapter 7

1. *Heart's Witness: The Sufi Quatrains of Awhaduddin Kirmani,* Trans. Bernd Manuel Weischer and Peter Lamborn Wilson (Tehran: Imperial Academy of Philosophy, 1978), p. 117.
2. *Selected Odes from the Divani Shamsi Tabriz,* trans. R. A. Nicholson (Cambridge: Cambridge University Press, 1898).

Photography Captions & Credits

Cover Photo
Decoration of dome in Prayer Hall, Lotfallah Mosque, Isfahan. Safavid dynasty, 1603-19.
Photo: SEF/Art Resource, NY

Page xxi
Decorated wall panel, Jameh Mosque, Isfahan. The mosque was first built during the Seljuq dynasty (11th-14th centuries).
Photo: SEF/Art Resource, New York.

Page xxii
Calligraphic hoopoe bird from the story of Solomon in the Quran. It reads, "It is in the name of God, the Merciful, the Compassionate" (27:30).
Photo: Bildarchiv Preussischer Kulturbesitz/Art Resource, New York.

Page xxiii
Interior of the Great Mosque in Cordoba, begun in AD 786.
Photo: Werner Forman/Art Resource, New York.

Page xxiv
View of the Shabistan, the winter prayer hall, Jameh Mosque, Isfahan.
Photo: Josephine Powell Photograph, Courtesy of Historic Photographs, Fine Arts Library, Harvard College Library

Page xxv
Stucco mihrab (niche marking the direction of prayer), built in 1310. Jameh Mosque, Isfahan.
Photo: Josephine Powell Photograph, Courtesy of Historic Photographs, Fine Arts Library, Harvard College Library

Page xxvi
Quranic leaf with the heading of Sura 29, possibly from Iraq, before 911. The leaf includes the end of Sura 28: "And call not upon another god with God; there is no god but He. Everything is perishing but His face; His is the judgment, and to Him you shall be returned." M. 712, f. 19v.
Photo: The Pierpont Morgan Library/ Art Resource, New York.

Page xxvii
Mevlevi dervishes performing the sama. Turkish miniature, 16th century.
Photo: Archivo Iconografico, S.A./ CORBIS.

Page xxviii
The Shah Mosque, Isfahan. Built by Shah Abbas I of the Safavid Dynasty, 1611-38.
Photo: SEF/Art Resource, New York.

Page xxix
Interior view of Jameh Mosque, Isfahan, with seated women.
Photo: SEF/Art Resource, New York.

Page xxx
Elias and Khizr at the Fountain of Life (inspired by Quran 18:60 ff.).
Photo: The Metropolitan Museum of Art, Cora Imken Burnett Collection of Persian Miniatures and Other Persian Art Objects, Bequest of Cora Timken Burnett, 1956 (57.51.28). Photograph ©1974 The Metropolitan Museum of Art

Page xxxi
Man admiring an illuminated manuscript. Late 17th century, India.
Photo: Bildarchiv Preussischer Kulturbesitz/Art Resource, New York.

Page xxxii
Geometric tile pattern from the wall of a building.
Photo: Eric Van Den Brulle © Getty Images

Page xxxiii
Mosque at the shrine of Ali ibn Abi Talib, 18th CE, Mazar-i Sharif, Afghanistan.
Photo: Scala/Art Resource, New York.

Page xxxiv
The Dome of the Rock, Jerusalem. Built in 688-92 CE, it is the oldest surviving intact Muslim monument.
   Photo: Tim Thompson © Getty Images

Page xxxv
The Dome of the Rock.
   Photo: Erich Lessing/Art Resource, New York.

Page xxxvi
The Ka'bah during the hajj.
   Photo: Nabeel Turner © Getty Images